Text Classics

PHILLIP FREDERICK EDWARD SCHULER was born in Melbourne in 1889. He was the only son of Frederick Schuler, the German-born editor of the *Age* from 1900 to 1926.

After completing compulsory military service, Phillip Schuler became a junior reporter at the *Age*. He volunteered in 1914 to sail to Egypt as the newspaper's war correspondent and photographer. En route, he became friendly with Australia's official war correspondent, C. E. W. Bean. In 1915 Schuler travelled to Turkey, where he was embedded with Anzac soldiers and filed a series of reports.

On his return home he wrote *Australia in Arms: A Narrative of the Australasian Imperial Force and Their Achievement at Anzac*, the first full-length account of Australia's role in the Gallipoli offensive, and the short illustrated work *The Battlefields of Anzac*. General Sir John Monash called *Australia in Arms* 'the best and fullest story...of the whole Anzac campaign'.

By the time the books were published, in 1916, Schuler had enlisted with the AIF. He was swiftly promoted and sent to Europe.

Phillip Schuler died in 1917 of injuries sustained in the Battle of Messines, Belgium. Bean's obituary described him as 'brilliantly handsome, bright, attractive, generous'. He is remembered as a pioneering Australian war reporter.

PAUL HAM lives in Sydney and Paris. For many years he was the Australian correspondent for the London *Sunday Times*. His acclaimed books include *Kokoda, Vietnam: The Australian War, Hiroshima Nagasaki, Sandakan* and *Young Hitler: The Making of the Führer*. Among his World War I works are *1914: The Year the World Ended* and *Passchendaele: Requiem for Doomed Youth*.

Australia in Arms

THE STORY OF GALLIPOLI

Phillip Schuler

Text Publishing Melbourne Australia

textclassics.com.au
textpublishing.com.au

The Text Publishing Company
Swann House
22 William Street
Melbourne Victoria 3000
Australia

First published by T. Fisher Unwin Ltd, London, 1916, as *Australia in Arms: A Narrative of the Australasian Imperial Force and Their Achievement at Anzac*
This edition published by The Text Publishing Company, 2018

Series and cover design by W. H. Chong
Cover photo by Private Victor Rupert Laidlaw, *In the Front Line, Anzac [Cove]*, c. 1915, State Library of Victoria, gift of Mrs E. Barker
Page design by Text
Typeset by Midland Typesetters

Printed and bound in Australia by Griffin Press, an accredited ISO/NZS 1401:2004 Environmental Management System printer

ISBN: 9781925603453 (paperback)
ISBN: 9781925626490 (ebook)

A catalogue record for this book is available from the National Library of Australia

This book is printed on paper certified against the Forest Stewardship Council® Standards. Griffin Press holds FSC chain-of-custody certification SGS-COC-005088. FSC promotes environmentally responsible, socially beneficial and economically viable management of the world's forests.

CONTENTS

PART III: THE GREAT ADVENTURE

Ever Generous, True as Gold
by Paul Ham

BETWEEN the covers of *Australia in Arms* you will find that rarity in our unchivalrous age: an account of Gallipoli by a young war correspondent who believed in notions of gallantry, liberty, heroism and self-sacrifice. He followed the men into the breach to tell their story, and then, slightly ashamed of being a mere scribbler, enlisted in the infantry.

Phillip F. E. Schuler was shot dead in Flanders in June 1917, just before the battle of Passchendaele. He was twenty-seven. He left behind this minor classic of the Gallipoli campaign, published a year earlier.

Schuler came from a prosperous literary family. His father was the editor of the Melbourne *Age*, which eased the lad's path to selection as a war reporter, and helped him secure a front-row seat at Gallipoli in 1915. He worked and played alongside the great Charles Bean, the official war correspondent. They met on board the *Orvieto* and visited the pyramids together. Bean would describe Schuler, after he was killed, as 'a brilliantly handsome, bright, attractive, [and] generous youngster'.

The extraordinary thing about Schuler's account of the Dardanelles is that it expresses without a trace of criticism or mockery the British and colonial effort at Gallipoli. Here is a man who utterly believed in the war and the men who led it. Most of the commanders he loved and respected. For him, the cause was right; the ends, just.

He was there during the journey out (where he witnessed the sinking of the *Emden*), at the Gallipoli landings, the battles of the Nek, Quinn's Post and Lone Pine, the charge of the Australian Light Horse and other fabled moments in the doomed invasion. And at the end of it all this young man was still able to see the battle not only as a worthwhile expression of duty done, but also as the forging of the nation: Australia, he writes,

> attained Nationhood by the heroism of her noble sons. 'Anzac' will ever form the front page in her history, and a unique and vivid chapter in the annals of the Empire. The very vigour of their manhood, the impetuosity of their courage, carried slopes that afterwards in cold blood, seemed impregnable.

Schuler is unflinching in his belief in the rightness of the Mother Country and in the sincerity with which he seeks to wrap the young Australian nation in the image of 'Anzac'. It never occurs to him to question that duty, to ask why Australia should have followed Churchill's crackpot plan, to invade the Turkish nation on the orders of Britain in an attempt to open a third front against Germany. Churchill rates just one mention in the book.

But we should not ask for such things in a work like this. It is not an analysis. It is reportage, written with sensitivity, awe and respect, by a man of his time. It is a historically accurate reflection of the ideals and feelings of most men and women of 1915, told in a voice that is at once sincere and ingenuous.

We are in Schuler's debt for that voice. It is authentic. His words cement the point that many Australians were *conscious* that they were building a new country in the crucible of war. That was not some pseudo-nationalist sentiment superimposed on Gallipoli with hindsight. In 1915 it was real; it was felt. And this authenticity deserves respect, whatever else you might feel about the project of trying to embed national identity in a military catastrophe.

Schuler was a journalist, not a historian, and yet his action-packed account of Gallipoli may indeed be read as the first draft of history. It is laden with vivid anecdote and well-chosen detail. Take his description of a crowd of enlisted men about to march off to war. He conjures the social gradations of an entire army through a snapshot of how they were shod and dressed:

> There were men in good boots and bad boots, in brown and tan boots, in hardly any boots at all; in sack suits and old clothes, and smart-cut suits just from the well-lined drawers of a fashionable home; there were workers and loafers, students and idlers, men of professions and men just workers, who formed that force. But—they were all fighters,

stickers, men with some grit (they got more as they went on), and men with a love of adventure. So they marched out to their camp at Broadmeadows—a good ten-mile tramp.

Schuler is unsparingly admiring of the Australian soldier, who was 'generous' to a fault and 'spoiled' the local Egyptians. Even on leave, when many Aussies were busy establishing their reputations as 'larrikins'—the timeless euphemism for drunken whore-mongering louts—the diggers were merely indulging in good old-fashioned masculine fun, the locker-room talk of 1915, 'innocent for the most part'. Hence Cairo was

> an orgy of pleasure, which only a free and, at the time, unrestrained city...could provide. Those men with £10 to £20 in their pockets, after being kept on board ship for two months, suddenly to be turned loose on an Eastern town—healthy, keen, spirited, and adventurous men—it would have been a strong hand that could have checked them in their pleasures.

His descriptive powers are well attuned to the tension of the moment. As the troopships approach the hilly shoreline of Gallipoli, he writes:

> The men were quietly singing the sentimental ditties of 'Home and Mother', or chatting in a final talk, yarning of the past—the future, so imminent now, left to take care of itself—until they were borne within a distance when silence was essential to success. Then they clenched their teeth...Over the whole of that army, 30,000 men, there hung a lifetime of suspense. Would the moon never go down!

x

As for the infamous error, of landing the troops at the wrong beach, Schuler cheerfully inquires,

> But was it so awful an error? Chance had carried in her womb a deeply significant advantage, for at the original point the beach had been carefully prepared with barbed wire, that ran down into the very water. Trenches lined the shore...So Chance guided the boats into a natural cove, certainly not very large—just a segment of a circle some 400 yards long. Never anticipating an attack at the foot of such a ridge, the Turks had dug but few trenches to protect this spot.

In other words, the mistake probably saved many lives during the landing, and yet the opening battles were as bloody as any during the seven-month campaign, thanks to the steep hills that met the wrong beach.

Schuler writes with a paintbrush, capturing a vivid scene wherever he goes: 'white hospital ships loomed like aluminium-painted craft in the fierce sun, and their yellow funnels seemed fairer still by the side of the darkened smoke-stacks of the panting destroyers.' The Turks' rifles sounded like 'thousands of typewriters'—perhaps an expression of a desire to exchange his for a rifle? And he sprinkles his prose with fascinating vignettes, such as the clandestine activities of the German commander: 'Under guise of a sergeant of the Red Crescent walked General Liman von Sanders, the German leader against Anzac, and he mixed with the burial parties.'

Some omissions are telling. There is no mention of John Simpson and his donkey, fabled heroes of Anzac popular history, suggesting that Simpson was no more or less feted than other stretcher bearers at the time. In this light, the donkey probably served the purposes of government propaganda more effectively than did Simpson.

To a man the commanders, Australian and British, in Schuler's telling, were brave and smart, and mucked in with the lads. In this case, Schuler's patriotism verges on the credulous: many of the officers were below average and some were disastrous. He diplomatically leaves out the names of the worst.

Yet he is spot on about the much-loved British General William Birdwood, leader of the Anzacs, and the only corps commander to oppose the evacuation. Birdwood rarely missed his evening dip, often within range of Turkish snipers: 'He bathed amongst his men, shedding off rank with his uniform...A quiet, very firm, but very friendly man was this leader of the Australians, who understood their character admirably.'

Of all the battles, the charge of the Australian Light Horse on 7 August most sharply spurred Schuler's pride in his countrymen:

> The whole line went. Each man knew that to leave those trenches was to face certain, almost immediate death. They knew it no less than the glorious Light Brigade at Balaclava...They charged. Lieut.-Colonel White had not gone ten paces when he fell dead, riddled with bullets. The first line of 150 men melted away ere they had gone half the distance to the trenches, and yet the second line, waiting and watching, followed them...What did the brigade do but its duty?—duty in the face of overwhelming

odds, in the face of certain death; and the men went because their leaders led them, and they were men. What more can be said? No one may ask if the price was not too great. The main object had been achieved. The Turks were held there.

And then, after Birdwood's August offensives failed, and reinforcements were denied, came the secret evacuation of the beaches. At dusk on 19 November, as the last phase of the withdrawal began, a mere six thousand men were left holding back fifty thousand Turkish troops, a fact of which the Turks were, for the Anzacs' sake, blissfully unaware.

Schuler offers this unforgettable portrait of the diggers retreating down the hills, to the safety of the departing boats:

> Their moving forms were clearly distinguishable in the glimmer from the crescent moon. The hills looked sullen and black. No beacon lights from dugouts burned. That first column began to leave Anzac shore at eight o'clock on the transports that were swiftly gliding from the shore...As the news broke on an astonished world, it was reported—and will be recorded—as one of the most extraordinary feats of naval and military history, that only three men at Anzac and two at Suvla Bay had been wounded in this astonishing masterpiece of strategy.

In another telling, the Anzacs abandoned the beaches in the dead of night, having been soundly defeated in a pointless campaign that had cost their force more than twenty-eight thousand dead and wounded.

And yet, it seems churlish to deny them the accolades of that astonishingly bloodless retreat, to puncture the youthful buoyancy of Schuler's vision of a proud nation at arms: 'Openhearted, ever generous, true as gold, and hard as steel, Australia's first great volunteer army, and its valorous deeds will live in history while the world lasts.'

Australia in Arms

To
the mothers of the heroes
who have fallen
I humbly dedicate these records of
glorious deeds

TO THE MOTHER COUNTRY

Because you trusted them, and gave them dower
Of your own ancient birthright, Liberty—
Forwent the meagre semblances of power
To win the deepest truth and loyalty—
Now, when these seeming slender roots are tried
Of all your strength, behold, they do not move;
The stripling nations hasten to your side
Impelled, as children should be, by their love.

And who shall grudge the pride of Motherhood
To this old Northern Kingdom of the sea?
Indeed our fathers' husbandry was good;
This is the harvest of our history;
Yet boast not. Rather pray we be not found
Unworthy those great men who tilled the ground.

F. D. Livingstone

PREFACE

One hot, bright morning early in the Dardanelles campaign, so the story goes, Lieut.-General Sir William Birdwood was walking up one of the worn tracks of Anzac that led over the hills into the firing-line when he stopped, as he very often did on these daily tours of the line, to talk with two men who were cooking over a fireplace made of shell cases. General Birdwood wore no jacket, therefore he had no badges of rank. His cap even lacked gold lace. Under his arm he had tucked a periscope. But the Australian addressed did not even boast of a shirt. Stripped to the waist, he was as fine a type of manhood as you might wish to see. He was burned a deep brown; his uniform consisted of a cap, shorts, and a pair of boots. His mate was similarly clad.

'Got something good there?' remarked the General as he stopped near the steaming pot of bully-beef stew.

'Ye-es,' replied the Australian, 'it's all right. Wish we had a few more spuds, though.' Conversation then branched off into matters relating to the firing-line, till at last General Birdwood signified his intention of going, bidding the soldier a cheery 'Good-day,' which was acknowledged by an inclination of the head. The General walked up the path to his firing-line, and the Australian turned to his mate, who had been very silent, but who now began to swear softly under his breath—

'You — fool! Do you know who you were talking to?'

'No!'

'Well, that was General Birdwood, that was, yer coot!'

'How was I to know that? Anyway, he seemed to know me all right.'

Those were the types of soldiers with whom I spent the first year of their entry into the Great War. I watched them drafted into camps in Australia, the raw material; I saw them charge into action like veteran troops, not a year later. Never downhearted, often grumbling, always chafing under delays, generous even to an alarming degree, the first twenty thousand who volunteered to go forth from Australia to help the Mother Country in the firing-line was an army that made even our enemies doubt if we had not deliberately 'chosen' the finest of the race. Since then there have been not twenty, but two hundred thousand of that stamp of soldier sent across the water to fight the Empire's battles at the throat of the foe.

This narrative does not pretend to be an 'Eyewitness' account. In most instances where I have had official papers before me, I have turned in preference to the more bold and vigorous stories of the men who have taken part in the stirring deeds.

I left Melbourne on 21st October on the Flagship of the Convoy, the *Orvieto*, that carried the 1st Division of Australian troops to Egypt, as the official representative of the *Melbourne Age* with the Expedition. I landed with the troops and went with them into the desert camp at Mena. It was then that I realised what staunch friends these young campaigners were. Colonel Wanliss and officers of the 5th Infantry Battalion insisted that I should become a member of their mess. I can never be grateful enough for that courtesy.

I wish also to gratefully acknowledge the kindly help and courtesy extended to me at all times by the Divisional Staff, and especially by Brigadier-General C. B. B. White, C.B. (then Lieut.-Colonel), Chief of the Staff, whom I always found courteous and anxious to facilitate me in my work as far as lay in his power.

It was while witnessing the welding of the Australasian Army in Egypt that I met Mr. W. T. Massey, representative of the *Daily Telegraph*, London, and Mr George Renwick, *Daily Chronicle*. We became a council of three for the four months we were together in Egypt, and it was a keen regret when Mr. Massey was unable to accompany me to the Dardanelles on the trip we had planned together, whereby, taking the advice of General Sir Ian Hamilton that we were 'free British subjects and could always take a ticket to the nearest railway-station to the fighting,' we had intended to witness together the landing. As it was, I went alone on a small 500-ton Greek trading steamer; but on arrival at Mitylene I was fortunate to find Mr. Renwick there and Mr. Stevens, who was now representing the *Daily Telegraph*, and they, having a motor-launch, invited me to join them in a little enterprise of our own. For a fortnight we watched the operations from the shores of Imbros and the decks of the launch, steaming up to the entrance of the Straits, living on what resources the island might deliver to us, which was mostly a poor fish, goat's milk, eggs, and very resinous native Greek wine. Eventually the motor-boat (and correspondents) was banished from 'The Zone' by British destroyers.

So I returned to Alexandria at the end of May, and was able to visit the hospitals and chat with the men from the firing-line. Then in July, General Sir Ian Hamilton—who had told us prior to his departure that he intended to do all in his power to help Mr. Massey and myself to visit the Anzac front—wrote from his headquarters at Imbros giving me his permission to come on to the famous battlefields.

In four hours I was on my way to the Dardanelles on a transport, and by stages (visiting the notorious *Aragon* at Mudros Harbour) reached Kephalos Bay, where the Commander-in-Chief had pitched his tent. The cordiality of General Hamilton's welcome will ever linger in my memory. I remember he was seated at a deal table in a small wooden hut with a pile of papers before him. He spoke of the Australians in terms of the highest praise. They were, he said, at present 'a thorn in the side of the Turks,' and when the time came he intended that that thorn should be pressed deeper. He advised me to see all I could, as quickly as I could.

I received a passport through the British and French lines and travelled from Helles to Anzac and Suvla Bay at will. Lieut.-General Birdwood and his Staff, Major-General Legge and the officers throughout the 1st Australian Division, and Major-General Godley and the leaders of the New Zealand Brigades, extended to me such courtesies as lay in their hands. I was able to witness the whole of the August offensive from the closest quarters, being in our trenches at Lone Pine during the engagement of the 6th.

At Anzac I was heartily welcomed by Captain Bean, the official correspondent with the Australian forces, who of all men was the most enthusiastic, painstaking, and conscientious worker that I have ever met, and I desire to acknowledge my debt to him for kindly criticism and good fellowship.

I would never be able to record the names of friends in the force, both in the firing-line and at the base, from whom I have received valuable suggestions and practical help.

I wish to express my gratitude to Mr. Geoffrey Syme, proprietor of *The Age*, for permission to use certain of the war dispatches I sent him for publication; to Mr. Osboldstone for permission to utilise some of the photographs he had already printed; and to the Minister of Defence for the reproduction or photographs and orders.

I am deeply indebted also to Mr. J. R. Watson for the spontaneous manner in which he offered to handle the manuscript for me in London while I was far across the water and corrected the proofs, thus enabling me to join the ranks of our Army. The apparent delight with which he entered on the work removed from my mind all thought of overtaxing a friendship.

Finally, I am most anxious to remove, at the outset, any suggestion that might be gained from this narrative that the Australians alone were the outstanding heroes of the Dardanelles campaign. When the history of the British forces—the magnificent 29th Division, the Lowland Division, and the Yeomanry—comes to be recorded, and the story of the French participation in the assault of Achi Baba told, it will be seen that, glorious as has been the name won by the Australians, heroically as they fought, proudly and surely as they held all they gained, they played a part in this 'Great Adventure,' and it is of that part that I have written because it was the only one of which I had full knowledge.

PHILLIP F. E. SCHULER
Melbourne, 5th April 1916

PART I

AUSTRALIA ANSWERS
THE CALL

CHAPTER I
THE TOCSIN IN AUSTRALIA

It is impossible to look back and recall without a glow of intense pride the instantaneous response made by the young manhood of Australia to the first signal of danger which fluttered at the central masthead of the Empire. As time goes on that pride has increased as battalions and brigades have followed one another into the firing-line; it has become now a pride steeped in the knowledge that the baptism of fire has proven the young nation, has given it an indelible stamp of Nationhood, has provoked from the lips of a great English soldier the phrase, 'These men from Australasia form the greatest army that an Empire has ever produced.' To-day that pride is the courage with which the people face and mourn the loss of their thousands of braves.

Let me recall the first dark days of August 1914, when the minds of the people of the Australian Commonwealth were grappling with and striving to focus the position of the British Empire in the war into which they had been so precipitately hurled. On Sunday, 2nd August, I well remember in Melbourne an army friend of mine being hastily recalled from a tennis party; and when I went to see him at the Victoria Barracks that same night, I found the whole place a glare of lights from end to end of the grim, grey stone building. It was the same the next and the next night, and for weeks, and so into the months. But even when the Governor-General, Sir Ronald Munro Ferguson, sent to the Prime Minister (Mr. Joseph Cook), at noon on 3rd August the telegram bearing the announcement that we all knew could not long be withheld, the strain seemed unlifted. 'England has declared war on Germany' was the brief but terrible message quickly transferred to the broadsheets that the newspapers printed at lightning speed and circulated, while the crowds in the streets cheered and cheered again as the message was posted on the display boards.

That night the streets were thronged (as they were for weeks to follow), and there was a series of riots, quickly subdued by the police, where raids had been made on German premises. Feeling was extraordinarily bitter, considering the remoteness of the Dominion. The Navy Office was barred to the casual visitor. Military motorcars swept through the streets and whirled into the barracks square. Army and Fleet, the new Australian Naval unit, were ready. More than one person during those grey days felt a thrill of satisfaction and comfort in the knowledge that of that Fleet unit the battle-cruiser *Australia* was greater and more powerful than any enemy vessel in Pacific waters.

Now it is no secret that arrangements exist with the British Admiralty under which the Commonwealth naval authorities receive at the first signs of hostilities a telegram in the nature of a warning. The second message simply says 'Strike.' The fact that the Navy Office in Melbourne received its warning cablegram not from the Admiralty, but from a message sent from H.M.S. *Minotaur,* then flagship of the China Squadron, asking particulars concerning the Australian unit, and 'presuming' that the naval authorities had received their warning, was only subsequently whispered. Where, then, was the Australian message? The original cable apparently was sent at the moment when Mr. Winston Churchill and Prince Louis of Battenberg between them took steps to keep mobilised the Grand Fleet in British waters, subsequent to the review, and sent them forthwith to their war stations. According to the prearranged understanding, the Australian unit was to pass automatically under the control of the Admiralty. Urgent wires were sent to the then Minister of Defence, Senator E. D. Millen, who was absent in Sydney, and the missing cablegram was brought to light in his possession. As soon as that final message came, the Australian ships, having coaled and prepared, moved to their war stations. It is not within the scope of this brief review to go further into this naval mobilisation, though I shall make reference later on to the Fleet unit and its war history.

On everybody's lips there now (4th August) arose the question of the young nation's part in the war. Would there be need of contingents? For the first period, at least, the Australian military authorities were too keenly occupied with home defence to vouchsafe much attention to this question, though high officers told me that it was inevitable that Australia would play her part very soon—to what extent and when, they could not judge. The immediate need lay in the mobilisation of part or all of the available forces at hand for coastal defence. The nervous tenseness of the situation was apparent on all hands; an underflow of intense uncertainty was plainly traceable in all the military movements. At the barracks day and night I found the military machine that Australia had so recently set running, rapidly speeding up.

All leave had been stopped on 1st August, and officers were hurrying back to their posts from various States of the Commonwealth. The defences of the ports along the coast were manned, and on the day when war was declared arrangements were completed for the extension of these defences to a mobile army, certainly of no great size as armies now are, to be used as shore patrols round the entrances of the great harbours of the capital cities. These men were the first draft of the Citizen Army that the Australian nation was training, and the rapidity with which they were mobilised, albeit it was only a small group, gave off the first spark from the machine, tested in a time of need. Yet the question that was ever to the fore during the first forty-eight hours after the declaration of war, and in fact until the following Wednesday, 10th August, was whether the whole of the Citizen Army was not to be mobilised. In other

15

words, would there be a general mobilisation, the plans for which were lying ready waiting to be opened all over the Commonwealth? The higher commands were told to hold themselves in readiness, and every one, from the youngest cadet to the Chief of the Staff, was expecting the word.

What would have been the need for such action? Remotely, of course, the position of the German High Sea Fleet and the integrity of the British Grand Fleet, but more closely the proximity of the German Pacific Squadron, consisting of two powerful cruisers, the *Scharnhorst* and *Gneisenau*, a number of smaller warships, colliers, and perhaps transports. Fortunately, the battle-cruiser *Australia* had been kept in Australian waters, and while she remained afloat, the German ships would not venture in her vicinity. But the possibility to which the military authorities looked was that of the German squadron eluding our patrols that stretched across the north of Australia from Darwin to the Marshall Islands, and convoying a landing party, arriving off our eastern or southern coasts. They might or might not land; they might content themselves with shelling the towns. At one time it was believed that secretly Germany had been pouring troops into German New Guinea and collecting stores there. That she had intended New Guinea or Papua as a base in the Pacific was evident enough. However, the worst fears were far from being realised. The British Fleet in the Pacific (now containing the Australian warships), and soon the Japanese Fleet co-operating, after an unsuccessful attempt to trap the enemy, edged them from the Australian coasts across the Pacific to South America, where they were eventually destroyed in the Falkland Islands engagement.

By this time the need for a general mobilisation in Australia was daily becoming less, as the enemy's ships were swept from the sea and the High Sea Fleet had been reduced to the category of floating forts. Accordingly the Government and military authorities turned their attention to the sending of an army to help the Motherland. German hopes had led them to suspect that the war would present for the people of the Commonwealth an excellent opportunity for revolt. Never did a young Dominion cling more closely or show its deep-rooted sense of gratitude and affection and responsibility to the parent nation. Having helped to secure herself, Australia immediately offered troops for active service overseas. A tremendous wave of enthusiasm swept over the land, and the acceptance by the Home Government of the offer was the occasion of great outbursts of cheering by the crowds that thronged the streets of the chief cities and eagerly scanned the news sheets and official announcements posted outside the newspaper offices. Recruiting began without delay. Already, in anticipation of events, the Defence Department had received names of officers and men from every State offering their services and anxious to join the first force. The composition of the force, after due consideration and consultation with the War Office, was to be a complete Division and a Brigade of Light Horse, 20,000 men in all. Depôts were established at the barracks, and soon in the suburban drill-halls—halls which were already the centres of the Compulsory Service movement in Home Defence—as well. The men poured into the depôts. There was the keenest competition for selection.

In making these drill-halls centres for recruiting the authorities were anxious to link up the regiments of the established Citizen Army with those that were going forth to battle across the seas, giving them in this way a tradition for all time. Young as the new army was, some 10 per cent, enlisted, those whose age was just twenty-one years. In this way, throughout the battalions was a sprinkling of the young Citizen Army, while the rest of the men were from the old militia regiments that had existed in past years. There were, I suppose, 60 per cent, of these men who flocked to the colours, and of these a proportion had seen service abroad, mostly in the South African War. Only a small number that went sloped a rifle for the first time.

Who would lead the force—Australia's first complete Division to take the field? No doubt seemed to cloud the minds of the General Staff, however much the mind of the Minister of Defence, Senator Millen, was swayed hither and thither. Brigadier-General Bridges was just entering on the fourth year of his command of the Duntroon Military College. The success of that college was already an established fact; the men who have left it have since proved that beyond question. It was, therefore, on Brigadier-General Bridges (raised to the rank of Major-General) that the choice eventually fell, and he at once handed over the control of the college to Colonel Parnell, Commandant of Victoria, and immediately commenced, on or about the 14th August, the selection of his higher commands for the force designated 'The First Australian Imperial Expeditionary Force.'

His task was no light one. Essentially a just man, but a man who demanded the utmost capacity from those beneath him in rank, he soon drew round him a brilliant Staff. The college, indeed, he robbed of most of its English leaders, and their places were filled by Australian officers. The Brigadiers were left the choice of their battalion commanders, and that choice fell on the men actively engaged in leading the young Citizen Army in the various centres, each State contributing its quota. The battalion commanders at first had free choice to select their officers, but subsequently a Board was established. Thousands of names were available, and, with one or two exceptions, it is with satisfaction I can write that every man chosen has proved himself in that force again and again as being worthy of the trust put in him, from high leaders to the most junior subalterns.

While recruiting went on apace, the Barracks remained illuminated day and night, and the tension remained for many weeks at a high pitch. Though the matter had been pondered over, the truth was, little or no provision had been made to form the nucleus of an Expeditionary Force. All Australia's energies had been devoted to preparing her Home Defence Army. Yet the machinery that had been created for that army now proved itself to be capable of such expansion as to provide all the mass of material necessary for the organisation and equipment of the Division under Major-General Bridges. The rapidity, the completeness, and efficiency with which that First Australian Contingent was equipped (referred to now by the men with such pride in comparison with other Empire troops) is eloquent enough praise in itself for the several war departments that met the strain, always remembering that in addition there

18

was the partially mobilised Citizen Army to equip and maintain, and the growing army of 30,000 young soldiers each year, to train. Much impatience was exhibited at the delay in getting the Expedition away from Australia. That delay was inevitable in the circumstances, though apparently comparing so unfavourably with the Continental armies that were in the field in a few days, and in three weeks numbered millions of men. Australia in times of peace had never contemplated raising an Expeditionary Force, and what reserve supplies she had were not intended for such an emergency as this. Nevertheless, the General Staff rose to the occasion in a manner which, as I have said, reflects on them not only the greatest credit but high praise. Too much cannot he said either of the manner in which the general public co-operated in the assembling of the army, and especially in regard to the gifts of horses for all branches of the service.

I consider myself indeed fortunate in having had an opportunity of witnessing the march through the streets of Melbourne of 4,000 Victorians who were to form the backbone of Victoria's contribution to the first 20,000 men. When I think of those lads on that bright August morning, and the trained army which General Sir Ian Hamilton reviewed in the desert in Egypt, one can laugh at those croakers who predicted the need for eighteen months' training to make these men real soldiers. I remember them on this morning, a band of cheerful youths (for the army is, and always must be, thought of as a young army—a mingling of freshness, vigour, eagerness, and panting zeal, the stuff that veterans are made of), headed by a band of Highland pipes and bugles that had volunteered to lead them, swinging with irregular, broken step along the main streets. Their pride swelled in their veins as they waved brown felt hats, straw-deckers, bowlers to their mates watching from office windows and roofs. It was the first sight of the reality of war that had come to really grip the hearts of the people, and they cheered these pioneers and the recklessness of their spirits. There were men in good boots and bad boots, in brown and tan boots, in hardly any boots at all; in sack suits and old clothes, and smart-cut suits just from the well-lined drawers of a fashionable home; there were workers and loafers, students and idlers, men of professions and men just workers, who formed that force. But—they were all fighters, stickers, men with some grit (they got more as they went on), and men with a love of adventure. So they marched out to their camp at Broadmeadows—a good ten-mile tramp.

As they swung round through the break in the panelled fencing of Major Wilson's property (placed generously at the disposal of the Government), there was weariness in their feet and limbs, but not in their spirits. Some shuffled now, and the dust rose from the attenuated column right along the undulating dusty road, stretching back almost to the city's smoke, just faintly visible on the horizon, where the smoke-stacks and tall buildings caught the last rays of the setting sun. And they found their tents pitched, and they had but to draw their blankets and break up into groups of eight or ten or eleven for each tent. Then they strolled round the green fields till the bugle called them to their first mess, cooked in the dixies. And the rising odour of well-boiled meat and onions whetted their appetite.

Then on the morrow they rose before the sun. Every morning they were thus early roused, were doing exercises with rifle and bayonet, and the drab black of their clothing changed to khaki uniforms; and as rapidly as this change came, so the earth was worn more brown with the constant treading of thousands of feet, and the grass disappeared altogether from the camp and the roads became rutted. More men and still more men crowded in and filled the vacant tents till other lines had to be pitched. The horses began to arrive, and motor-lorries with immense loads thundered across the paddocks to the stores, where huge tarpaulins covered masses of equipment and marquees tons of meat and bread. From four thousand the army grew to ten; for fresh contingents were offered, accepted, and sent into training. Tents peeped from between pine-trees that enclosed a field, and guns began to rumble in and were parked in neat rows pointing to the road. They waited for the horses which the gunners were busily lashing into control. It was rapid, effective housebreaking that I saw in this artillery school, where the animals were left to kick logs till they tired, and then were compelled to drag them, in place of the valuable artillery pieces.

The foam gathered on their haunches at such times and they flung themselves to the earth—and then they threw their riders for a change—until at length they grew weary of the play and subsided as fine artillery horses as ever dragged guns

Into the jaws of death,
Into the mouth of Hell.

All around the hills were green still. Each day they were covered with lines of moving troops. Infantry passed the guns on the road, and Light Horse passed the infantry and wheeled in through the same break in the panelled fence. The Commandant, Colonel Wallace, inspected the units in the making, so did the Brigadiers and the General himself or his representative. Then the State Governor, Sir Arthur Stanley, took a part, and the Governor-General spent an afternoon at the camp and reviewed the whole of the troops. The people flocked in thousands on holidays and Sundays to see their soldier sons. The camp each night was full of visitors till dusk, for those few precious hours permitted after the day's duties were done when family ties might be drawn close just a little longer. Every train and tram was filled with bands of soldiers; the traffic on the roads showed its quota of khaki. Bands turned the people's thoughts to war with their martial music, as they woke the troops with their persistent beating in the early morning.

What it was in Melbourne, so in every State capital of the Commonwealth, where the camps lay scattered on the outskirts of the suburbs. Each State trained its own men for a common interest for the First Division, and in each State the method, like the routine, was the same.

The time was approaching for departure. Camps were closed to the public. All leave was stopped. Nobody knew the date of going, and yet everybody knew it and chafed under the wait. But before the men went they showed 'the metal of their pastured.' In one never-to-be-forgotten glistening line they swept through the centres of the cities, marching from end to end. What once had been a heavy day—the march out to camp—they made light of

21

now; and while the Light Horse headed the columns, the horses prancing and dancing to the drums, the guns rumbled heavily with much rattling after the even, infantry lines. And still it was not farewell. Those tender partings were said in the quiet of the hearth. It could only be taken as the cities' greetings and tributes to the pioneers—those men of the 1st Australian Division—who went quietly, silently, without farewells to the waiting transports in the bright mid-October sunlight—train after train load of them—down to the wharves.

And the people who wanted them go were a few hundreds.

CHAPTER II
THE ASSEMBLY

While it was general knowledge that the First Australian Contingent was about to leave its native shores—26th September—no exact date was mentioned as the day of departure. For one very sound reason. The German cruisers had not been rounded up and some of them were still known to be cruising in Australian waters. They could be heard talking in the loud, high-pitched Telefunken code, but the messages were not always readable, lucky as had been the capture early in the war of a code-book from a German merchant ship in New Guinea waters. The newspapers were prohibited by very strict censorship from giving any hint of the embarkation of troops, of striking camps, or of anything that could be communicated to the enemy likely to give him an idea of the position of the Convoy that was now hurrying from the northern capitals—from, indeed, all the capital cities—to the rendezvous, King George's Sound, Albany. That rendezvous, for months kept an absolute official secret, was, nevertheless, on the lips of every second person, though never named publicly. It was apparent that the military authorities had an uncomfortable feeling that though they had blocked the use of private wireless installations, messages were leaving Australia. I will say nothing here of the various scares and rumours and diligent searches made upon perfectly harmless old professors and others engaged in peaceful fishing expeditions along the coastal towns; that lies without the sphere of this book. It seemed almost callous that the troops going so far across two oceans, the first great Australian army that had been sent to fight for the Mother Country, should be allowed to slip away uncheered, unspoken of. For even the final scenes in Melbourne, where there were some four or five thousand people to see the *Orvieto*, the Flagship of the Convoy, depart, formed an impromptu gathering, and for days before great liners, with two thousand troops aboard, had been slipping away from their moorings with only a fluttering of a few handkerchiefs to send them off. Still, the troops had crowded into the rigging and sang while the bands played them off to 'Tipperary.' In every port it was alike. How much more touching was the leaving of the Flagship, when the crowd broke the barriers and rushed the pier, overwhelming the scanty military guards and forcing back Ministers of the Crown and men of State who had gone aboard to wish Major-General Bridges success with the Division. It was unmilitary, but it was magnificent, this sudden welling up of the spirit of the people and the burst of enthusiasm that knew no barriers. Ribbons were cast aboard and made the last links with the shore. Never shall I for one (and there were hundreds on board in whose throat a lump arose) forget the sudden quiet on ship and shore as the band played the National Anthem when the liner slowly moved from the pier out into the channel; and then the majestic notes of other anthems weaved into one brave throbbing melody that sent the blood pulsing through the brain.

Britons never, never will be slaves

Blared the bugles, and the drums rattled and thumped the bars with odd emphasis till the ribbons had snapped and the watchers on the pier became a blurred impressionist picture, and even the yachts and steamboats could no longer keep pace with the steamer as she swung her nose to the harbour heads.

All this was, let me repeat, in striking contrast to the manner in which the ships in Sydney Harbour, in Hobart, in Port Augusta, and from other capitals had pulled out into the stream at dusk or in the early hours of the cold September mornings and hastened away to the rendezvous. Before the final departure I have just described on the afternoon of 21st October there had been a false alarm and interrupted start. The reasons for this delay are certainly worth recording. The Flagship was to have left Melbourne—the last of the Convoy from Eastern waters—on 29th September. That is to say, by the end of the month all the details of the Division had been completed, and were embarked or ready for embarkation. Indeed, some had actually started, and a number of transports left the northern harbours and had to anchor in Port Phillip Bay, where the troops were disembarked altogether or each day for a fortnight or more. For the reasons of this we have to extend our view to New Zealand. It was not generally known at the time that a contingent of 10,000 men from the sister Dominion were to form portion of the Convoy, and that two ships from New Zealand had already left port, when a hasty message from the Fleet drove them back. Now it became the Navy's job, once the men were on the ships, to be responsible for their safety—the safety of 30,000 lives. It had been arranged that the New Zealand transports should be escorted across the Southern Ocean to Bass Straits by the little cruiser *Pioneer*—sister ship of the *Pegasus*, later to come into prominence—and another small cruiser, as being sufficient protection in view of the line of warships and destroyers patrolling the strategic line north of Australia, curving down to the New Zealand coast. The German cruisers, admittedly frightened of an encounter with the *Australia*, had been successfully eluding that battle-cruiser for weeks, and were skulking amongst the islands or the Pacific destroying certain trading and wireless stations, and apparently waiting for an opportunity strike at the Convoy. One scare was, therefore, sufficient. The Dominion Government refused to dispatch the troops without adequate escort, and in consequence all the programme was thrown out of gear, and the *Minotaur*—flagship of the escort—went herself with the *Encounter* and the two original cruisers to New Zealand and brought across the whole Maoriland Contingent. The alteration in the plans resulted in a delay of three weeks, for the warships had to coal again before proceeding across the Indian Ocean. However, it was better to be safe than sorry, and the delayed Australian Convoy was released in the third week of October and the ships commenced to gather at the appointed rendezvous.

Yet I am loath to think that this alone was the reason for the delay. One can read now into events happening at the heart of Empire a very significant cause for hesitancy to send this Australian Contingent to England for Service in France. For matters in Turkey were already unsatisfactory. On 25th September messages had reached London of the preparations of the Turks on the Sinai Peninsula and the activity of the Germans in the Ottoman Empire, led by that extraordinary personality Enver Pasha. It was certain that every effort was being made by Great Britain to preserve peace with the Turks, but the Porte was taking a high hand, and it appeared that war would become inevitable. How far the Australian Government was taken into the confidence of the Foreign Office one can only guess. It must be supposed that Major-General Bridges, the Prime Minister, and Minister of Defence, together with the Governor-General of the Commonwealth, were in possession of the main points of the diplomatic relations between Great Britain and Turkey. Matters, too, in the Persian Gulf were very unsatisfactory in the beginning of October, and by the time that the last ship of the Convoy had left port it was certain from the attitude of Turkey, as reflected in the reports of Sir Louis Mallet, British Ambassador at Constantinople, that war would be declared. Military preparations pointed to an attack on the Suez Canal being pushed forward with all speed, and it was therefore necessary to have a large defending force available to draw on. So far as it is possible to read the inner history of events, this was the actual reason for the holding up (strange paradox as it may sound) of the Convoy until the destination of the 30,000 men should be determined. For it must be conceded that, with the Cape route open, not very much longer and far safer, with the venomous *Emden* raiding

26

Indian waters and the German Pacific Fleet ready to dart out from the Northern islands, it was more feasible than using the Suez Canal with such a vast convoy of ships. As a matter of fact, this was the route chosen. True enough, when the time came, the landing of this army in Egypt for training 'and war purposes' must have carried great significance to the Turks; and the plea of the badness of the English climate at the time preventing training in England, served as good an excuse as did the German cruiser menace in New Zealand waters. For while there may have been a lingering suspicion in Lord Kitchener's mind that perhaps the camps at Salisbury might not be ready, it was a trump card to have a body of 30,000 troops ready to divert either at once or in the near future to a strategic point against Turkey. Be all this as it may, the combined Convoys did not leave Australian waters until 1st November, and on the 30th October Sir L. Mallet had been told to ask for his passports within twelve hours unless the Turkish Government dismissed the German crews of the *Goeben* and *Breslau* from Constantinople. So actually when leaving the last port the Convoy were directed against Turkey, Yet I suppose no one for a moment read in all the portents of the future even a remote possibility of the landing of the Australian troops in Turkey. Later it was admitted that while training they would simply defend Egypt—to German plotting the one vital point to strike at the British Empire.

Let us return, however, with an apology for the digression, to the gathering up of the Convoy. King George's Sound, the chosen rendezvous of the fleet, is a magnificent harbour, steeped already in historical associations. It offered as fine an anchorage as could be wished for the forty transports and escorting warships. The harbour might have easily held three or four times the number of ships. Yet was this host of forty leviathians sufficient to find no parallel in history! True, the Athenians in ancient times, and even the Turks in the sixteenth century, had sent a fleet of greater size against the Order of St. John at Malta, had entered on marauding expeditions, but hardly so great an army had they embarked and sent across the Mediterranean. Here was a fleet crossing three seas, still disputed—though feebly enough, it is true.

Of many thrilling scenes it needs no great effort of memory to recall that Albany Harbour as those on the flagship saw it first through the thick grey mists of the early morning of 26th October. Almost the last of the Australian ships to enter port, the wind drove the waves over her bows and cast the spray on the decks. Most of the Divisional Staff, barely daylight as it was, were on deck, peering through the mists to catch the first glimpse of the host that they knew now lay at anchor in the harbour. First it was a visionary, fleeting glimpse of masts and funnels, and then, as the coast closed in darker on either bow and the beacons from the lighthouses at the entrance flashed, I could see ships gradually resolving themselves into definite shape, much in the way a conjuror brings from the gloom of a darkened chamber strange realities. The troops were astir and crowded to the ships' sides. They stood to attention as the liner glided down the lines of anchored transports, for the mass of shipping was anchored in ordered lines. The bugles rang out sharp and clear the assembly notes, flags dipped in salute to the General's flag at the mast-head. It was calm now inside this refuge. A large warship was creeping under the dark protection of a cliff like a lobster seeking to hide itself in the background of rocks, and the men learned with some surprise it was a Japanese cruiser, the *Abuki*. She remained there a few days and then steamed out, lost in a cloud of dense black smoke, while in her place came the two Australian cruisers, the *Melbourne* and *Sydney*. Each night the troops watched one or others of these scouts put to sea, stealing at dusk to patrol, and not alone, the entrance to the harbour wherein lay the precious Convoy.

On the morning of the 28th the New Zealand Convoy, consisting of ten ships, arrived, and anchored just inside the entrance of the harbour. From shore the sight was truly wonderful. Three regular lines of steamers, each crammed with troops and horses, were lying in an almost forgotten and certainly neglected harbour. What signs of habitation there were on shore were limited to a whaling station on the west and a few pretty red-roofed bungalows on the east; while the entrance to an inner harbour, the selected spot for a destroyer base of the Australian Navy, suggested as snug a little cove as one might wish. Opposite the main entrance behind the anchored Convoy was the narrow channel leading to the port where the warships anchored, protected from outer view behind high cliffs from which frowned the guns of the forts. It was from these forts, commanded then by Major Meekes, that I looked down on to the ships—that was after nearly being arrested as a spy by a suspicious vigilant guard. Each day three ships entered the port to coal, until the bunkers of the whole fleet were filled to overflowing, to carry them across the Indian Ocean. All was in readiness. It only needed the signal from the Admiralty to the Convoy and its escort and the army of 30,000 would move finally from Australian shores. This was the mustering of a complete Division for the first time in the history of the young Dominion. It had not as yet even been operating as an army in the field, but here it lay, taking thirty ships to transport (with ten more ships for the Maorilanders), in the same historical harbour where as early as 1780 a British frigate had put in for refuge from a storm and for water. It was this port, too, that two Princes of royal blood had visited; while later, at the beginning of the present century and a new era for Australia— the Commonwealth era—the King of England, then the Duke of York, had come. His visit was as unavoidable as certainly it was unexpected, for he had sought refuge, like the ancient British frigate from a violent storm; but, liking the spot, the King decided to stay, and festivities were transferred to Albany in haste. In 1907 the American Atlantic Squadron, under Rear-Admiral Speary, during its visit to Austral shores, had anchored in the broad bay. Thus had tradition, in which this assembly of the First Australian Expeditionary Force marked so deep a score, already begun to be formed round the beautiful harbour.

It will not be out of place to quote here the disposition of the troops and the ships bearing the men of the Contingent. It was the largest of any convoy during the war, steaming over 6,000 leagues. The records need no comment beyond pointing out that the indicated speeds of the ships show how the speed of the Convoy had to be regulated by the speed of the slowest ship—the *Southern*— and that the arrangement of the three divisions of transports was based on the pace of each, the object of which is apparent when viewed in the light of the necessity of the Convoy scattering on the approach of enemy ships, and avoidance of slow ships hindering those of greater speed.

In the closing days of October the message was flashed through the fleet that the Convoy should get under way on 1st November, and that right early in the morning, for Major-General Bridges, no less than Captain Gordon Smith, who had command of the Convoy (he was Second Naval Member on the Australian Naval Board), was anxious to be off to his destination. That that point was to some degree fixed when the ships left port I have no doubt, though the masters of the transports actually did not know the route until they were some hundred miles clear of the coast and the *Minotaur* set the course to the Equator. Incessantly all through the night previous the tug-boats had churned the waters round our vessel's sides, darting off now to the uttermost ship of the line—the *Miltiades* (she had English reservists on board), now to return from the lighted town which lay behind the Flagship with rebellious spirits, who had come near to being left behind, to explain away their return now as best they might. To and fro panted the motor-boats, with their eyes of red as if sleepy from overwork. The General of the Division, in fact all his Staff, were up late settling these cases. I wondered at the matters that needed his personal attention; even though the ships were to be together for weeks, still they were in a sense isolated. When the last tug had departed and the last lingering soldier been brought from the shore and sent off to his own ship, there stole over the whole sleeping fleet a great peace. It was Sunday morning.

Heaving up her anchor at six o'clock by the chimes of the distant clocks on shore, the Flagship led the way from port. The waters were calm. No white-winged yachts came to circle round the fleet, only a tug with a cinematographer on board waited for the ships as they slowly went forth on to the perilous deep, each ship dipping its flag, paying tribute to the General on the Flagship, even down to the New Zealand transports, painted all a dull warship grey. The cruiser *Melbourne* lay in harbour still, while the other warships had gone ahead to the open sea, the *Minotaur* and *Sydney* gliding gracefully through the dull waters, leaving in their wake a terrible wash of foam, as warships will. The bugles still rang in our ears, though the wind from the south blew the notes astern. Amongst a group of officers I was standing on a skylight of the dining saloon watching the moving panorama behind. To bring the fleet, anchored facing the head of the Sound, into motion meant the gradual turning of each ship so that they passed one another, and because the entrance to the harbour was not quite wide enough, the Flagship went out first, barely making 10 knots, followed by the *Southern*, and the others in their line behind. We watched her bows buried in the sea one minute and then the red of her keel, and saw her speed cone at the mast-head. We smiled at the efforts of this craft to keep pace, a smile which later in the voyage became wry at the mention of the ill-speeded vessel's name. Gradually on either quarter there crept towards us the leaders of the other lines or divisions, the *Euripides* and *Wiltshire* and their nine followers. Each ship was coaling and threw her smoke in the air, and each ship that left made a smoky trail, till the harbour became obscured like in a fog. As the *Orvieto*, following the course of the *Minotaur* half a mile ahead, now turned to the westward, astern we saw nothing but a bank of dark grey cloud, and from it masts and funnels and sometimes the bows of a ship protruding. It was all so smoothly and finely planned that it seemed almost unreal, as the ships took up their positions, our central line slowing down to permit of the other ships making up leeway. As I looked down the lines of ships each became a little smaller and a little more indistinct, until the last was scarcely more than 'hull up' on the horizon. On either hand a warship; ahead a warship. The coast faded to a dim blue, more distinct once the sun rose over the hills, but soon vanishing over the swelling horizon. It was the last link with the Homeland, and who knew how many would see those shores again—and when! It was at last the real start.

Two days out—on the 3rd November—during the afternoon, the last two transports joined the fleet, escorted to their places by the Japanese cruiser *Ibuki* and the *Pioneer*. They came through a storm, I remember, and slipped into line without the least fuss.

The *Minotaur* had signalled across to the Convoy, and soon we saw the warships that brought our escort up to five. This is how they lay beside the Convoy: the *Minotaur* a mile ahead marked the course (at night we steered by a stern light); the *Ibuki* on our right and starboard beam, a mile away; the *Sydney* on the left a similar distance. The *Melbourne* was a mile astern of the last New Zealand ship that followed hard in the track of the Australian Convoy, their ten ships ranged up on either side of the central division. The *Pioneer* turned back. Each transport was two cables length ahead of the one following; each division (on parallel courses) four cables from the other. So went the fleet with its precious Convoy into the Indian Ocean.

CHAPTER III
ADVENTURES ON THE CONVOY

Now the course set by the *Minotaur*, once the Convoy was well clear of the Western Australian coast, was not the ordinary trade route to Colombo. In the first place we steamed farther west, and then shaped a course to pass some 60 or 70 miles to the east of Cocos Islands. This was on the opposite side of that group to the ordinary track of the mail steamers. The reason for the change of route was to ensure protection. Other courses were open to us; for instance, the one which would have led us amongst the Deia Garcia Islands off the Madagascar coast. However, our destinies were guided by information received by wireless on the Flagship from the Admiralty. The troops were not aware of it, but there was a Japanese squadron operating round the coasts of Java and in this distant way protecting our flank. The speed of the Convoy varied from 9½ to 11 knots an hour, though the usual run for a day was about 244 knots.

The black sheep of the fleet—if one may call a vessel such—was the *Southern*, the 4,000-ton vessel which I have already referred to as following the *Orvieto*, the Flagship of the central line. She became the cynosure of every eye, regarded in turn with interest, mirth, derision, and finally anger and compassion. There was something in the attitude of the steamer with her great heavy bows that suggested she was always doing her best to keep up, and always she seemed to be stoking. One pictures her ghost stalking each night along her confined decks looking with alarm at the terrific pace! (10 knots) and wondering for how long it would continue. Not the least amusing part was that sometimes, gathering speed, she made spurts, and all but 'came aboard' the *Orvieto*, taking this opportunity of hauling her speed cone part way down the mast, with an arrogance that she hastily had to abandon some ten minutes later. It was never quite understandable why she was chosen as a transport, and I have heard since that it was a hasty bargain of the Government when an early departure of the force was contemplated. The Medical Board had condemned certain ships as overcrowded, and this ship was taken on as an extra vessel, thereby reducing the speed of the Convoy by at least a knot an hour. The shortsightedness of this policy will be apparent when one calculates that the ships were hired by the day. With the *Southern* absent, one and a half knots an hour would have been added to the speed of the Convoy. This meant the dropping of 36 knots in a day, which in a voyage of thirty-five days was the same as two days wasted. Now, reckoning coal at 15s. a ton, as a Government price, the cost of that first Convoy a day was at least £6,000. That is to say, probably a great deal more than £12,000 was flung away by keeping the *Southern*. I cannot help including this incident. Captain Kiddle, of the *Minotaur*, had been given power by the Navy Office to discard the vessel if she was a nuisance, and it was thought at one time of turning her into a hospital ship at Colombo; in fact, that zealous officer signalled to Captain Gordon Smith, commanding the Convoy, telling him 'to distribute the horses and men when you get to Colombo, and then allow her [the *Southern*] to return to the obscurity from which she should never have emerged.' Unfortunately, for some reason this was not done, and she remained there faithfully with us till the end of the voyage—the constant source of our gibes.

Routine on the transports was not a very strenuous affair after the hard days of drill in the training camps and the long marches.

To begin with, there was very little marching; only on the *Orvieto* and ships like the *Euripides*, where there was a certain length of deck available, did it permit of companies of men being marched round the ship. Many is the time I have sat writing in my cabin listening to the steady tramp of unbooted feet along the decks above, and the bands, stationed amidships, thumping out march after march. Never, however, could I grow accustomed to the distant squeal of the bagpipes, a band of which we were unfortunately enough to have with us. One threw down one's pen and tried to piece together some melody in the panting pipes.

Each day the men roused out at réveillé, sounded at six o'clock, and did physical jerks (exercises) before breakfast. Then they cleaned ship and prepared for the ten o'clock inspection by the officer in command of the troops, who went round with the Medical Officers and the Captain. The troops by this time would be mustered on deck, gathered in groups, learning all about rifles, machine guns, signalling, listening to lectures by the officers on trenches and the way to take cover, sniping, observation, and even aiming at miniature targets realistically made by enthusiastic leaders. At 11.30 the main work was over for the day. For an hour or two in the afternoon there were more exercises, but as the ships steamed into the tropics this afternoon drill was relaxed. The officers attended classes, and regular schools were formed and an immense amount was done to advance their technical knowledge. Besides all this, there were boat and life-belt rills and occasional night alarms to vary the monotony—but a precaution very necessary indeed. As the Convoy for the greater part of the six weeks' voyage steamed without lights, or only lights very much dimmed, work for the day ceased at dusk. Always there were guards and orderly duties, for the correct running of the ship, which occupied about a hundred men on the largest transport with a definite duty each day.

It was on the voyage that the skin sun-tanning process began, to be carried to perfection in Egypt, and later on the Gallipoli Peninsula. A pair of 'slacks' (short pants) and a shirt and white hat was enough for the men to wear on deck. They did not put on boots for three weeks, and their feet became as hard as those

35

of the mariners. One heard them stumping round the deck with muffled tramp. But the physical exercises regularly given, the rifle exercises and the earlier training, and high standard demanded on enlistment, made this first contingent into a force of young athletes.

It was the raiding *Emden* that rendered the precautions taken on the first Convoy that left Australia so very essential—a matter which subsequent contingents knew nothing of, with the German commerce and warships swept from the seas. The anxiety of Captain Gordon Smith—the naval officer on the Flagship of the Convoy responsible for the safe conduct of each transport, as the *Minotaur*'s captain, and subsequently Captain Silver of the *Melbourne*, was responsible for the whole fleet—at times turned to exasperation as he watched the lines of transports through his telescope. The dropping out of a ship from the long column through a temporary engine defect, the losing of position, the constant disregard by the New Zealand transport of instructions (they pulled out of the line deliberately to engage in target practice), and other matters, caused caustic, and characteristically naval, signals to go flying up and down the divisions. Once, when boxes and the like were being thrown overboard, providing ample evidence to the enemy, if found, of the track of the Convoy, the signal was made: 'This is not a paperchase.' At night too, when some ship incautiously showed lights through an open porthole, or a saloon door was left open on deck, after certain warnings, would buzz the message: 'You are showing too much light; turn off your dynamos.' When it came to the merchant skippers steering by stern lights hung over each vessel just above the propeller, throwing a phosphorescent light on the whitened waters, it was a task at the same time their terror and their despair, especially when orders came to draw closer together, during the nights' steaming in the vicinity of Cocos Islands. The transports were forbidden to use their wireless, and a buzzer was provided, with a 'speaking' radius of about 15 miles, for intercommunication throughout the fleet. Relative to the tension at this period, I will make an extract from my notes written on the *Orvieto*:

36

So we sailed on, drawing nearer and nearer into the middle of the Indian Ocean. Looking at the chart each day, I feel that while we are a large fleet, the largest that has ever crossed this ocean, after all the seas are very broad. There is comfort as well as uneasiness in the thought. It will be as difficult for a foreign ship to find us as for us to run into a foreign ship by some chance. However, the lads are taught to grow accustomed to meet any emergency and to muster on deck with lights out . . . . It was on the night before we reached Cocos Islands— to he exact, 7th November—shortly after our evening meal, while the troops were lying about the decks loath to turn in on such a hot night, that the lights suddenly went out altogether. I remember wandering out of the saloon, having last seen the glowing end of General Bridges' cigar, and stumbled on companies of troops falling into their lines. I got to my station amidships, and remained there for what seemed hours, but which in reality was fifteen minutes, while I could only hear whispering voices round me, and just make out dim, silhouetted figures and forms. There were muffled commands. It was eerie, this mustering in the dark. I had been in alarms at night in a darkened camp, when I had risen from warm blankets and the hard ground and stumbled over guide-ropes to one's company down the lines, but to feel one's way round a crowded deck was a very different proposition. Over the whole fleet had been cast this shadow, for, in turn, each of the ships disappeared from sight. I hardly like to contemplate what would have happened to the soldier who ventured, thoughtlessly, to light a cigarette at this moment. The Australian is a good talker, and it seems impossible to absolutely stifle conversation. The ship was strangely quiet. However, the alarm was exceedingly well carried out . . . . Yet little did we dream that this testing was shortly to be put into stern actuality. On the following Saturday night, while we were steaming with very dimmed lights, cabin shutters closed, making the interior of the ship intensely stuffy, all lights went out. Yet that night, with a single light thrown on the piano, we held a concert. But the very next night the evening meal was taken before dusk, and at 7.30 all lights were again extinguished. In not one of the ships was a dynamo generating. The fleet had become almost invisible, like phantom ships on a still sea. One undressed in the dark, and felt one's way from point to point, bumping into people as one went. A few candles stuck in heaps of sand flickered in the smoke-room. It did not take long to get round that the reason for this drastic step was because it was thought that, if any danger threatened—which none of us thought it did, with the escort of warships around us—then to-night was the night . . . .

How we passed the *Emden* on this very evening, quite ignorant of our danger and of that daring cruiser's destruction, needs to be related in a separate chapter.

CHAPTER IV
THE FIRST PAGE OF AUSTRALIAN
NAVAL HISTORY

I. FROM THE DECKS OF THE CONVOY

Taking events in their chronological order, I halt here in the narrative of the advance of the Australian Contingent into Egypt to deal with the incidents relating to the chase and destruction of the notorious raiding cruiser *Emden* by the Australian cruiser *Sydney*, which, together with her sister ship, the *Melbourne*, at the time of the action was part of the Convoy. It was singularly significant that this first page of Australia's naval history— a glorious, magnificently written page—should have occurred in the very presence, as it were, of an Australian army. Well did it merit the enthusiasm and relief that followed the exploit not only throughout India, but through the Straits Settlements and amongst all the Allied merchant service that sailed the seas. About this time the *Minotaur*, till then the Flagship of the escort, had departed and was over 300 miles away on the route, I believe, to the Cape of Good Hope to replace the *Good Hope*, sunk by the German Pacific Squadron off Valparaiso a few days before. She left at 5.30 on the evening of the 8th November with the parting message: 'Off on another service. Hope Australians and New Zealanders have good luck in Germany and give the Germans a good shaking.' This had reduced our escort to the two Australians cruisers and the *Ibuki*. It was, however, very evident that there was nothing now to fear from German ships after their short-lived victory off the South American coast, so only the *Emden* remained at large (the *Königsberg* meanwhile having been successfully bottled up on the South African coast). At the risk of tiring the reader's patience I will tell first of the relative position of the Convoy, believing that the knowledge that this great fleet, carrying 30,000 Australasians, had so narrow an escape will strengthen the dramatic interest of the naval battle when it shall be told. I intend to quote from a letter written at this time, but which the Censor in Australia, for some reason I have been unable to discover, refused to allow to be published, although approved by the naval officers directly connected with the fight and the escort. In consequence of which action, I may mention, much nonsense appeared in the Press from time to time relating to the closeness of the *Emden* to the fleet.

Little did the people in Australia, when the news of the victory was announced, know of the danger which their transports had run. The bald announcement made some days later by the Minister of Defence (when the news leaked out) that the Convoy had been within 100 miles of the sea fight, was the only information vouchsafed. Sea romances have been written by the score, but I doubt if there is any more thrilling than the tale from mid-Indian Ocean of a fight to the finish which took place quite unexpectedly in a calm tropical sea on a bright morning in November. It seemed, indeed, nothing short of a fairy-tale (Captain Silver's own words were: 'It seems like a fairy-tale just to think that when we are trying out utmost to avoid the *Emden* we should run across her tracks') that the ship for which the fleet—and no mean fleet—was seeking high and low, which had eluded capture so long, should be caught red-handed in the very presence of a Convoy of forty ships that were creeping across the ocean, anxious above all else to avoid such an awkward meeting.

In the light of what actually occurred, events previous to the fight (which I described in the last chapter) had a curious significance. I suppose that none of us at the time fully appreciated the reasons which actuated the very drastic precautions against detection which were taken three days before we reached Cocos Islands. We had boat drills and day and night alarms. 'On the evening of the 8th,' I find I wrote, 'we were called to our evening meal earlier than usual, and by dusk the fleet was plunged in darkness for the whole night. Of all conjectures for this action, the one which gained most support was that before dawn we would reach the danger-point of our voyage—the Cocos Islands—the only possible rendezvous for a hostile ship in mid-Indian Ocean. We knew that our course would carry us 50 miles to the eastward of the islands and was far away from the ordinary trade route, but still danger might lurk at this spot. Even mast-head lights were extinguished, and not a gleam could be seen from any ship. So they travelled through the night, while barely three hours ahead of them the *Emden* was crossing their path, silently, very secretly, bent on a very different mission from what she might have undertaken had she known of the proximity of the fleet. One, however, can only conjecture what might have happened had the lights not been doused.'

On Monday morning, 9th November, the troops were already astir when they saw, at seven o'clock, the *Sydney* preparing for action. Half an hour previously they had watched the *Melbourne*, then in charge of the Convoy and at the head of the line, dart away towards the south-west. Captain Silver had not gone far on this course when he remembered he was in charge, and there remained for him but to stay at his post and send forward the sister ship, the *Sydney*, into action. It was a sad blow for him and for the keen crew on board, who saw thus the opportunity for which they had been longing snatched from under their eyes. Nevertheless, he honourably stuck to his post, and I saw him gradually edge his cruiser towards the Convoy until it almost came alongside the *Orvieto*, the Flagship. Meanwhile the searchlight on her forward control was blinking speedily, in the pale, chill morning air, messages in code that sent the *Sydney* dashing away to the south from the

41

position she had held on the port beam of the Convoy. In less than ten minutes she disappeared behind a cloud of smoke. When the troops saw, as I could with good glasses, a warship travelling at 26 knots an hour with a White Ensign run up to her fore-peak, an Australian ensign at her truck, and the Union Jack floating from her after-mast, with the decks being cleared for action, they realised that some trouble was brewing, though the Convoy as a whole knew nothing very definitely for hours. On the Flagship we knew that a strange warship had been seen at the entrance to the harbour of Keeling Island, then 40 miles away. As the officers came on deck at 7.30, the *Melbourne* was still signalling and the *Ibuki* was preparing for action. The wireless calls for help had ceased abruptly, and we could see nothing but the two threatening warships. For all on board it was a period of supreme suspence and suppressed excitement. Captain Gordon Smith, Mr. Parker (Naval Secretary), and General Bridges were on the bridge waiting for the messages coming through from the *Sydney* as she raced south. Scraps of news were reaching me as they were taken by the operators in the Marconi-room amidships. 'It was Cocos Island that had called, about 50 miles away—it might not be the *Emden*, but some other ship—probably there was more than one, perhaps five!' Who was the enemy? Would the *Sydney* reach her in time? Would the other ships go? Those were the thoughts drumming in our ears. The *Melbourne*, quite near us again, was semaphoring rapidly, and then she darted away between the lines of ships to a position 10 miles on our port-beam, lying almost at right angles to the course we were taking. Obviously she was waiting to catch any messages and act as a shield against the approaching enemy should she escape the *Sydney* and try and push in on the Convoy.

Meanwhile the Japanese cruiser *Ibuki* presented a magnificent sight. Long shall I remember how her fighting flags were run up to the mast-heads, as they had been on the *Sydney*, where they hung limp until the breeze sprung up and they floated out great patches of colour. The danger was imminent enough for her to move, slowly at first, and then rapidly gaining speed as she swept across our bows towards the west. So close did she pass that I could see plainly enough the white figures swarming over her decks. They worked in squads of twenty or thirty and very rapidly, standing on the gun-turrets and on the fire-control stations fastening the sand-bags and hammocks round the vulnerable points to stop the flying splinters of the shells. The sun caught the dull colour of the guns and they shone. Masses of thick smoke coiled from her funnels, growing denser every minute. Each thrust of the propeller she was gaining speed. As the cruiser passed, there flew to the truck of her after-mast the national ensign, with another at her peak, half-way down the mast. Lit by the sun's rays, these flags looked blood-red streaks on a background of white. In battle array the cruiser won the admiration of all. Barely ten minutes after being signalled was she ready. The breeze was so light that the smoke rose in a column 40, 60 feet in the air; but as she gathered way the wind caught it, and drew it back behind, just as it caught and stretched the limp flags. And all the while were the great 12-in. guns being turned this way and that, as if anxious to nose out the enemy. We watched them swing in their heavy turrets.

Both *Melbourne* and *Ibuki* during the hours of the battle were constantly changing their course, the latter turning and twisting, now presenting her broadside, now her bows only, to the direction in which the *Sydney* had disappeared. Both were edging farther away, but always lay between the enemy and the Convoy. Warning had come from the *Sydney* that the enemy was escaping northward, and a thrill ran through the watchers on board as it was spread round. It seemed as if any moment the Japanese guns might boom with their long range of fire. At five minutes to ten we heard from the Australian cruiser, 'I am engaging the enemy,' and again that 'The enemy is escaping north.' In suspense for another hour we waited, until the message arrived at 11.20, 'Enemy ran ashore to save sinking.' Though sent to the *Melbourne*, these signals were received on the *Orvieto*, being the Flagship of the Convoy, and knowing the code, as we had the chief naval transport officer on board, they were quickly interpreted. At 11.28 we heard, 'Enemy beached herself to save sinking; am pursuing merchant collier.' Meanwhile the *Minotaur* had been asking for information, and accordingly the *Sydney* sent the message, '*Emden* beached and done for' at 11.44 to that cruiser, which, I believe, had turned back ready to give assistance if needed. A cheer rose from the troop decks and spread through the fleet as the message, definitely stating it was the *Emden* that was destroyed, was semaphored from ship to ship down the lines. By noon flashed the message across the calm, vivid blue waters that our casualties had only been two (later three) killed and thirteen wounded. I well recall what relief that news brought, no one daring to hint how much the *Sydney* had suffered. I thought, as I watched the troops talking excitedly on deck, of Wordsworth's line:

Smiles broke from us, and we had ease.

That tense two hours had bathed us all in perspiration. The troops had broken from their drill to look longingly in the direction of the battle which was raging 50 miles away. Not even the distant rumble of a gun reached us on the transports. A little calculation showed that the *Sydney* must have steamed nearly 70 miles in the three and a half hours before she dispatched her quarry. The victory seemed to draw us all closer together. A kind of general thaw set in. That night at mess, besides the toast of 'The King,' General Bridges proposed 'The Navy, coupled with the name of the *Sydney*.' Need it be related how it was honoured by soldiers?

Now that it was known that the other enemy ship was but a collier, there was no need for the other cruisers to remain in fighting trim. But before I saw the fighting flags stowed away on the Japanese cruiser there was yet another instance of the fine spirit which animated our Ally. From the captain of the *Melbourne* she sought permission a second time to enter the fight and join the *Sydney*, with the request, 'I wish go.' Indeed, at one time she started like a bloodhound straining at the leash towards the south, believing that her services were needed, when Captain Silver reluctantly signalled, 'Sorry, permission cannot be given; we have to rest content in the knowledge that by remaining we are doing our duty.' So in accordance with that duty she doubled slowly, and it seemed reluctantly, back, and went, unbinding her hammocks and sandbags, to her former post. Now, early in the morning there had come the same message sent from Cocos Island from the *Osaki*, a sister ship of the *Ibuki*, which ship, too, had picked up the call for help. This led us to the knowledge that a Japanese squadron was cruising off the coast of Java, a few hundred miles on our right, as part of that net which was gradually being drawn round the *Emden*.

It will be realised that amongst the crews of the two warships excluded from a share in the fight there should be a certain disappointment. Captain Silver's action showed that high sense of, and devotion to, duty of which the Navy is justly proud. And feeling for brother officers, Captain Gordon Smith, as officer in charge of the Convoy, sent across to the two cruisers the typically facetious naval message:

'Sorry there was not enough meat to go round.'

II. The Destruction of the *Emden*

It may indeed be considered a happy omen that the first chapter of Australia's naval history should be written in such glowing colours as those that surrounded the destruction of the German raider *Emden*, for whose capture no price was deemed too high to pay. Hearing the recital of that chapter by Captain Glossop in the cabin of the *Sydney* two days after the engagement, I consider myself amongst the most fortunate. In the late afternoon I had come on board the *Sydney*, then lying in the harbour of Colombo cleaning up (having just twenty-four hours before handed over the last of her prisoners), from one of the native caïques, and except for the paint that had peeled from her guns and the wrecked after fire-control, I saw, at first glance, very little to suggest an action of the terrific nature she had fought. But as I walked round the lacerated decks I began to realise more and more the game fight the *Emden* had put up and the accuracy of her shooting (she is alleged to have been the best gunnery ship in the German Fleet). On the bow side amidships was the yellow stain caused by the explosion of some lyddite, while just near it was a dent in the armour-plated side where a shell had struck without bursting. The after control was a twisted wreck of darkened iron and steel and burnt canvas. There were holes in the funnels and the engine-room, and a clean-cut hole in an officer's cabin where a shell had passed through the legs of a desk and out the cruiser's side without bursting. The hollows scooped out of the decks were filled with cement as a rough makeshift, while the gun near by (a shell had burst on it) was chipped and splattered with bullets and pieces of shell. Up in the bow was a great cavern in the deck, where a shell had struck the cruiser squarely, and had ripped up the decks like matchwood and dived below, where it burst amidst the canvas hammocks and mess tables, splintering the wood and riddling a notice board with shot. A fire had been quickly extinguished. Mounting then to the top of the forward fire-control, I saw where the range-finder had stood (it had been blown away), and where the petty officer had been sitting when the shell carried him and the instrument away—a shot, by the way, which nearly deprived the *Sydney* of her captain, her range-finding officer, and three others. Returning to the after deck we found Captain Glossop himself. He was walking the decks enjoying the balmy evening, and he went with Captain Bean, the Australian Official War Correspondent, and myself below to his stateroom, where he told us in a beautifully clear and simple manner the story of the action. I saw, too, the chart of the battle reproduced here. After what we then heard, what we had already seen and learned from the officers at mess later that evening (they sent us off to the *Orvieto* in the picket boat), we hastened back to set down the story of the fight. Perusal of reports, plans, and data obtained from one source and another leads me now to alter very little the first impressions I recorded of that famous encounter, which, I may add, was taken in a spirit of modesty mingled with a genuine and hearty appreciation of the foe by all the officers and crew of the *Sydney*.

It is quite beyond the region of doubt to suppose that the *Emden* knew anything of the approach of the Convoy, or of the presence of Australian cruisers in Indian waters. What she did believe was that the warship she saw approaching her so rapidly was either the

Newcastle or *Yarmouth*, and right up to the concluding phases of the action she believed this. On the other hand, the *Emden* herself had been mistaken for the *Newcastle* by the operators at the wireless station on Cocos Islands when she had put in an appearance on the evening before the action, 8th November, just at dusk. The coming of the cruiser to the island at sunset had not excited the suspicions of the people on shore, for her colour was not distinguishable, and she had apparently four funnels similar to the *Newcastle*. Having reconnoitred the harbour and seen all was safe, the *Emden* had lain off all night, and next morning before dawn had steamed into the harbour and dropped anchor close inshore. Still the people at the station were unsuspicious until by some mischance (I have heard also, by orders) the astonished islanders saw one of the funnels wobble and shake, and then fall to the deck in a heap. It was the painted dummy canvas funnel. Meanwhile the *Emden* had sent off a landing party, and there was just time for the operators to rush to their posts and send through the message by wireless which the Convoy had received, and which the *Melbourne* and *Sydney* had heard: 'Strange cruiser at entrance to harbour' and the S.O.S. call. At the same time the cable operator was busy sending over the cable message after message, which was being registered in London, of the approach of the landing party, ending with the dramatic: 'They are entering the door'—and silence.

This revelation of the identity of the vessel at once explained to the operators where the German wireless signals, that had been choking the air overnight, had been emanating from. The endeavour of the cruiser to drown the calls for assistance by her high-pitched Telefunken waves was frustrated, and, as I have said, the arrival of the landing party put a stop to further messages. Still, the call had gone forth and was picked up at 6.30 a.m. by the Convoy, with the result that the *Sydney* went into action steaming considerably over 20 knots an hour, and at each revolution of the propeller gaining speed until she was tearing through the water, cutting it with her sharp prow like a knife. It was not long before the lookout on the cruiser saw lights ahead from the island and the tops of palm-trees, and almost at the same moment the top of the masts of the 'strange warship.' Quickly the funnels rose over the horizon, and by the time the whole ship came into view there was very little doubt that it was the *Emden*. Yet the enemy showed no signs of attempting to escape and make a long chase of it (which she might have done, being a ship with a speed of 25 knots) and a dash for liberty, although the *Sydney*'s smoke she must have seen come up over the rim of the seas, probably long before she saw the ship itself. Even with the knowledge that her guns were of smaller calibre than her antagonist, she dashed straight at the *Sydney* and tried to close.

The *Emden* opened fire at 9.40 at the extreme range of her guns, slightly under 10,000 yards. She let loose a whole broadside, but while this was in the air our guns had been trained on her and had fired too—the portside batteries coming into action. With a shriek the German shells went over the heads of the men and the masts of the *Sydney*, while it was seen that the *Sydney*'s shots had also carried over the chase by about 400 yards. The next broadsides from both ships fell short, and the water was sent into the air like columns of crystal before the eyes of the gunners. Within the next few salvos both ships found the range, halving the first ranges, and hit the target. The air was filled with the sickening swish of the shells and the loud, dull explosions. As the German opened fire an exclamation of surprise broke from the lips of the officer in charge of the *Sydney*'s range-finder. That a cruiser with such light guns was able to open and engage a cruiser carrying 6-in. guns at such extreme range was disquieting. With the next shell his cap was almost raised from his head as it whistled past between him and his assistant and carried away the range-finder that was immediately behind him in the centre of the control. The man seated there was instantly killed, while the captain and another officer, a few feet away, were flung back against the sides of the control station. Lucky it was that this shell, the blast of which had scorched the men, passed through the starboard side of the lofty station and, without exploding, over the side of the ship. It was shells from this salvo, or ones following hard on it—for the Germans were firing at a furious rate, and three of their shells would be in the air at one time—that made the most telling hits on the *Sydney*. A shell had searched the after control and gouged a cavity the size of a man's body along the wall nearest the after funnel, and passed on without exploding there, but it struck the deck, scooping out a huge mass of iron before it ricocheted into the water. The five men had been thrown to the floor of the control, wounded in the legs, and while still stunned by the impact another shell tore its way through, completely wrecking the control and bursting inside as it struck the opposite wall. As the enemy's guns were firing at extreme range the angle of descent was steep, and therefore the impact not so great, for the *Sydney*, with a superior range of fire, kept edging off from the *Emden*, still trying to close. Again the enemy scored, and the next minute a shell blew two holes in the steampipe beside the funnel and exploded behind the second starboard gun, killing two of the gun crew and wounding others, while it ignited a quantity of guncotton and charges lying on deck. That, due to the remarkable coolness of a gunner, was at once thrown overboard and the fire extinguished. Great gashes were made in the deck where the bits of the shell (it was high explosive) had struck, and the gear of the gun itself was chipped all over, while one of the breech pins was blown away. At the time the gun was not in action, and when the *Sydney* doubled, as she soon did, conforming with the move by the *Emden*, the gun was ready again for firing, worked by the portside crew. Meanwhile shells had hulled the cruiser, and there had been a shudder through the vessel as a shell burst through the deck just below the forward control and wrecked the mess deck. But so intent on the enemy were the gunners that none I have talked to, seemed to have noticed the shells very much.

But what of the *Emden*? The greater power of our guns and the appalling accuracy of our fire had, in that first half-hour— when the air was thick with shot and shell and the stench of lyddite fumes filled the nostrils, when faces were blackened by the smoke from the guns and funnels—wrought fearful havoc in the enemy's ship. The *Sydney* was not firing so rapidly as her opponent, bur her fire was surer, and the shells went swifter, because more directly, to their mark. It was, I believe, the third or fourth salvo when the fore funnel of the *Emden* went with a terrific crash over the side, dragging with it stays and rigging. Each of our salvos meant five guns aimed, and each of these appeared to be finding the mark. The water round the cruiser was alive with shell that sent the spray over her decks. In another few minutes a whole broadside hit the stern by the after port-holes. The shells—there must have been fully three of them—exploded in the interior of the ship, blowing and bulging up the deck, and twisting the iron plates as if they had been so much cardboard instead of toughened steel. Fires broke out from all points astern, and it has been learned since that this salvo wrecked the steering gear and communication system. After this the *Emden*'s speed appreciably diminished and she was compelled to steer by her propellers. In this manner were the whole of the after guns put out of action, and, indeed, one of the gun's crew was blown into the water by the shock of the impact and the blast of the arriving shells. The ship trembled in her course, and shuddered over her whole length. In between decks the fires were gaining, licking up the woodwork and the clothing of the crew. Smoke enveloped at this time the whole of the stern. It gushed from the hatches and the rents in the side, smothering the wounded that lay about the decks. The iron plates became white hot, and the crew were forced further and further forward as other fires broke out. Then, too, the after funnel came crashing down, cut off near the deck, and the inner funnel fell out and dragged in the water. Already the after control had gone by the board, and another salvo shot the foremast completely away, wrecking the whole of the forward control and bringing the rigging, iron plates, sandbags, and hammocks tumbling down to the decks on the crew below, mangling them in an indistinguishable, horrible heap.

By this time the *Emden*'s fire had slackened considerably, as the guns were blown out of action. In the first quarter of an hour the Germans had been firing broadside after broadside as rapidly as the shells could be crammed into the breeches of the guns. The ship had doubled like a hare, bringing alternate broadsides into action, but the *Sydney*, unscathed as to her speed, and her engines working magnificently (thanks to the work of the chief engineer), at one time topped 27 knots, and was easily able to keep off at over 6,000 yards and, taking the greater or outside circle, steam round her victim. On the second time of doubling, when the fire from the *Emden* had died down to an intermittent gun fire, the *Sydney* ran in to close range (4,000 yards) and fired a torpedo. The direction was good, but it never reached its mark. It was seen that the enemy was beaten and must soon sink. A fresh burst of fire had greeted the Australian cruiser, which continued to pour salvo after salvo into her foe, sweeping the decks and riddling her sides until she crawled with a list. Early in the action a lucky shot had flooded the *Emden*'s torpedo chamber, and in this regard she was powerless. Fires now burst from her decks at all points, and smoke indeed covered her from stem to stern. For one period she was obscured from view by a very light yellow smoke that seemed to the *Sydney*'s gunners as if the ship had disappeared, as she had stopped firing. The gunners ceased fire.

'She's gone, sir—she's gone!' shouted the men, their pent-up feelings for the first time bursting forth. 'Man the lifeboats!' Cheers filled the air, but the next minute the *Emden* emerged from the cloud, fired, and the men returned to serve their guns. It was then that the third and last remaining funnel went by the board. It was the centre one of the three, and it came toppling down, and lay across the third and after funnel, which had fallen over to port. The fires had driven the crew into the bows, which were practically undamaged, but the ship was in flames. The decks were unbearably hot. The German shells were falling very short, the guns no longer accurate. The *Sydney* had ceased to fire salvos, and for the last half-hour individual gun fire had been ordered. The end came when the *Emden*, already headed for the shores of the north Keeling Island, struck on the reef and remained with her bows firmly embedded in the coral. It was just 11.20, and while the *Emden*'s flag was still flying Captain Glossop decided to give the foe two more salvos, and these found a target below the waterline. Still the German ensign flew at the after mast-head.

In the meantime the enemy's collier, ignorant of the fray, had come up (it was arranged that the *Emden* should coal at Cocos at 1 o'clock), and soon showed herself bent in some way or other on assisting the cruiser. The *Sydney* kept guns trained on her, and now, when there was breathing space after an action lasting an hour and forty minutes, she gave chase, and at ten minutes past twelve caught up with the collier and fired a shell across her bows. At the mast-head was flown the international code signal to stop. This the Germans proceeded to do, first having taken measures to scuttle the ship by removing the sea-cock, and to make doubly sure they destroyed it. An armed crew put off from the *Sydney* to the collier, which was now found to be the captured British merchantman S.S. *Buresk*. They finding it now impossible to save the ship, her crew were brought off, offering no resistance. There were eighteen Chinamen aboard, an English steward, a Norwegian cook, and a prize crew from the *Emden* consisting of three officers, one warrant officer, and twelve men. When these had been taken in tow by the *Sydney*'s boats, the cruiser fired four shells into the collier, and she quickly subsided beneath the waves.

Turning south again, the *Sydney* proceeded back to the *Emden* and picked up some survivors of the battle who were struggling in the water. They were men from the after guns who had been blown into the water when the salvo had struck the *Emden*, doing such fearful execution to her stern. These men had been in the water from ten o'clock, and were almost exhausted. As the waters hereabout are shark infested, their rescue seemed all the more remarkable. Arriving now back before her quarry at 4.30, the *Sydney* found the *Emden* had still her colours flying. For some time she steamed back and force, signalling in the international code for surrender, but without obtaining any answer. As the German flag still fluttered at the mast, there was nothing to do but to fire further broadsides, and these, with deadly accuracy, again found the target. It was only when the German captain hauled down his ensign with the Iron Cross in the middle and the German Jack in the corner and hoisted a white flag that the firing ceased. As it was after five o'clock, the *Sydney* immediately steamed back to pick up the boats of the *Buresk* before it grew dusk, and returning again, rescued two more German sailors on the way. A boat was sent off, manned by the German prize crew from the collier with an officer. Captain Müller was on board, and he was informed that the *Sydney* would return next morning to render what assistance was possible. To attempt rescue work that night was impossible for one reason above all others—that the *Königsberg* might still have been at large and coming to the scene. The German cruiser was an absolute wreck on the southern shores of the island, and the surf beat so furiously that it would have been dangerous for boats to have approached in the dusk. The island itself was quite deserted.

Leaving these unfortunate men of war, let me turn to a section of the chapter which is really a story within a story. For, as the *Sydney* approached the cable station on Direction Island, the largest of the Cocos Group, she learned for the first time that much had been happening on shore. The Germans had at daybreak that eventful morning landed a crew, consisting of three officers (Lieutenants Schmidt, Kieslinger, and Capt.-Lieutenant Von Möcke) and fifty men, including ten stokers, with four maxims, in charge of the first officer of the *Emden*, for the purpose of taking possession of the cable station and wireless plant. The majority of the men were the best gunners from the cruiser. Not having met with any resistance, as the population of the island is in all not more than thirty-eight whites (it belongs to the Marconi Company), the Germans proceeded leisurely with their work until they found the *Emden* signalling furiously to them. They had no time to get away to their ship in the heavy boat before she up-anchored and steamed out to meet the smoke that was soon to resolve itself into the *Sydney*.

With the other people on the station the Germans then proceeded to the roof of the largest of the cable buildings, where they watched the fight from beginning to end. With absolute confidence they seemed to have anticipated a victory for the *Emden*, and it was not till the broadsides from the *Sydney* carried away the funnel that the inhabitants were hurried below and placed under guard. With what feelings the gunners must have seen their cruiser literally blown to pieces under their eyes can but be imagined. They hardly waited until the *Sydney* went off after the collier before they seized a schooner lying in the harbour. She proved to be the

Ayesia, of 70 tons burden only. She had no auxiliary engine, so that if the raiders were to escape, which they had now determined to attempt, their time was very limited. The party, on landing, at first had proceeded to put out of action the cable and wireless instruments, which they smashed, while they managed to cut one of the cables. Fortunately, a spare set of instruments had been buried after the experience of a station in the Pacific, raided some weeks before by the German Pacific Squadron. Beds were next requisitioned, and supplies taken for a three months' cruise. Water was taken on board, and the schooner was loaded, so that just before dusk she slipped out and round the southern end of the island at what time the *Sydney* was again approaching from the north after her last shots at the *Emden*. In fact, had not the *Sydney* stopped to pick up another German sailor struggling in the water, she in all probability would have sighted the escaping schooner, which was later to land this party of Germans on the coast of Arabia. Having learned of the situation, the *Sydney* was unable to land any men on the island, as it was imperative that she should lie off and be ready for any emergency, such as I have already hinted. This prohibited her going to the aid of the Germans on the vanquished *Emden*. All night she cruised slowly and her crew cleared away the wreckage, while the doctor tended to the wounded and made what arrangements were possible for the reception of the prisoners and wounded next day. The space on a cruiser is always cut to a minimum, so not much could be done. Fortunately, her own casualties had been slight for such an action. There were three killed, five seriously wounded (one of whom subsequently died), four wounded, and four slightly wounded.

Early next morning the *Sydney* once again steamed back to the *Emden*. The task before her was as difficult as it was awful. The ship was a shambles and the decks too appalling to bear description. The Germans lent what assistance they could, but the whole ship was in the most shocking condition. The men who remained alive on board were either half-mad with thirst or so stunned and stupefied with the detonation of the guns that they did not comprehend anything at all, or were unable to appreciate their position. They had all been without water for almost two days, as the *Sydney*'s salvos had wrecked the water-tanks. The fires had to burn themselves out, and though the decks were now cooled, the charred bodies that lay around showed only too plainly what an inferno the vessel must have been when she ran shores. 'At 11.10 a.m.,' writes an officer, 'we arrived off the *Emden* again in one of the cutters. Luckily, her stern was sticking out beyond where the surf broke, so that with a rope from the stern of the ship one could ride close under one quarter with the boat's bow to seaward. The rollers were very big and surging to and fro, and made getting aboard fairly difficult. However, the Germans standing aft gave me a hand up, and I was received by the captain of the *Emden*.' Nevertheless, it was a work of the utmost difficulty getting the wounded (there were fifteen bad cases), and even those who were only slightly injured, into the boats. Water was what the men wanted most, and a cask was hauled on board and eagerly drunk. The boarding party found the stern of the cruiser a twisted mass of steel, and her decks up to the bows were rent and torn in all directions, while plates had buckled, bolts had sprung, and the vessel was falling to pieces in some parts. Nearly every gun had been put out of action, and whole gun's crews had been incinerated inside the armoured shield. Our lyddite had done appalling, even revolting, execution. The aim of the gunners was deadly in the extreme. As one prisoner quite frankly admitted to an officer, 'Your artillery was magnificent.'

The last man was rescued from the ship at 5 p.m. The captain and a nephew of the Kaiser, Prince Joseph of Hohenzollern, who was torpedo officer and just twenty years of age, were amongst those who had not sustained any injuries. During the absence of the *Sydney* a party of twenty Germans had managed in some way to get ashore to the island. Either they had scrambled from the bows of the wrecked cruiser on to the reef and taken their chance in the surf or they had been washed ashore. It was, at any rate, too late that evening to rescue these men, and it was not till the next morning that a cutter and some stretchers were put off and ran up on the westward side of the island on a sandy beach, just at 5 a.m. The Germans on shore were in a terrible state. They had been too dazed to attempt even to get the coconuts for food and drink. The ship's doctor, through the strain, had insisted on drinking sea-water, and had gone mad and had died the previous night. In the meantime the *Sydney* had returned overnight to Direction Island and brought another doctor to tend the wounded. She was back again off Keeling Island by ten o'clock, and the remaining wounded and prisoners embarked at 10.35 and the *Sydney* started to steam for Colombo.

On the *Sydney*'s decks the men were laid out side by side and their wounded attended to as far as possible. The worst cases were given accommodation below, the doctor of the *Sydney* with the German surgeon working day and night to relieve the men of their pain. The heat from the ship and from the tropical sun made the conditions dreadful. The prisoners had in most cases nothing but the clothes they stood up in. One man, who had received a gash in his chest, had tied a kimono in a knot and plugged the wound with it by tying round a piece of cord. Otherwise he was naked. The death-roll on the cruiser had been appalling. There were 12 officers killed and 119 men. The wounded taken on board numbered 56, while there were 115 prisoners, including 11 officers. Many of the wounded subsequently died of their wounds. The prisoners were placed in the bows, with a small guard over them. The cruiser, at no time meant to carry extra men, was horribly congested. The less seriously wounded were removed to the *Empress of Russia*, which had passed the Convoy, hastily summoned from Colombo, about 60 hours' steam from that port, and this gave some relief.

It was only after close inspection that I realised the full extent of the *Sydney*'s scars, which her crew point to now with such pride. A casual glance would hardly have detected a hole, about as big as a saucer, on the port side. This was the result of one of the high trajectory shots that had made a curious passage for itself, as I described earlier. This tracing of the course of the shells was most interesting. I saw where the paint had been scorched off the fire-control station, and where the hammocks that were used to protect the men from flying splinters had been burned brown, or black, or dyed crimson with blood. I saw, too, the shape of a man's leg on a canvas screen where it had fallen. Looking in at the door of one of the petty officers' mess-rooms below, I was told I was just in the same position as one of the crew who had been standing there when a shell struck the side of the ship opposite him and tried to pierce the armoured plate, though he himself had not waited long enough to see the great blister it raised, almost as large as a football, before it fell back spent into the sea. The men were below, writing home, when I went through to the bows to see the damage done by the shells that had torn up the decks. They laughed as they pointed to places now filled up with cement, and laughed at the notice board and draught-flue, riddled with holes. So far as the interior of the ship was concerned, there was nothing else to suggest the stress she had been through. The only knowledge the engineers had of the action was a distant rumbling of the guns and a small fragment of shell that tumbled down a companion-way into the engine room. And I wonder if too great praise can be bestowed on the engineers for their work in this crisis. From 9.20 a.m., which was when the cruiser sighted the *Emden*, until noon, when she left the *Emden* a wreck, the *Sydney* steamed 68 miles at speeds varying between 13 and 27 knots.

As I grew accustomed to look for the chips off the portions of the ship, I marked places where shells must have just grazed the decks and fittings. All the holes had been filled with cement till the cruiser could get to Malta to refit. Stays had been repaired and the damaged steam-pipe was working again. The only break had been a temporary stoppage of the refrigerating machinery, owing to a shell cutting the pipe. So I went round while the officers accounted for fourteen bad hits. I wondered how many times the *Emden* had been holed and belted. Our gunners had fired about 650 rounds of ordinary shell, the starboard guns firing more than the port guns. The German cruiser had expended 1,500 rounds, and had practically exhausted all the ammunition she carried.

I am unwilling to leave the story of the battle without reference to the action of a petty officer who was in the after fire-control when it was wrecked, at the beginning of the fight. It will be recalled that there were two shells that got home on this control, and the five men stationed there were injured, in some extraordinary way, not seriously. The wounds were nearly all about the legs, and the men were unable to walk. Yet they knew their only chance for their lives was to leave this place as soon as possible. Shells were streaming past, the ship was trembling under the discharge of the guns. Less badly damaged than his mates, a petty officer managed to stand, and though in intense pain, half-fell, half-lowered himself from the control station to the deck, about 5 feet below. The remainder of the group had simply to throw themselves to the deck, breaking their fall by clinging to the twisted stays as best they might. All five of them pulled themselves across the deck, wriggling on their stomachs until they reached the companion-way. They were all making up their minds to fall down this as well, as being the only means of getting below, when the gallant petty officer struggled to his feet and carried his mates down the companion-way one by one. As a feat alone this was no mean task, but executed under the conditions it was, it became a magnificent action of devotion and sacrifice.

Before concluding this account, let me say that Major-General Bridges was anxious that the *Sydney* should be suitably welcomed as she steamed past the Convoy on her way to Colombo, and sent a request to Captain Glossop asking that she might steam near the fleet. The answer was: 'Thank you for your invitation. In view of wounded would request no cheering. Will steam between 1st and 2nd Divisions.' The same request to have no cheering was signalled to Colombo, and it touched the captain of the *Emden* deeply, as he afterwards told us. But the Convoy were denied the inspiring sight, for it was just 4.30 in the morning and barely dawn when the *Sydney* and the *Empress of Russia*, huge and overpowering by comparison with the slim, dark-lined warship, sped past in the distance. Once in port, however, when any boats from the fleet approached the *Sydney*, hearty, ringing cheers came unchecked to the lips of all Australasians.

CHAPTER VI
UP THE RED SEA

At Colombo the Australian troops found the sight of quaint junks, and mosquito craft, and naked natives, ready to dive to the bottom for a *sou*, very fascinating after coming from more prosaic Southern climes. Colombo Harbour itself was choked with shipping and warships of the Allied Powers. There was the cruiser *Sydney*, little the worse for wear, and also several British cruisers. There was the five-funnelled *Askold*, which curiously enough turned up here just after the *Emden* had gone—the two vessels, according to report, had fought one another to the death at the very beginning of the war in the China seas. There was a Chinese gunboat lying not far from the immense Empress liners, towering out of the water. The Japanese ensign fluttered from the *Ibuki* (now having a washing day), her masts hung with fluttering white duck. There were transports from Bombay and Calcutta and Singapore, with ships bringing Territorials from England, to which now were added the transports from Australasia. Most of these latter were lying outside the breakwater and harbour, which could contain only a portion of that mass of shipping.

So after two days' delay the great Convoy, having taken in

coal and water, steamed on, and a section waited by the scorched shores of Aden for a time before linking up again with the whole.

On the evening of the 27–28th November the destination of the Convoy, which was then in the Red Sea, was changed. A marconigram arrived at midnight for Major-General Bridges, and soon the whole of the Staff was roused out and a conference held. It had been then definitely announced from the War Office that the troops were to disembark in Egypt, both the Australians and New Zealanders, the purpose being, according to official statements, 'to complete their training and for war purposes.' The message said it was unforseen circumstances, but at Aden I have no doubt a very good idea was obtained that Egypt was to be our destination, owing to the declaration of war on Turkey, while it seems quite probable that the G.O.C. knew at Albany that this land of the Nile was most likely to be the training-ground for the troops. The message further announced that Lieut.-General Sir William Birdwood would command. He was in India at the time.

That the voyage was going to end far sooner than had been expected brought some excitement to the troops, though most had been looking forward to visiting England. None at this time believed that the stay in Egypt would be long. It was recognised that the climatic conditions would be enormously in the army's favour, which afterwards was given out as one of the chief reasons for the dropping down like a bolt from the blue of this army of 30,000 men, near enough to the Canal to be of service if required. There, too, they might repel any invasion of Egypt, such as was now declared by the Turks to be their main objective, and which Germany, even as early as October, had decided to be their means of striking a blow at England—her only real vulnerable point.

But I hasten too fast and far. Arrangements, of course, had at once to be made for the distribution of the ships and the other of their procedure through the Canal (Alexandria was to be the port of disembarkation owing to lack of wharf accommodation at Suez). At the last church parade on Sunday the troops began to appear in boots and rather crumpled jackets that had been stowed away in lockers, and the tramp of booted feet on deck, with the bands playing, made a huge din. But the troops were looking marvellously fit—such magnificent types of men. The Flagship hurried on, and was at Suez a day before the remainder of the Convoy, so as to disembark some of the Staff, who were to go on to Cairo to make arrangements for the detraining and the camp, which of course was already set out by the G.O.C. in Egypt, General Sir John Maxwell. On 30th November, in the early morning, the *Orvieto* anchored at Suez, and during the afternoon the rest of the ships began to come in, mostly New Zealanders first, and by three o'clock our ship started through the Canal. By reason of the nearness of the enemy an armed party was posted on deck with forty rounds each in their belts, for it was just possible that there might be raiding parties approaching at some point as we went slowly through, our great searchlight in the bows lighting up the bank. Before it was dusk, however, we had a chance of seeing some of the preparations for the protection of the Canal and Egypt, including the fortified posts and trenches, which are best described in detail when I come to deal with them separately when discussing the Canal attack.

A general impression I shall give, though, indicative of the feelings of many Australians travelling for the first time this great waterway. Not half a mile from the entrance to the Canal, with the town of Suez lying squat and white on the left, is the quarantine station of Shat. It was surrounded by deep trenches, out of which now rose up Indian troops, Sikhs and Gurkhas, and they came running across the sand to the banks of the Canal, where they greeted us with cheers and cries, answered by the troops, who had crowded into the rigging and were sitting on the ships' rails and deckhouses. Close beside the station was a regular, strong redoubt, with high parapets and loopholes and trenches running along the banks of the Canal, connected up with outer posts. About 20 miles farther on we came across a big redoubt, with some thousands of men camped on either side of the Canal. They belonged to the 128th Regiment, so an officer told us, as he shouted from a punt moored alongside the bank. It was just growing dusk as the transport reached this spot. The hills that formed a barrier about 15 miles from the Canal were fading into a deep vermilion in the rays of the departing sun that sank down behind a purple ridge, clear cut, on the southern side of the Canal outside of the town of Suez. Between it and the Canal was a luxurious pasturage and long lines of waving palm-trees. It was deathly still and calm, and the voices broke sharply on the air. 'Where are you bound for?' asked an officer, shouting through his hands to our lads.

'We're Australians, going to Cairo,' chorused the men eagerly, proud of their nationality.

'Good God!' commented the officer; and he seemed to be appalled or amazed, I could not tell which, at the prospect.

Then there came riding along the banks a man apparently from a Canal station. A dog followed his ambling ass. 'Get any rabbits?' shouted the Australian bushmen, and the man with the gun laughed and shouted 'Good luck!'

The desert sands were turning from gold into bronze, and soon nothing but the fierce glare of the searchlights lit up the banks. The bagpipes were playing, and this seemed to rouse the instincts of some of the Indian tribesmen, whom we saw dancing, capering, and shouting on the parapet of trenches as we swept slowly and majestically on. The troops on shore cheered, and our troops cheered hack, always telling they were Australians, and, in particular, Victorians. We came across a sentinel post manned by Yorkshiremen, who spoke with a very broad accent. One such post, I remember, had rigged up a dummy sentry, and a very good imitation it was too. Out in the desert were hummocks of sand which had been set up as range marks for the warships and armed cruisers which we began now to pass anchored in the lakes. We asked one of the men on the Canal banks, who came down to cheer us, were they expecting the Turks soon to attack across the desert, and the answer was in the affirmative, and that they had been waiting for them for nights now and they had never come. Various passenger steamers we passed, and the Convoy, which closely was following the Flagship (almost a continuous line it was, for the next twenty hours), and they cheered us as we went on to Port Said, reached just after dawn.

In those days Port Said was tremendously busy; for there were a number of warships there, including the French ships the

Montcalm, *Desaix*, and *Duplex*. The strip of desert lying immediately to the north of the entrance to the Canal, where there had been great saltworks, had been flooded to the extent of some 100 square miles as a safeguard from any enemy advancing from the north by the shore caravan route. Beside which protection there were patrol and picket boats, which we now saw constantly going up and down the coast and dashing in and out of the Canal entrance. On the 1st December I watched the transports as they tied up on either side, leaving a clear passage-way for the late arriving ships that anchored further down towards the entrance to the Canal, near the great statue of De Lesseps that stands by the breakwater overlooking the Mediterranean. Amongst the transports were the warships, and a few ordinary passenger steamers outward bound to India. I remember that they were landing hydroplanes from a French 'parent' ship, and we could see three or four being lifted on to a lighter, while others were tugged, resting on their floats, up to the hangar established at the eastern end of the wharves. Coaling was an operation that took a day, and gave the troops plenty to occupy their time, watching the antics of the Arabs and causing endless confusion by throwing coins amongst them, much to the distress of the chief gangers, who beat the unruly lumpers until they relinquished their searchings.

The *Desaix* and *Requiem* were lying just opposite to the *Orvieto*, and also an aeroplane ship, so M. Guillaux, a famous French aviator, who was on board, told me. It carried only light guns, but had stalls for camels on the forward deck and a workshop amidships. It was altogether a most curious-looking vessel. The *Swiftsure* was a little further down, and one of the 'P' class of naval patrol boats, with Captain Hardy, of the Naval Depôt, Williamstown, curiously enough, in charge. As I went on shore to post some letters, for the first time I saw at the Indian Post Office written 'The Army of Occupation in Egypt,' and proclamations about martial law and other military orders, rather stern to men coming from the outskirts of Empire, where such things were unnecessary as part and parcel of dread war. I heard here rumours of the approach of the Turkish Army to the Canal, and it was in this spirit, and amidst thoughts of a possible immediate fight, that the troops looked forward to disembarking.

It is impossible, almost, to describe the excitement amongst the troops on board (steadily growing and being fomented during the 1st and 2nd December) as the transports came past one another close enough for friends to exchange greetings. Each ship saluted with a blare of trumpets, and then the bands broke into a clatter. Never shall I, for one, forget the departure for Alexandria, twelve hours' steam away.

The men, to add to their spirits, had received a few letters, one or two scattered throughout the platoons, and, as soldiers will in barrack life in India, these few were passed round and news read out for the general company. On the afternoon of the 2nd December the Flagship drew out and passed down between lines of troop-ships. Bugles challenged bugles in 'salutes'; the bands played 'Rule Britannia,' the National Anthem, and the Russian Hymn, while the characteristic short, sharp cheers came from the French and British tars on the warships, in appreciation. We must have passed eight or ten ships before the entrance was cleared. The men, so soon as the salute had been duly given, rushed cheering to the sides to greet their comrades and friends, from whom now they had been separated some seven weeks.

Early next morning the Flagship reached Alexandria Harbour, and by the tortuous channel passed the shattered forts (that British guns had smashed nearly forty years before), and at length, at eight o'clock, the long voyage came to an end. The men, their kitbags already packed and their equipment on, rapidly began to entrain in the waiting troop trains. It was the 5th—I call them the Pioneer 5th Battalion, under Lieut.-Colonel Wanliss, who landed first, while at adjacent wharves the *Euripides* disgorged New South Wales Battalions and the New Zealand transports landed their regiments. Thus I saw three troop trains away into the desert before, with the officers of the 5th, I boarded one for the camp at Cairo.

CHAPTER VII
THE CAMPS AROUND CAIRO

Mena Camp, when I saw it at daybreak on the morning of 4th December, consisted of a score of tents scattered about in a square mile of desert, and perhaps a thousand men lying in their great-coats, asleep in the sand, their heads resting on their packs. The men of the 5th Battalion—those that are left of them—are not likely to forget that march out from Cairo on the night of the 3rd–4th, and the subsequent days of settling down to camp, and the greetings they gave to regiment after regiment as they came crowding into the camp. On the night the first troop trains came into Abbu Ella station, near Cairo, which was the siding on the southern side of the city, it was cold and sharp, but a bright moon came up towards midnight. Outside the sprinkling of Staff officers present to meet the train was a line of dusky faces and a jabbering crowd of natives. Electric trams buzzed along outside the station yard, and after the men had been formed up and detrained, they had a few minutes to get, from a temporary coffee-stall, some hot coffee and a roll, which, after the journey, was very much appreciated. It was nine o'clock. Guides were ready waiting. Territorials they were, who had been in Cairo for some time, and they led the men out on a long 10-mile march to Mena Camp. Baggage was to go by special tram, and it went out, under guard, later.

Less a company of the 5th which had been sent forward as an advance party from Port Said, the battalion set out, pipes and bands playing, through the dimly seen minaretted city. These Australians will remember the long, hearty cheers they got as they tramped past the Kasr El Nil Barracks, situated on the banks of the River Nile, where the Manchester Territorials turned out to do honour to the new army in Egypt. Across the long Nile bridge and through Gezirah, down a long avenue of lebbock-trees, out on the main road to the Pyramids, the troops marched, singing, chipping, smoking, their packs getting a wee bit heavier at each step. Life on board ship had not made them as hard as they believed, and by the time they left the gem-studded city behind and turned on the road that ran between irrigated fields they began to grow more silent. Overhead, the trees met in a vast arabesque design, showing only now and then the stars and the moon. The shadows on the path were deep, dispersed for a few seconds only by the passing electric trams, which the men cheered. Then they began, as the early hours of the morning drew on, to see something of the desert in front of them and the blurred outline of the Pyramids standing there, solemn sentinels, exactly as they had stood for over six thousand years. They grew in hugeness until the troops came right to the foot of the slope which led up to their base. Their thoughts were distracted from the sight by the advance party of their own battalion coming to meet them and conduct them through a eucalyptus grove (what memories of a fragrant bush!) along a great new-made white road, and through the sand for the last quarter of a mile to their camp lines. Was it any wonder, therefore, in the face of this, that when at dawn next morning I came amongst the troops they were still lying sleeping, and not even the struggling rays of the sun roused them from their slumber?

How cheery all the officers were! Gathered in one tent, sitting on their baggage, they ate the 'twenty-niners,' as they called the biscuits ('forty-threes' they had been called in South Africa), with a bit of cheese and jam and bully beef. There was the Padre,

Captain Dexter, and the Doctor, Captain Lind, Captain Flockart, Major Saker, Captain Stewart, Lieutenant Derham, and Lieutenant 'Billy' Mangar, and scores of others, alas! now separated by the horror of war. That morning their spirits were high, and as soon as possible most of the regiments set out on what might be called an exploration expedition to the ridges of hills that ran along the eastern side of the camp, and above which peeped the Pyramids in small triangles. That day, I must say, little effort was made to settle down to camp, and the 5th, pioneers that they were, was the first Australian regiment to scramble over the ancient holy ground of Mena, the City of the Dead and burial-place of the forgotten monarchs of ancient Egypt. But what could be done? Tents had not yet arrived, and it was, indeed, weeks before all the troops were under canvas, though in the meantime they made humpies and dugouts for themselves in the sand with the help of native matting.

I turned back from the hill, dotted with whooping Australians, to watch another battalion march into camp, one of the New South Wales regiments of Colonel M'Laurin, and saw the wheeled transport drawn by mules (the horses, of course, being yet unfit for use after so long a sea voyage) almost stick in the sand, until shoulders were put to the wheel and they got the heavy vehicles to the lines. The whole camp had been laid out by the engineers on the Staff of the General Officer Commanding (General Sir John Maxwell) the week before. It must be remembered that barely a week's notice was given of the landing of the great overseas force, and it was one of the happy features of the troops' arrival in Egypt that they found arrangements so far advanced as they were. I remember walking along the white road, which a couple of steam-rollers were flattening, into the desert. The stone was being brought on a string of camels from quarries in the hills. Lines of small white stones marked where the road was going to lead right through the centre of the camp. It was a rectangle at that time, branching off from the Mena road through an orchard belonging to the Mena House Hotel, where the main road ended abruptly at the foot of the Pyramids; hard it was, too, as any cement, and each day lengthening, with cross sections sprouting out further into the desert. A loop of the electric tramway was being run along by one side of it, a water-pipe by the other, to reservoirs being constructed in the hills. Nevertheless, I cannot help commenting that the site of the camp lay in a hollow between, as I have said, two rows of hills running south into the desert and starting from a marsh in the swampy irrigation fields. Later on, the follies of such a site were borne out by the diseases that struck down far too high a percentage of the troops during their four months' residence there.

Day after day, enthralled, I watched this encampment growing and spreading out on either side of the road, creeping up the sides of the hills, stretching out across the desert, until the furthermost tents looked like tiny white-peaked triangles set in the yellow sand. The battalions filed into their places coming from the seaboard, where twelve ships at a time were discharging their human cargoes; while each day ten trains brought the troops up 130 miles to the desert camps. After the men came the gear, the wagons, the guns, the horses. For this was the divisional camp, the first divisional camp Australia had ever assembled. It was, also, the first time that Major-General Bridges had seen his command mustered together. With his Staff he took up his headquarters in a section of Mena House for use as offices, with their living tents pitched close by. This was the chance to organise and dovetail one unit into another, work brigade in with brigade, artillery with the infantry, the Light Horse regiments as protecting screens and scouts. The Army Service Corps, Signallers, Post Office, all came into being as part of a larger unit for the first time. The troops became part of a big military machine, units, cogs in the wheel. They began to apply what had been learnt in sections, and thus duties once thought unnecessary began to be adjusted and to have a new significance.

Of course, it could not all be expected to work smoothly at first. For some six weeks the horses were not available for transport work, and so the electric tramway carried the stores the 10 miles from the city, and brought the army's rations and corn and chaff for the animals. Donkeys, mules, and camels were all to be seen crowding along the Pyramid road day and night, drawing and carrying their queer, ungainly loads.

Besides Mena Camp, two other sites had been selected as training areas for the army corps, which, as I have said, was commanded now by Lieut.-General (afterwards Sir William) Birdwood, D.S.O. One of these was at Zeitoun, or Heliopolis, some 6 miles from Cairo, on directly the opposite side of the town—that is, the south—to the Mena Camp; while the other was situated close to an oasis settlement, or model irrigation town, at Maadi, and lying just parallel with Mena Camp, but on the other (eastern) side of the river, and some 12 miles distant from it. Zeitoun was the site of the old Roman battlefields, and later of an English victory over an Arab host. In mythology it is recorded as the site of the Sun City. The troops found it just desert, of rather coarser sand than at Mena, and on it the remains of an aerodrome, where two years before a great flying meeting had been held. For the first month, only New Zealanders occupied this site, both their infantry and mounted rifles, and then, as the 2nd Australian and New Zealand Division was formed, Colonel Monash's 4th Brigade (the Second Contingent) came and camped on an adjacent site, at the same time as Colonel Chauvel's Light Horse Brigade linked up, riding across from Maadi. Then into the latter camp Colonel Ryrie led the 3rd Light Horse Brigade.

As sightseers I am satisfied that the Australians beat the Yankee in three ways. They get further, they see more, and they pay nothing for it. Perhaps it was because they were soldiers, and Egypt, with its mixed population, had laid itself out to entertain the troops right royally. It must not be thought I want to give the impression that the Australian soldier, the highest paid of any troops fighting in the war, saved his money and was stingy. On the contrary, he was liberal, generous, and spoiled the native by the openness of his purse. Some believe that it was an evil that the troops had so much funds at their disposal. It was, I believe, under the circumstances—peculiar circumstances—that reflects no credit on the higher commands, and to be explained anon. It would be out of place just at the moment to bring any dark shadow across the bright, fiery path of reckless revelry that the troops embarked on during the week preceding and the week following Christmas.

It was an orgy of pleasure, which only a free and, at the time, unrestrained city such as Cairo could provide. Those men with £10 to £20 in their pockets, after being kept on board ship for two months, suddenly to be turned loose on an Eastern town—healthy, keen, spirited, and adventurous men—it would have been a strong hand that could have checked them in their pleasures, innocent as they were for the most part.

In all the camps 20 per cent leave was granted. That meant that some 6,000 soldiers were free to go whither they wished from afternoon till 9.30 p.m., when leave was supposed to end in the city. Now, owing to lax discipline, the leave was more like 40 per cent, and ended with the dawn. Each night—soft, silky Egyptian nights—when the subtle cloak of an unsuspected winter hung a mantle of fog round the city and the camps—10,000 men must have invaded the city nightly, to which number must be added the 2,000 Territorial troops garrisoning Cairo at the time that were free, and the Indian troops, numbering about 1,000. The majority of the men came from Mena and from the New Zealand camp at Zeitoun. The Pyramids Camp was linked to the city by a fine highway (built at the time of the opening of the Canal as one of the freaks of the Empress Eugénie), along the side of which now runs an electric tramway. Imagine officials with only a single line available being faced with the problem of the transport of 10,000 troops nightly to and from the camps! No wonder it was inadequate. No wonder each tram was not only packed inside, but covered outside with khaki figures. Scores sat on the roofs or clung to the rails. Generally at three o'clock the exodus began from the camps. What an exodus! What spirits! What choruses and shouting and linking up of parties! Here was Australia at the Pyramids. Men from every State, every district, every village and hamlet, throughout the length and breadth of the Commonwealth, were encamped, to the number of 20,000, in a square mile. An army gains in weight and fighting prowess as it gains in every day efficiency by the unitedness of the whole. Now, the true meaning of camaraderie is understood by Australians, and is with them, I believe, an instinct, due to the isolated nature of their home lives

71

and the freedom of their native land. When the troops overflowed from the trams, they linked up into parties and hired motor-cars, the owners of which were not slow to appreciate the situation. They tumbled ten or twelve into these cars, and went, irrespective of speed limits, hooting and whirring towards the twinkling city. And when the motors gave out, there was a long line of gharries (*arabehs*), which are open victorias, very comfortable, and with a spanking pair of Arab steeds, travelling the 10 miles to the city.

Imagine, therefore, this Pyramid road arched with lebbock-trees that made a tunnel of dark living branches and green leaves. By five o'clock night had fallen, coming so suddenly that its mantle was on before one realised the sun had sunk behind the irrigated fields, the canals, and the waving sugar-canes. Imagine these men of the South, the warm blood tingling in their veins (and sovereigns jingling in their pockets), invading the city like an avalanche!

So much was novel, so much strange and entrancing in this city of Arabian fables. Cairo presents the paradox of the Eastern mind, and the reverse nature of events and incidents amused and excited the imaginations of the Australians.

By midnight had commenced in earnest the return of the troops along that great highway, an exodus starting each night at nine o'clock. Again was the tram service inadequate, nor could the motors and gharries cope with the rush of the men back to the lines before leave expired. Donkey-men filled the breach with their obstinate asses, and the main streets were crowded with wild, shouting troops as a drove of twenty or thirty donkeys went clattering past, whooping Australians on their backs, urging on their speed to a delicate canter. But it was hard work riding these donkeys, and a 10-mile ride brought resolutions not to again overstay leave or, at least, to make adequate arrangements for return by more sober and comfortable means. The main highway such nights became a stream of flickering fire. The motors picked their way at frantic speed through the traffic, past the burdened camels and loaded carts of rations and fodder for the camp. No speed was too high; the limit of the engines was the only brake. By great good fortune no disaster occurred: minor accidents were regarded as part and parcel of the revels.

Whatever may have been the attitude of the military authorities when the troops landed and up till Christmas week, the very first day of the New Year saw a vast change in the discipline of the camp. It was really a comparatively easy matter, had a proper grip been taken of the men, to have restrained the overstaying and breaking of leave that occurred up till New Year's Day. Mena Camp, situated 10 miles from the city in the desert, with only one avenue or practicable approach, required but few guards; but those guards needed to be vigilant and strong. True, I have watched men making great detours through the cotton-fields and desert in order to come into the camp from some remote angle, but they agreed that the trouble was not worth while. Once, however, the guards were placed at the bridge across the Canal that lay at right angles to the road and formed a sort of moat round the south of my camp, and examined carefully passes and checked any men without authority, leave was difficult to break. From 20 it was reduced to 10 per cent of the force. General Birdwood's arrival resulted in the tightening up of duties considerably, while the visit of Sir George Reid (High Commissioner for the Commonwealth in London) and his inspiring addresses urging the troops to cast out the 'wrong uns' from their midst, at the same time bringing to their mind the duty to their Country and their King that lay before them still undone, settled the army to its hard training. He, so well known a figure in Australia, of all men could give to the troops a feeling that across the seas their interests were being closely and critically watched. After a few weeks of the hard work involved in the completion of their military training, even the toughening sinews of the Australians and their love of pleasure and the fun of Cairo were not strong enough to make them wish to go far, joyriding.

CHAPTER VIII
RUMOURS OF THE TURKS' ATTACK

News in Egypt travels like wildfire. Consequently, during the end of January, just prior to the first attack on the Canal and attempted invasion of Egypt by the Turks, Cairo was 'thick,' or, as the troops said, 'stiff,' with rumours, and the bazaars, I found from conversation with Egyptian journalists, were filled with murmurs of sedition. It was said hundreds of thousands of Turks were about to cross the Canal and enter Egypt. The Young Turk party, no doubt, were responsible for originating these stories, aided by the fertile imagination of the Arab and fellaheen. So were passed on from lip to lip the scanty phrases of news that came direct from the banks of the Canal, where at one time rather a panic set in amongst the Arab population.

Naturally these rumours percolated to the camps, and, with certain orders to brigades of the 1st Division and the New Zealanders to get equipped and stores to be got in as quickly as possible, it was no wonder that the troops were eagerly anticipating their marching orders. They would at this time, too, have given a lot to have escaped from the relentless training that was getting them fit: the monotony of the desert had begun to pall.

At any rate, on 3rd January the 3rd Company of Engineers, under Major Clogstoun, had gone down to the Canal to assist the Royal Engineers, already at work on trenches, entanglements, and pontoon bridges. To their work I shall refer in detail later on, when I come to deal with the invasion. In the first week of February the 7th Battalion, under Lieut.-Colonel Elliott, and 8th Battalion, under Lieut.-Colonel Bolton, V.D., and the whole of the New Zealand Brigade of Infantry were hastily dispatched to the Canal, and were camped side by side at the Ismailia station. Meanwhile the New Zealand Artillery had already been sent to take up positions on the Canal banks.

During January the Buccaneer Camel Corps, under Lieutenant Chope, met, during reconnoitring and patrol duty, a strong party of Arabs, Turks, and Bedouins, to the number of 300, and he gallantly engaged them and carried on a running fight in the desert for miles, successfully putting to flight the enemy and capturing some of their number, while they left dead and wounded on the sand. For this Lieutenant Chope was decorated with the D.S.O.

Fresh rumours began now to float into Cairo as to the estimate of the Turkish force and the number of Germans likely to be in it. Djemal Pasha was known to be in command, but it was said that he was under the German General Von der Goltz, who had stiffened the force with about 300 of his barbarians, mostly non-commissioned officers and officers. The Turkish force, which was certainly a very mixed host, was declared to number about 80,000, which was more than four times the number that actually made the raid on the Canal, though I have no reason to doubt that there were that number on the borders of Egypt, ready to follow up the attack were it successful. Some dissent existed amongst the Turkish force, and was faithfully reported to the War Office in Cairo, and many Arabs and some Indians captured on the Canal told how they had been forced into the service and compelled to bear arms. Serious trouble had occurred with a party of Bedouins in Arabia, who brought camels to the order of the Turkish Government, and who found their animals commandeered and no money given in payment. On this occasion a fight occurred, and the Bedouins promptly returned to their desert homes.

Summing up the opinion in Egypt at that time, it appeared tolerably certain, in the middle of January, that the Turkish attack was to be made. In what strength it was not quite known, but it seemed unlikely to be in the nature of a great invasion, as the transport troubles and the difficulties of the water supply were too great. One day the Turks would be said to have crossed the Canal, another that the Canal was blocked by the sinking of ships (from the very outset of the war one of the main objects of the invaders, using mines as their device). I suppose that British, Indian, and Egyptian troops (for the Egyptian mounted gun battery was encamped on the Canal) must have numbered over 80,000, not including the force of 40,000 Australians held as a reserve in Cairo, together with a Division of Territorials.

If ever troops longed for chance to meet the enemy, it was these Australians. The Engineers had been down on the Canal, as I have said, since January, and it was rumoured every day towards the end of January that there was to be at least a brigade of Australians sent down to the Canal. Imagine the thrill that went through the camp, the rumours and contradictions as to which brigade it should be. Finally, on the 3rd February the 7th and 8th Battalions, under Colonel M'Cay, Brigadier of the 2nd Infantry Brigade, were dispatched, and encamped outside of Ismailia. I saw these troops go from the camp. They were enormously pleased that they had been told off for the job, not that other battalions did not believe they would soon follow. As they marched out of the Mena lines (and from the desert, for they had to go at a moment's notice right from drill, with barely time to pack their kits) they were cheered lustily by their comrades, who deemed them 'lucky dogs' to get out of the 'blasted sand'. However, they were going to be far worse, and no tents; but then there was before them the Canal and a possible fight, and, anyway, the blue sea and a change of aspect from the 'everlasting Pyramids.' They entrained in ordinary trucks and got into bivouac somewhere about midnight. They found the New Zealanders there, two battalions of them. On the way down they passed a large Indian encampment, which I subsequently saw, where thousands of camels had been collected, ready to go out to meet the invaders or follow them up in the event of their hasty retreat. The camp lay sprawled out over miles of desert, and, just on the horizon, about 4 miles from the Canal, was an aeroplane hangar. I used to watch the aeroplanes going and coming on their reconnaissances out over the desert to the Turkish outposts and concentration camps. The Territorial guns, 15-pounders, were already in position round, or rather to the east of, Ismailia.

On the 2nd February the attack began to develop. It was important enough, rather for its significance than its strength or result, to be treated at length.

CHAPTER IX
FIRST SUEZ CANAL BATTLE

The Turkish Army, gathered under the direction of General Liman von Sanders, the German Military Governor of Turkey, was composed of Turks, Bedouins, Arabs, refugees from Asia Minor, and a few Germans. About 20,000 men in all, under the command of Djemal Pasha, they crossed the peninsula, dashed themselves vainly against the defences of the Canal, and fell back broken into Turkey again. Very briefly, or as concisely as is consistent with accuracy, let me review the Canal and the approaches to the waterway, and the troops that the Turks had available. Small as was the operation in actual degree of numbers, its purpose, likely to be repeated again, was to dislocate the machinery of the British Empire. The link that narrow waterway, 76 feet wide, means to Australia, is something more than a sea route. It was, therefore, not inappropriate that Australians should have taken part in its defence then, as well as later.

One day, talking to a British officer who knew well the character of the Sinai Peninsula, he remarked, 'This is a race to water for water.' He was not sanguine of any success attending an attack, though he remembered the crossing of the desert by 10,000 men under the Egyptian General Ibraham, and without a railway line near the frontier at the end of his journey. But I do not want to convey the idea that the desert tract of 150 miles which lies between the Suez Canal and the Borderland of Turkey is waterless, or that it is level. On the contrary. During January and February, when the chief rainfall occurs, there are 'wadis,' or gorges, where the water runs away in raging torrents until at length it disappears into the sand. So it comes about there are any number of wells, some good, some rather bad; but if carefully guarded, protected, and additional bores put down, the wells would make a sufficient water supply for any invading host, even up to as many as 40,000 men. Now this figure was, I believe, about the actual number of the army that took part in the attempt to pierce the line of the Canal. It was a quarter of the army stationed in Syria, and contained some of the finest, as it did some of the poorest, of the Turkish troops at that time under arms. It was impossible for the Turkish military authorities to draw away from the coast-line of the Mediterranean all of the army that had to be kept there in anticipation of a British landing at such spots as Gaza and Adana, where the railway to Constantinople runs close to the coast. Nor was the army well trained or well equipped. On the contrary, scouting parties that were captured, were in tattered garments and often without boots. Throughout the army the commissariat was bad in comparison with what it was when the Gallipoli campaign started.

Now, the Canal is approached by caravan routes from three points, a northern, southern, and central zone. Gaza might be said to be the starting-point of the northern route, and it runs just out of artillery range along the coast until El Arisch is reached. It was along this sea route that Napoleon took his 10,000 men in retreat from Egypt. From this last town the route branches south towards El Kantara. The intervening space between that important crossing and Port Said is marshy, and is occupied with saltworks. In order to make Port Said impregnable these were flooded, giving a lake of some 300 miles in area and about 4 feet or 5 feet deep. Kantara therefore remained the most vital northerly spot at which the Canal could be pierced, and next to that, Ismailia. The northern route lies along almost level desert. But the further one gets south, the loftier become the curious sandstone and limestone ridges that, opposite Lake Timsah, can be seen, 12 or 14 miles from the Canal, rising up to 800 feet in height. Southwards from this point there lies a chain of hills running parallel to the Canal, with spurs running towards the central portion of the peninsula, where the ranges boast mountain peaks of 6,000 and 7,000 feet in height. There are gullies and ravines of an almost impassable nature, and the route winds round the sides of mountains, which features made the armies on the march hard to detect, as I learned our aviators reported.

Maan may be described as the jumping-off point for the starting of any expedition against the central and southern portions of the Canal. The Maan leads a railway, and it runs beyond down past the Gulf of Akaba, parallel with the Red Sea. From Maan the caravan would go to Moufrak, and from thence to Nekhl, high up in the hills and ranges of the desert. Nekhl is not a large settlement, but, like most Arab and Bedouin villages, just a few mud huts and some wells, with a few palms and sycamore-trees round them. But when the end of January came there were 300 Khurdish cavalry there and a great many infantry troops. Nekhl is exactly half way on the direct route to Suez, but the force that was to attack the Canal branched northward from this point until it came over the hills by devious routes to Moiya Harah, and over the last range that in the evening is to be seen from the Canal—a purply range, with the pink and golden desert stretching miles between. Just out of gun range, therefore, was the camp which the Turkish force made. I am led from various official reports I have read to estimate that Turkish force here at nearly 18,000. A certain number of troops, 3,000 perhaps, came by the northern route, and linked up on a given date with the forces that were destined for the attack on Ismailia, Serapuem, and Suez. That is to say, half the army was making feint attacks and maintaining lines of communication, while the remainder, 20,000 men, were available to be launched against the chosen point as it turned out, Toussoum and Serapeum. But one must remember that, small as that force was, the Turkish leader undoubtedly reckoned on the revolt of the Moslems in Egypt, as every endeavour had been tried (and failed) to stir up a holy war; and that at Jerusalem there must have been an army of 100,000 men ready to maintain the territory won, should it be won, even if they were not at a closer camp.

Therefore, the Turks overcame the water difficulty by elaborating the wells and carrying supplies with them on the march, and they got the support of artillery by attaching caterpillar wheels to get 6-in. and other guns through the sand towards the Canal (I am not inclined to believe the statements that the guns were buried in the desert years before by the Germans, and had been unearthed for the occasion), and for the actual crossing they brought up thirty or forty pontoons, which had been carried on wagons up to the hills, and then across the last level plain on the shoulder of the men. It was in very truth the burning of their boats in the attack if it failed. They had no railway, such as they had built in the later part of 1915, but relied on the camels for their provision trains. The rainfall in January, the wet season, was the best that had been experienced for many years, and so far as the climatic conditions were concerned, everything favoured the attacks.

This brings us down to the end of January 1915. For the whole of the month there had been parties of Turkish snipers approaching the Canal, and in consequence, the mail boats and cargo steamers, as well as transports, had had to protect their bridges with sandbags, while the passengers kept out of sight as far as possible. On all troopships an armed guard with fifty rounds per man was mounted on the deck facing the desert. It was anticipated that the Turkish plan of attack would include the dropping of mines into the Canal (which plan they actually succeeded in), and thus block the Canal by sinking a ship in the fairway.

Skirmishes and conflicts with outposts occurred first at the northern end of the Canal defences, opposite to Kantara. The Intelligence Branch of the General Staff was kept well supplied with information from the refugees, Frenchmen, Armenians, and Arabs, who escaped from Asia Minor. They told of the manner in which all equipment and supplies were commandeered, together with camels. This did not point to very enthusiastic interest or belief in the invasion. By the third week in January the Turkish patrols could be seen along the slopes of the hills, and aeroplanes reported large bodies of troops moving up from Nekhl.

On 26th January the first brush occurred. It was a prelude to the real attack. A small force opened fire on Kantara post, which was regarded as a very vital point in the Canal line. The Turks brought up mountain guns and fired on the patrols. At four o'clock on the 28th, a Thursday morning, the attacks developed.

The British-Indian outpost line waited purely on the defensive, and with small losses to either side, the enemy withdrew. Minor engagement occurred from this time on till the attack, which synchronised with the main attack—40 miles away— on 3rd February. Reinforcements were observed entrenched behind the sand dunes. Now, that night the Indian outposts successfully laid a trap for the Turks by changing the direction of the telegraph line and the road that led into Kantara. They led the Turks, when they eventually did come on, into an ambush. At this post was stationed the 1st Australian Clearing Hospital, and very fine work was performed by it. Sergeant Syme, though contrary to orders, drove a motor ambulance out under fire and brought in a number of wounded.

Never have new troops won quicker appreciation from their officers than did the companies of Australian Engineers, under Major H. O. Clogstoun, who began in January to build up the defences of the Canal. They were a happy, hard-working unit, and showed rare skill and adaptability in making a series of bridges at Ismailia. You would see a large load of them going up the Canal perhaps to improve trenches, and they began a friendship (that Anzac cemented) with the Indian troops, which I doubt if time will do anything but strengthen. There were seventeen to twenty pontoons, or rowing boats, which they applied to the purpose, constructed, while the materials for other floating bridges were obtained from iron casks. In, I believe, eleven minutes these bridges could be thrown across the width of the Canal. Tugs were available to tow the sections to whatever point they might be required. As the traffic of shipping was heavy, the bridges were constantly being joined and detached again. Bathing in the Canal was a great luxury, and the men at the time, and the infantry later on, took full advantage of it. Before passing on, let me give the comment of Colonel Wright, the Engineer officer on General Maxwell's Staff, on a suggestion of removing these Engineers back to Cairo after having completed the bridges:

> I sincerely hope that you are not going to take this company from me until the present strife is over. They are simply invaluable, both officers and men, and have thoroughly earned the excellent reputation they have already acquired everywhere they have been.
>
> They have worked up till 2.30 by moonlight. Their work has been excellent. The men have been delighted with the work, and they have been exemplary in their conduct. Even if you can produce other companies as good, I should be rather in a hole if No. 3 were to be taken away.

Thus we arrive at the day before the main attack was delivered. It was intended by the Turkish and German leaders that there should be feints all along the 70 miles of fightable front, and that between Tousson and Serapeum the main body would be thrown in and across the Canal. Plans were formulated to deceive the defenders as to the exact point of the attack, troops marching diagonally across the front (an operation which had brought disaster to the German Army at the Marne), and changing position during the days preceding the main venture; but, nevertheless, this manoeuvre was limited to a 20-mile section, with Ismailia as the central point.

The Turks commenced on the afternoon of Tuesday, 2nd February, to engage our artillery at a point some miles north of Ismailia, called El Ferdan, but there was little force in the attack. Really it seemed only designed to cover the movement of bodies of troops which had been massed at Kateb el Kheil, and which were now with camel trains proceeding south and taking up position for the attack. A party of British and Indian troops moved out to locate, and silence if possible, the artillery, but a sandstorm of great violence compelled both the Indian and Turkish forces to retire within their camps.

On the morning of the 3rd the main attack was delivered. I was enabled to visit the defences at Ismailia, and was taken through the Ismailia ferry post round through the long length of communication trenches that led to the forward positions and back to the banks of the Canal, many hundred yards farther north. I saw the extraordinary pits that had been dug by the Gurkhas, in the centre of which had been placed spiked iron rails, on which many of the enemy subsequently became impaled. There were flares and trip wires round the lines, making, even on the darkest night, a surprise attack an impossibility. Ismailia post, like, for that matter, all the posts I saw along the Canal, was exceedingly strong. The trenches were 10 feet deep, and many of them protected with overhead cover, with iron and wood and sandbags. Extreme care had been taken to conceal the exact contour of the trenches, and from two or three hundred yards away out in the desert I would never have suspected that there was a post bristling with machine guns on the edge of the yellow desert dunes behind which lay the blue waters of the Canal. For at this place, like so many spots along the Canal, the banks are as much as 80 feet high, which, while they serve as a protection, do not always enable the warships to fire over the banks. Gaps, however, were to be found, and the Bitter Lakes presented suitable stations for the battleships that took part in the battle, as I shall indicate.

Before dawn on the 3rd, therefore, between Toussoum and Serapeum, at each of which places there were posts held by Indian troops, the main attempt was delivered and failed, though it was pressed home against a weak spot with some force. In choosing this point to drive in their wedge the Turks had borne in mind that the Suez-Cairo Railway was within a few miles of the Canal, and that one of the branches of the great Freshwater Canal, that supplies the whole of the length of the Canal settlements, lay not a mile away. Weather conditions favoured the Turks. It was cloudy and overcast. One would not say that the defenders were unprepared, for there had been too much quite apparent preparation by the enemy on the previous days. What was not known was the exact point of launching the attack. No doubt Djemal Pasha, who was present in person, gained much information from his spies, but he seems to have been rather wrongly informed. An early move of this adroit leader was an attempted bluff some days before the attack, when a letter was received by General Sir John Maxwell suggesting that, as the Canal was a neutral zone, and that shipping should not be interrupted, the fight should take place on ground to be selected on the Egyptian or western side of the Canal. One can picture the Turkish General, tongue in his cheek, writing the note.

As regards the defence works: at the point of attack there was a post at Toussoum, which lies not 3 miles from the southern extremity of Lake Timsah and about 6 or 8 miles from Ismailia. A series of trenches had been dug on the east bank of the Canal. They were complete and strong, practically intended as a guard for the Canal Company's station of Toussoum, on the west bank. A ferry was in the vicinity, close to the station on the side next to the lake. A mile south was Serapeum, another post on the east bank, with trenches on the western bank and a camp. At Serapeum proper was a fine hospital.

The alarm was sounded at 3.25, when sentries noticed blurred figures moving along the Canal bank not 100 yards distant from the Toussoum post. It was soon reported that the enemy were coming up in considerable strength on the south side (see point marked 47, on map) of the post. Therefore it may be taken that the enemy approach was carried out very quietly and silently, for two pontoons were already in the water when they were fired on from the groups of Indian troops entrenched on the western bank, and were sunk. This was the signal for launching the great effort, and immediately firing broke out in tremendous volume from Toussoum post. Artillery firing soon opened from both sides; the air was noisy with shell. Curiously, though the Turkish gunners had at first the range, they soon lengthened it, evidently in the belief that they would cut off reinforcements; their shells went high and little damage was done. The Toussoum guard-house escaped with a few hits only, and bullets riddled posts and rafters. Vainly about 1,000 Turks endeavoured to seize Toussoum post, while three times that number launched the pontoons, which had been carried on the shoulders of thirty men across the soft sand to the bank. There were places here suitable for the launching, for V-shaped dips or gullies enabled the enemy to approach, protected on either flank, though exposed to a murderous frontal fire from the opposite Canal bank, which apparently they had not expected. At the distance-post at 47/2 the first launching was attempted, but almost simultaneously came the launching for an attack at 47/6. Shouts of 'Allah!' were now started by the enemy south of the Toussoum post. At once machine guns came into action and the shouting of 'Allah!' died away. By this time the Turks got their machine guns into action, and were ripping belts of lead into the British post, making any attempt at a flanking movement impossible. This was, however, unnecessary to foil the main plan; for the pontoons that had been carried with such terrible difficulty across the desert were being sunk almost as they were launched. A few reached midstream—the rowers were riddled with bullets, the sides of the pontoons ripped, and they sank almost immediately with their freight. Two only reached the opposite bank. One was sunk there immediately and the Turks killed. From the other the men scrambled and entrenched themselves, digging up the soft mud in their desperation with their hands. Next morning they capitulated. Four men alone reached the upper portion of the shore and escaped, only to be captured a few days later in the villages.

An hour after the first shot was fired, the 5th Battery Egyptian Mounted Artillery came into action from the opposite bank, and the Turkish position and head of the wedge being definitely determined, companies from the 62nd Punjabis from the reserve at Serapeum opened fire from midway between the two stations on the west Egyptian bank. The noise of rifles and the intense popping of machine guns resounded up and down the banks of the Canal between the two posts. The ground across which the Turks had made their final dash was tussocky, and behind these tussocks they gained some shelter and entrenched themselves, once the crossing had so dismally failed.

It is estimated that some eighteen pontoons were launched. Some were dropped in the water over a low rubble wall that had been left close to the water's edge, others were brought down part of the bank less steep, and which offered easy access. Four boatloads of the enemy were sunk in midstream, the boats riddled with bullets, either from the shore batteries or from a torpedo-boat destroyer that came down from Serapeum at a quarter to eight. As daylight came, the Turks who still were in the water or struggling up the banks were shot down, while some few, as related, managed to dig themselves in on the west bank. The remainder of the attackers (killed, wounded, and prisoners numbered nearly 3,000), about 3,000, retired some hundred yards. As far as those in command at Toussoum and Serapeum can estimate it, after reading Turkish captured orders, a whole brigade of Syrians, Armenians, and Turkish troops, some the flower of the Army, took part in the attack; but for some reason not explainable the main body, about 12,000 men, never came into action. The initial attack failed to push back the resistance offered, and the Turks, one supposes, became disheartened, though actually the troops guarding those posts were barely 2,000. Boat after boat the enemy had hurried up till daylight broke, but often the bearers were shot down as they reached the Canal bank and pinned under their own pontoons. Dawn, no doubt, brought realisation to the enemy that the attack had signally failed. All their boats were gone. They had lost eggs and baskets as well. New Zealand infantry companies were in the trenches on the west bank, and they kept up a withering fire directly opposite on the entrenched foe. In the meantime the *Hardinge* and the *d'Entrecasteaux* opened fire with 5- and 8-inch guns, and soon silenced the 6-inch battery which the Turks had dug in, some 5 miles from the Canal, between Toussoum and Ismailia. But, entrenching, the Turks continued to fight all through the morning and afternoon of the 3rd. The British received reinforcements shortly after noon and the position was safe. But the last phase of the attack was not ended quickly.

At twenty minutes to nine that morning five lines of the enemy were seen advancing on Serapeum post, with a field battery of four 15-pounder guns in support. Their objective was evidently a frontal attack on Serapeum. Our Indian reinforcements crossed the Canal at that post, and the 92nd Punjabis moved out from the post and were ordered to clear up the small parties of Turks believed to be still amongst the dunes on the banks. About the same time a number of the Turkish troops amongst the hummocks commenced to retire. It was evidently done with a view to massing their forces; at the same time the enemy deployed two brigades in two lines some 3 miles from Serapeum, west and facing that post. The Punjabis met this attack. As supports there had been sent the Gurkha Rifles. The Punjabis occupied a ridge about 500 yards from the Serapeum post in a south-easterly line. An hour later three battalions of the enemy seemed to be advancing on the post in close order, with wide intervals between each battalion. That attack was never pressed home.

A mile north, on the Toussoum flank, the battle still raged. Lieut.-Colonel Thomas Glover, just before noon, led a force of 92nd Punjabis in an attempt to dislodge the enemy from our day trenches, which they had occupied to the east of Toussoum post. At noon seven battalions of the enemy, with numerous field guns, could be seen about 3,500 yards away. Curiously enough, these units were halted. So the Indian troops' work of clearing the day trenches, continued, the Turks sending no reinforcements to their doomed comrades. It was here that occurred an incident which was thought to be treachery, but which perhaps may have been a misunderstanding on the part of the men in the trench. As it was related officially it is stated: 'The enemy in the trenches made signs of surrender several times, but would not lay down their arms. Finally, some men of the left counter-attack got within 20 yards of the enemy's trench, and one machine gun took up a position enfilading it at point-blank range. The enemy's commander came across and made signs that they would surrender. He then returned to his own trench, seized a rifle, fixed a bayonet, and fired a shot at our men. Several of the enemy aimed at our troops. The machine gun opened fire at once, killing the commander, and the remainder of the enemy laid down their arms and were taken prisoners. Many prisoners were wounded, and fifty were dead counted by this post, where some pontoons were also found.'

Thus late in the afternoon the trenches near Toussoum were free; all pontoons in the vicinity had been destroyed; there remained but the enemy opposite the Serapeum position to deal with. Fresh British reinforcements began to arrive at dusk, including the 27th Punjabis. It was cold and raining, and during the night the enemy showed no disposition to renew the attack, though an intermittent fire was kept up. The enemy still held a small point on the cast bank at 47/8, which seemed to indicate a fresh attempt to cross. None was made, and evidently the party was sacrificed while preparations were made for flight of the main army and orders could be circulated over the 90-mile front.

At daylight on the morning of the 4th the enemy could be seen still digging themselves in opposite the ridge near Serapeum, occupied by the 92nd Punjabis. Successful steps were immediately taken to capture the few enemy remaining in the trenches on the east bank, and Captain Cohran in charge, with two companies, moved up in extended formation. Progress was slow. The enemy was very scattered, and the sand dunes uncertain. Again there were signs of treachery on the part of the enemy intimating surrender. Considerable British reinforcements had been sent up, and Major MacLauchlan, who had taken over command, at once ordered a charge at a moment when the enemy commenced to stand up, apparently about to charge themselves. Fire was directed immediately against them, and they quickly got down again into the trenches. Shortly after this six officers and 120 men surrendered.

Little more remains to be told. At the height of the engagement a Prussian officer, Major von den Hagen, was shot, and a cross marks the place of his burial, and can be seen to-day from passing steamers on the top of the Canal bank. On him was found a white flag folded in a khaki bag. It was some 2 feet square, and, while it might have been merely a night signalling flag, it is more probably that it was carried for the purpose of trickery.

The enemy lost some 600 killed and about 3,000 wounded or taken prisoner. The British losses were comparatively light, about 50 killed and 200 wounded.

Once the main Turkish Army started to retire they fled hurriedly, retreating precipitately to the south-east, while the main body withdrew into the hills. Many people have wondered since that the opportunity of trapping the Turkish Army by a rapid pursuit, when all the cavalry was available, and when camel trains were ready to move off in support, was not seized. As a matter of fact, orders were issued for a pursuing force to leave on the evening of the 4th, but early in the morning of the 5th countermanding orders came through. As the Australian troops and the New Zealanders I referred to as being in reserve near Ismailia station were to form a part of the pursuing force, it was to them a keen blow. I rather suspect that the countermanding came from the War Office and Lord Kitchener, who understood the Moslem mind so clearly. For I have it from the lips of the officer, Lieut.-Colonel Howard, who was out on many reconnaissances to the eastern hills, that it was probably a good thing that the counter-attack had not been persisted in, for the Turks, on the evening of the 4th, when the whole of the main body so unexpectedly withdrew to the ridges, took up a thoroughly well entrenched position, which he thought it was reasonable to regard as an ambush. Patrols subsequently went into the hills and destroyed some of the wells that had been sunk, cleared up many points of doubts about the attack, and captured camel trains and provisions. By the end of the week not a Turk was within 60 miles of the Canal.

PART II

THE ANZAC CAMPAIGN

CHAPTER X
THE PLAN OF ATTACK

The first bombardment of the Turkish forts at the entrance to the Dardanelles by British and French squadrons started at 8 a.m. on 19th February 1915, and at dusk the warships had to be withdrawn, with the Turkish Kum Kale batteries still firing. On the 25th operations were resumed with the *Queen Elizabeth*, *Agamemnon*, and *Irresistible* in the fight. By 4th March the outer forts had been silenced, and the way lay clear to the inner ring of forts in the vicinity of Dardanus. Meanwhile the Turks had brought down howitzer batteries, which they carefully entrenched amongst the hills round the shores of Erenkeui Bay, and peppered the warships. For the next week there was a systematic bombardment from the ships inside the Straits, with indirect fire from the *Queen Elizabeth*'s 15-in. guns, and the *Agamemnon* and *Ocean*, from the Gulf of Saros near Gaba Tepe, across the peninsula. Though the Turkish forts (9-in. and 10-in. guns) at Seddul Bahr, Morto Bay, and Kum Kale had been destroyed, the Turks had entrenched themselves round the ruins of the forts, and no landing was possible.

Now, about this time there arose what will probably be recorded in after years as the great conflict of opinion between Admiral

Carden and Admiral De Robeck as to the advisability of forcing the Dardanelles with the ships now assembled. To this conference of Admirals came General Sir Ian Hamilton, having travelled by the swift destroyer *Phaeton* to the Dardanelles, arriving on 17th March at Tenedos, the headquarters of the fleet at that time. There he was met by General D'Amade, who had also arrived with 20,000 French troops to join the Army Expedition. One may picture that council of three Admirals and two army leaders. Admiral Carden the same day resigned for 'health reasons.' He did not favour the direct attack, and Admiral De Robeck, who did, took command. General D'Amade had sided with the retiring Admiral, while General Hamilton and the French Admiral, Guepratte, were in favour of the immediate strong attack.

Consequently, the following day this operation was launched. General Hamilton saw it from the decks of a destroyer, on which he went into the thick of the fray. Later I heard his description of that fight, and the manner in which the *Bouvet* had steamed to her doom in two minutes as she left the firing line, while the British ships *Irresistible* and *Ocean* sank more slowly and their crews were rescued.

Close as had the ships crept to the towering forts of Point Kephez, there was no silencing the forts, and the attempt was given up—a failure. The *Gaulois* and *Inflexible* had both been badly damaged, and sought refuge near Rabbit Islands.

It was not till after the campaign that the Turks were prepared to admit that a little more force and the forts would have fallen— a little grater sacrifice of ships; yet I learned from General Hamilton's Staff that the Allies expected, and were prepared, to lose twelve ships.

So under such inauspicious circumstances the military operation began: yet not immediately. With all speed General Hamilton returned to Alexandria, having found in the meantime—I have, no doubt, to his chagrin and disgust—that the ships ready to embark troops contained certainly the equipment and gear, but all wrongly packed. A rearrangement was essential. This delay caused a revision of the whole of the plans of the Allies. Instead of there being a force immediately available to support the action of the ships which had battered the forts and crushed down the Turks, an intermittent bombardment, as the weather permitted, had to be kept up for a month, to prevent the Turks repairing effectively their destroyed forts, while the whole of the army was properly arranged and the transports collected. General Hamilton's army, therefore, became an invading host instead of a supporting force, landed to hold what the fleet had won. It was very patent to the War Council that now to force the Dardanelles by sending ships forward alone (even with the mine fields cleared) was impossible, and, committed to a campaign, resort had to be made to a landing.

The Turks during the month's respite, in March–April, commenced thoroughly to entrench the Gallipoli Peninsula against the execution of the Allies' plans. These plans, speaking broadly, may be thus briefly described, leaving the story of the landing to explain the details: the peninsula, regarded from its topographical aspect, was naturally fortified by stern hills, which reduced the number of places of possible landings. So in the very nature of things it was necessary for the leader of such an expedition to attack at as many landings as possible and to push home only those which were most vital. This would prevent the enemy from being able to anticipate the point where the attack was to be delivered and concentrate troops there. During April the army was assembled at Lemnos—British, Australian, French, and Indian troops, drawn from Egypt. To the British was assigned the task of taking the toe of the peninsula; to the French the feint on the Kum Kale forts and the landing along the Asia Minor coast. The Australians were to thrust a 'thorn' into the side of the Turks at Gaba Tepe, which was opposite Maidos, the narrowest portion of the peninsula. Certain other troops, mostly Australians, were to make a feint at the Bulair lines, while feints were also planned by warships at Enos and Smyrna. Two attacks only were to be pushed home—the Australians at Gaba Tepe and the British (afterwards to be supported by the French) at Cape Helles, at the toe of the peninsula.

Officers of all the forces inspected the coast-lines in the various sections allotted them, from the decks of the warships bombarding the entrenchments and fortifications, which it was only too apparent that the Turks had effected in the months of warning and interval that had been given them. It looked, as it was, a desperate venture. Everything certainly hung on the successful linking up of the two landed armies round the foot of the great Kelid Bahr position, that lay like another rock of Gibraltar, protecting the Turkish Asiatic batteries at Chanak and Nagara from direct fire from the warships hammering at the entrance to the Straits and from the Gulf of Saros. But once the communications to this fortified hill were broken, it was regarded as certain that the Narrows would be won, and once field guns began to play directly on the rear of the forts at Kelid Bahr, unable to reply behind them up the peninsula, that the position would be gained.

Anxious not to miss the scene of the landing, I had made plans with my friend Mr. W. T. Massey, the correspondent of the *Daily Telegraph*, to reach an island nearest to the entrance to the Dardanelles—Imbros. It was while trying to make these plans that one day we saw General Hamilton, from whom we had already received courteous replies to letters asking for permission to witness the landing. The Commander-in-Chief told us it was outside his power to grant this request. What he told us later is worthy of record. The same wiry leader, energetic yet calm, his voice highly pitched, as I had remembered it during many trips with him as the Inspector-General of the Oversea Forces, round the camps of Victoria, he now greeted me cordially and spoke of his regret at being unable to offer us his help. As he spoke he paced up and down the bare room, with just a writing-desk in it, in a building situated in the centre of the town of Alexandria, which was the first base of the great Mediterranean Expedition.

'I believe that the Press should have representatives with the forces,' he began, 'to tell the people what is being done. If the war is to succeed, you must interest the democracy first, for it is the democracy's war. By all means have censorship, but let your articles be written by a journalist, and not literary men who think they are journalists. The trained man who knows how to interest people in things that cannot matter to the army is the fellow needed.

However, it has been decreed otherwise, and I can do nothing. You are free British subjects, nevertheless, and can always take a ticket to the nearest railway-station. If it is possible, I shall do all I can to help you.'

We wished the General success and left him, receiving then, as always, the greatest courtesy in all our dealings with the General staff. It was an encouraging attitude, we felt, and for this reason we decided to land on Imbros and wait an opportunity to reach the mainland after the troops had advanced. I may say here that General Hamilton, true to his promise, did make a great exception for me later, and I was enabled to spend July and August on the peninsula itself. For the present, on a Greek steamer of uncertain tonnage, carrying a mixed cargo that included onions, garlic, and much oil and fish, I left for the islands lying round the entrance to the Dardanelles. I quitted the vessel at Castro, the capital of Lemnos Island (if a wretched little township with a decayed fort dominating it might be called a capital); and curiously enough, just afterwards that vessel was boarded by a British destroyer and sent to Malta for carrying flour to Dedeagatch, a Bulgarian port. Flour had been declared contraband since we had left Alexandria, for Turkey had obtained enormous supplies, 500,000 tons I was told it was estimated at, through the agency of King Ferdinand.

My experiences of being in 'The War Zone' were only beginning. At Castro I was arrested on landing, and asked if I did not know that the island was under the command of the Admiral. This was the British Admiral, Admiral de Robeck, though I did not know, but might easily have guessed, for the whole of the assembled fleet of transports, as well as the Allied battleships, were sheltered at Mudros at this time, waiting for the day to be determined on for the landing—this event subject now to the weather. Once already plans had been postponed. It was not until the 25th it was agreed that it would be possible to have a sufficiently long and fine spell of calm seas and a favourable phase of the moon to make the attempt. I had already experienced something of the storms of the Mediterranean on my journey north. For two days the sea had been running high and we were tossed about like a cockleshell.

What, then, of small destroyers and landing-barges! By the time, however, we had passed the Dardanelles on our way to Lemnos the sea had grown perfectly calm again, and in the distance I could hear the boom of the guns—a solemn, stately knell it seemed at that time, as of a Nation knocking at the door of another Nation, a kind of threat, behind which I knew lay the power of the army.

I managed at Castro to assuage the worst fears of the British officer, that I was a spy, and to assure him that I had a friend in General Hamilton, and that I had merely come for a 'look round.' Yes, I was told, I might go to Mudros Harbour, since I seemed to know the fleets were there, but I should be detained there pending the pleasure of the authorities, who were to determine when it would be safe to release me with the news I might obtain. The Greek gendarmes heartily cooperated in detaining me under observation until the next morning, and then I was permitted, on giving an undertaking not to visit Mudros, to set out for the hot springs at Thermia with the object of taking a bath.

At this spot was a mountain, Mount Elias, and from it I, marvelling at the sea power of Great Britain, looked down on to the wonderful crowded harbour of Mudros. I saw the vast fleet lying placidly at anchor. With powerful glasses I could detect the small boats and the men landing on the slopes and dashing up the shore for practice. How far the real from this make-believe! Reluctantly, after hours of watching, I left this grandstand, having seen trawlers, warships, transports, coming and going along the tortuous channel to the harbour, which was protected by skilfully placed nets and guarded by active little patrol-boats.

I found trace of the 3rd Australian Brigade round this charming valley at the foot of the mountain, for they had visited the springs for the same purpose that I had done—the luxury of a warm bath—and left a recommendation with the proprietor, which he treasures to this day, as to the value of the mineral waters. In the distance I could always hear the slow booming of the guns at the Dardanelles. I returned to Castro, satisfied that the time was nearly ripe, and forthwith determined to leave the island, where, obviously, I was cramped and would find no means of seeing the landing.

It rained, to make matters more miserable; but my stay was not without interest. One day the Greek Admiral came ashore in his yacht and was received by the Governor of the island. From the inhabitants, many of whom were Turks, who knew all about the peninsula, having tended their flocks for many years at the Dardanelles shores, I gained my first knowledge of the fields of battle I was later to visit. These Turks were mostly taken up with living in the cafés and singing and dancing to curious rhythmic music, not unpleasantly tuned, but played by some execrable violinists. Most of the dances showed a distinct Russian trait.

Let me remark here in passing that the Greek caïques, or sailing-boats, were all this time leaving this harbour for Bulgarian and Turkish posts along the coast (one offered to land me on the Gulf of Saros). The British officer at Castro told me he was there to stop the leakage of news. I asked if he thought it possible for information to be smuggled from the island. He replied in the negative; but I told him that I thought he was mistaken; for I had obtained much information of a general character about the fleet and about other correspondents interned at Mudros at the time, from various Greeks who had come across as traders to the capital, and it seemed to me to have been an easy matter for news to have been taken by the caïques to the Bulgarian coast. In fact, one man I now suspect of having been a spy (he was selling wine and came back with me when I left the island). I said so to the British officer, but he only smiled and advised me to leave for Salonika, as being the most suitable spot for me in the Ægean. As a matter of fact, I half-suspect that he had orders to 'remove the correspondent,' and that satisfied me that, as the Tommies would say, 'there was something doing.' I left for Mitylene, an island close to the Asia Minor coast, where I had learned that more news was to be obtained and could be got away. Moreover, it enabled me to write what I had learned on the undelectable island of Mudros. Long will I remember those four days.

I knew now, however, that the plans were ripe, that the day was close at hand for the landing. The whole island knew it, and I have no doubt (having watched the officers travelling on the warship up and down the coast of Gallipoli while the bombardment continued, by which means the leaders learned the nature of their task) that the Turks gained the same information as well, if, indeed, the actual plans had not been already betrayed by the Queen of Greece into the hands of her august and Germanic brother, William.

ANZAC! In April—a name unformed, undetermined: June—and the worth of a Nation and Dominion proved by the five letters— bound together, by the young army's leader, Lieut.-General Sir W. Birdwood, in the inspired 'Anzac'—Australian, New Zealand Army Corps.

In reality, the first battle of Anzac began when the transports commenced to steam out of the great harbour of Mudros on Saturday afternoon, 24th April. All that was needed for the swift commencement of the deep-laid plan was a perfectly calm sea. This condition General Sir Ian Hamilton had, as he sent forth, under the care of the Navy and Rear-Admiral Thursby, his fine army of Australians and New Zealanders. Already on the evening of the 23rd, the covering force for the British landing at Cape Helles, which had been entrusted to the 29th Division, had steamed to Tenedos, where the fleet lay enchained as in the story of ancient Troy, waiting for the remainder of the ships, which on the morning of the 24th began to stand off Tenedos. It was as if the shipping of the Levant had been suddenly diverted to lock the gates of the waterway leading to the heart of the Turkish Empire, for the sea was covered with ships—ships one-funnelled, two or four-funnelled; ships that were guarded by giant battleships and destroyers and escorted up to the land; and tiny little ships—scouts, picket boats, pinnaces, and trawlers.

The majestic battleships led the lines from the great harbour amidst the beating of drums and ringing cheers from the crowded French and British transports that formed a channel down which each Division steamed from the port. With their minds set to the last task, the very test of themselves as soldiers, the Australians lay most of the night on the decks of the transports. On the battleship *Queen*, 1,500 of the finest men of the 3rd Brigade attended a short service held by the Padre, and heard the stirring message from the Admiral and the Army. Then for six hours of ease and smoke and chat with the Navy. Here was the beginning of the mutual admiration that grew in the hearts of the two services—in the one for England's mariners of old, in the other for the spirit of the young, vigorous, and physically great Nation.

By dusk on that April evening, as calm as any spring night, and as cool as the troops would know it in Melbourne, a long string of transports, battleships, torpedo boats, pinnaces, and row boats were slipping through the waters round the western headland of Imbros Island, where a lighthouse blinked its warning, towards the mountainous shores of Gallipoli.

In a bight in the land the ships lay awhile, their numbers increasing as the hours drifted on. Down on the troopships' decks the men were quietly singing the sentimental ditties of 'Home and Mother,' or chatting in a final talk, yarning of the past—the future, so imminent now, left to take care of itself—until they were borne within a distance when silence was essential to success. Then they clenched their teeth. Leaders, instructed in the plan, knew exactly what their objectives were to be, though nothing but dark, hazy hills could they see in the dropping rays of the moon. Again and again they had rehearsed it, had placed their fingers on the knolls that the enemy held—just then in what numbers they did not know, but could only guess—went carefully through each operation of getting the troops from the ships to the shore and on those hills. Once finally now they went over it all, calmly, ever so calmly, calculating every step that they were to advance.

Midnight. The moon still hung obstinately above the horizon, tipping with silver the island mountain peaks towering over the fleet. The smoke trickled from the funnels of the huge battleships that surrounded, and mingled between the transports; it rolled in thick, snaky coils from the funnels of the low destroyers panting alongside the ships, ready for their mission. Over the whole of that army, 30,000 men, there hung a lifetime of suspense. Would the moon never go down! On the battleships, where companies of the 3rd Australian Brigade—the covering party—were waiting quietly, parting instructions were given. The voices of the high officers sounded crisp and deathly calm in the night. Against the grim, grey decks of the warships the waiting men were as patches of deeper shadow, circled by a ring of luminous paint. That line separated them into boat loads. Down the steel sides silently were dripped the rope ladders. So soon as the moon would descend, so soon would the men go down these into the destroyers—as elsewhere off that Gallipoli Peninsula, thousands would go over the sides of other destroyers waiting to dash to the shore.

Three o'clock and still the moon was above the horizon, but just above it. It dipped. The opaque light faded from the sky. That intense darkness which precedes dawn settled on the sea. It blotted out even the faint line of the hills. The transports steamed forward to their appointed stations off the coast. The mystery of it! The silent, terrible power of an organised fighting machine! The wheels set in motion! Alongside of each ship came the destroyers, and alongside them in turn drifted the strings of boats into which the troops had to go on the last stage of their journey. Already the men, fully equipped with their heavy packs, greatcoats, and weapons of war, were drawn up on the decks. No unnecessary word was spoken now. I believe that the troops had so much to think of, that the thought of bullets did not enter their mind at that time. Those that did not carry a pick, had a spade; and every man carried a special entrenching tool. All had bags for filling with sand, wire-cutters, to say nothing of three days' rations in their haversacks, and their packs besides. They had 200 rounds of ammunition per man. Their rifles they tucked away under their arms, gripping them with their elbows. This left their hands free. So down four ladders they dropped over the sides of the battleships and transports on to the decks of the destroyers. They were crowded there; no room to move at all. To the unknown hostile strand they went. The last 2 miles was a race against time, for soon now the Turks would know of the landing. At least, they knew not at which point it would come, so they prepared the whole of the beaches. Later I shall tell you exactly how. It was four o'clock in the morning, and bitterly cold. The men said they remembered that much, and the last warm breakfast of coffee and rolls that they had on deck; they remembered little else than that. They had a rifle and no target that they could see.

Now the Army Corps had, as I have told elsewhere, a covering force chosen specially and assiduously practised in landing on Mudros beaches—the 3rd Brigade, under Colonel Maclagan. This daring force was to blaze the way, or brush aside, in a military sense, any obstruction of the enemy; barely 3,500 men, on whom the reputation of an army and a Nation was staked.

To be more exact. At 2.30 a.m. the transports, together with the tows and the destroyers, steamed in to within 4 miles of the coast. The moon was sinking slowly, and the silver haze it cast in the heavens, back of the island of Imbros, may have silhouetted the ships dimly and served as a warning for the Turks. Probably the ships came undetected, but no sight of land could be seen, not even a signal light. From the battleship *Queen*, lying but a mile off the promontory of Gaba Tepe, all directions were given and the attack commanded.

Six bells and 'All's well' still with the adventure. No smoking is allowed. Fierce oaths rap out at thoughtless soldiers who, by a simply act, might imperil the lives of all. Has a signal light on shore any significance? Nothing happens; so all believe it was not. The murmurs of the men had been lowered to whispers as they had last talks and confidences and chats over the 'game afoot.' It was only 12 miles across from Imbros to the intended point of disembarkation, but at a slow 4-knot speed, what length those three hours! Suddenly in the midst of all the whisperings and lapping of the waves on the black fleet, a ray of light stretches like a gaunt white arm far into the sky, and begins to sweep round stiffly behind the rugged hill. It rests down south at the entrance to the Straits, and then, as if satisfied in its search, roves idly along, until suddenly as it appeared, it vanishes. Yes, the fleets had escaped detection surely, for the light came from Chanak Fort, where the restless Turk spent another night in trembling anticipation. Often after did we see that wandering restless ray, with others, go streaming down the Straits in search of victims on which to train the fortress guns. That night, so well planned was the attack, it found naught of the ships lying concealed behind Tenedos, and which so few hours later, were to set forth, British manned, at the time the Australians were hurling themselves ashore on the narrow cove that goes down to history named after them—Anzac.

Only a general idea of the shore on which the army corps was to set foot had been gained by the leaders from the decks of warships. It revealed to them, just north of Gaba Tepe, a short strip of beach, little more than a hundred yards in length, with a low plain behind it, out of which rose up the ridges and foothills, ending in the great ridge of Sari Bair and culminating in Koja Chemin Tepe (Hill 971), the objective of the Army Corps. There was to be a descent on this beach, so it was planned, and a turn north-east up along a plateau or ridge that rose rapidly to the crowning hill. Gaba Tepe itself was a headland in which the Turks had concealed batteries of machine guns to enfilade this landing and other beaches, but which same point had served for weeks as a good target for the warships. This point was to be stormed and held.

The 2½-knot current that sweeps along the coast from the mouth of the Straits, bore the bows of heavily laden but shallow draft lifeboats and barges down the Gulf farther than was intended, and so the landing beach was mistaken in the dark. The attack once launched, there was no withdrawal or remedy, so the troops began to pour ashore a mile farther along the coast to the north than was intended; not, on landing, to reach a plain, but to be faced with terrible hills and deep ravines. But was it so awful an error? Chance had carried in her womb a deeply significant advantage, for at the original point the beach had been carefully prepared with barbed wire, that ran down into the very water. Trenches lined the shore—making similar obstacles to those the British troops faced 9 miles at Helles. So Chance guided the boats into a natural cove, certainly not very large—just a segment of a circle some 400 yards long. Never anticipating an attack at the foot of such a ridge, the Turks had dug but few trenches to protect this spot, more so as the whole of the beach might be commanded by machine guns, concealed in certain knolls. Around the northern point of the cove, however, the breach broadened out again into what, in winter, was a marsh about 200 yards wide, which eventually, towards Suvla Bay, opened out into the marshes and plains of Suvla Bay and the valley that leads up to the Anafarta villages.

Unwittingly, into the cove and around its northern point, Ari Burnu, the first boats were towed by destroyers and pinnaces until, the water shallowing, the ropes were cast off and a naval crew of four, with vigorous strokes, pushed on until a splutter of rifles proclaimed that the Turks had realised the purpose. The battle opened at 4.17 a.m. The racket of the rifles reached the ears of the other brigades, locked still in the transports, while the 3rd Brigade, men of the 9th, 10th, 11th, and 12th Battalions, went ashore to form the screen for the landing army—the 9th (Queensland) Battalion led by Lieut.-Colonel Lee, the 10th (South Australian) led by Lieut.-Colonel Weir, the 11th (West Australian) led by Lieut.-Colonel J. L. Johnston, and the 12th (from S.A., W.A., and Tasmania) led by Lieut.-Colonel Clarke, D.S.O. It was a terrible duty, but a proud position, and Colonel Sinclair Maclagan had command. The men had orders not to fire. They had to judge for themselves, and leap into the water when they were nearing the shore. So the men jumped from the boats into the icy Ægean, up to their armpits sometimes, their rifles held above their heads, and slowly facing the stream of lead, waded to the shore. Eager to be free of action, they at once dropped their packs and charged. Some Turks were running along the beach to oppose them. These were killed or wounded. At other places round the northern extremity of the cove the boats were drifting in, and along the broader shore were grounding on the beach, only to be shattered and the whole parties in them decimated by the machine guns in Fisherman's Hut and the low hills above his enemy post.

So the Turks found the attack on them before they realised its proximity and strength. A few companies of the enemy were manning shallow trenches on the foothills, others were on the ridges overlooking the beach. Firing spread from end to end of the beaches, the machine guns spluttering a deadly line. Against this opposition, with a yell and cheers, the Australians dashed into their first action. 'Impshee,* Impshee, Yallah—you black devils!' was the cry that broke from a thousand throats. Louder and still louder grew the crack of the rifles, and when the Turks turned, not waiting for the army that now tumbled on to the beach, and ceased firing, the guns from behind the ridge and from Gaba Tepe point, took up the tale. Shrapnel soon began to burst over the beach, flicking to foam the waters between the now dimly visible transports and the water's edge. It was fortunate the Turkish gun fire went high in that first hour's fighting, and only fell harmlessly into the water, the men ashore escaping hurt as they swiftly advanced through the bushes, routing the Turks on the beach. Then, faced by almost perpendicular cliffs, these fearless fighters turned half-right (they had bayoneted for few Turks that remained) and went up the side of a high ridge—Maclagan's Ridge, 200 feet high—and paused only for want of breath. On they went a moment later, the officers leading what squads of men they could gather up, on to a plateau, known afterwards as 'Plugge's Plateau,' and down into a great ravine or *dere*—Shrapnel Gully.

Only men in perfect health and of the physique of these troops could have accomplished the scaling of those hills and still charge on, their vigour unabated. That climb had been amongst firs and holly bushes, over carpets of poppies, anemones, and wild flowers. The troops fired now from the ridges into the running Turks, whom

---

* Egyptian: 'Get out!'

they could not well see, but could hear crashing away ahead of them. It was the first step in a great charge. The Turks had not been numerous, but their position might well have been called impregnable. I do not suppose more than 500 to 800 Turks composed the force that manned the heights, but they had trenches, machine guns in positions, and had but to turn their fire on the water's edge that gently lapped the shore. They knew they had many thousands in reserve at Maidos, Bogali, and Kojadere, the nearest camp, but fearful of the landing host, they had turned and gone hack to the gully, where, joined by reserves, they waited the next onslaught. These enemy lines too, now the gallant 3rd Brigade, spreading out in a thin line, drove before them. Raked by machine guns from other ridges, the bullets came whistling through the leaves of the bushes round them. It was no use to pause in the valley—bullets came from behind, as snipers waited while the onward rush went over them, and then fired into the rear of the advancing parties— only to push on and on. Terrible work this was, crashing through the undergrowth, down, down into a valley, the bottom of which could not be seen, over broken ground, to reach at last creeks, and then to climb the hill outlined faintly in irregular silhouette before the advancing dawn.

As it grew lighter the enemy in great numbers could be seen running along these ridges, or establishing themselves in hasty entrenchments. Had they attacked, 4,000 strong as they were, they must have dispersed our isolated parties, driving them back at least. But the fierceness of the landing had shaken the nerve of the Turkish army; for the moment, I believe, the attack was paralysed. For an hour the Turks had ceased firing—between 5.30 and 6.30. Oh, thrice blessed hour, that gave the landing army time to gather its strength! The main gully was intersected by many smaller gullies, and down each of these parties of shouting Australians went, wherever they could find a leader—a sergeant, a South African veteran, or officer—to lead them. Some waited for word to go on, others went on till they were lost to their comrades for ever in the distant ridges.

In the early hours Major Brand, Brigade-Major of the 3rd Brigade, directing the right of the line that was working east, led a party across a crest, and, on the hillside below, saw a redoubt and earthworks, on which, after opening rapid fire, without delay he charged. The Turks fled, leaving as a prize to fall into our hands a three-gun battery of Krupp guns. One cannot overestimate the gallantry of this small party, who lost no time in spiking the guns and destroying them as best they could. For already the Turkish first counter-attack was developing, and it became necessary for Colonel Maclagan, while waiting for the new regiments, to contract his front. Major Brand had to retire to the hill crest, and for this deed and other heroism that morning he obtained the D.S.O.

Hours ere this had fled by, and meanwhile other regiments were pouring from the transports. Still the darkness hung over the shore. Only with the faint streaks of dawn could it be definitely learned that the brigade that had landed had won and held the heights. As one section of transports, having discharged its human freight, moved out, others filed in to take their places. The flashes of rifles could be seen on the cliffs, the error of the landing—that fortunate error—realised with a gasp of horror, surprise, and fear. All need for silence now ended, the orders rang out sharp and clear. Torpedo-boats bumped alongside, swiftly brought to rest, while the troops dropped down on to their decks, only to find there wounded men who had returned, never having set foot ashore.

'Hullo, mates, stung!' called some men from the transports to the wounded men.

'Blasted bad luck!—months of training, and never got a shot at the blighters, and only twenty minutes of fighting.'

Wounded were being lifted gently on board by the slings; others lay on the torpedo-boats, the time too precious to render anything but first aid while the task of disembarking still remained unfinished.

How magnificent the attitude of the Navy now that the strain was lifted, and a silent, stern air had given place to a jaunty assurance. Boys ran pinnaces up to grim transports and took command of hundreds of men, fearing death as little as any tried veterans. Reckless of danger, they never flinched. Let me only tell of one such midshipman hailing a transport (the skipper told me the story himself later), saying:

'Admiral's orders, but you will move in to — position, closer in shore.'

'Is there any danger?' bellowed back the skipper, thinking of the safety of his ship and the shells that threw towers of water up over his decks.

'Danger, sir! What is danger?' came back the piping reply.

And those men a little more senior, commanding the destroyers, the adventure of it all appealed to their deep-rooted instincts—the instincts of the Navy.

'Well, where do you want to go to?' asked a destroyer commander of a young infantry officer with his hundreds of men as he came aboard from the liner towering above the squat little warship.

'Good God!' exclaimed the officer, and, turning, shouted up to his commanding officer, still on board the transport, 'He does not know where to take me!'

'That is all right,' laughed the naval man. 'I went a bit north last time. I'll try a little higher up.' And his engine-room bell tinkled and they were off.

Amongst the boats and barges and small craft, as the dawn grew bright, the shells from the Turks fell, and the bullets from the hills raked them and killed the rowers at the oars.

Major Jackson, in command of a company of the 7th Victorians, related to me his experience, that, in the words of a soldier, most vividly tells the adventures of all those regiments landed about six o'clock in the pale morning light:

We had few oars—not enough to get quickly out of the hell fire once the pinnaces had cast us off, nearly 100 yards from shore. All the men who could crouched low in the boat, while the others rowed or sat by me on the gunwale. Then one lad caught a crab, and I commenced to curse him till, taking one more stroke, he fell dead across his oar, shot through the head. The bullets were ripping against our sides and the boat was filling with water. Many of us had to jump out while still the water was up to our armpits and push the boat inshore; many could never leave the boat. I formed up all the men I could from my own and other boats, and was directed up to the hills. But I can tell you that in many boats few men came out, and others lay at the bottom jammed beneath their dead comrades, who crushed them down.

Surely no words can describe the gallantry of troops who, without a murmur, bore their wounds. They joked while in the boats, talked of the nearness of the shot and shell, laughed as bullets flicked caps and jackets. Their attitude to death roused the enthusiasm of the sailors. 'They believe they are still on a picnic!' exclaimed a naval officer, and as the outline of the cliffs grew more distinct, 'Hell!' he exclaimed. 'They are up there! Good on you, Australians!' It was the beginning of the knowledge to the Navy what fighters the young Nation had, and they welcomed them and henceforth anything in their power was too little to help men who could face death with a cheer and a smile. Portions of the 5th, under Colonel Wanliss, and 6th battalion, under Colonel M'Nicol, came inshore on large lighters that remained almost stationary off shore, with the shrapnel bursting over them, till lines were passed to the beach and their comrades hauled them in. Major Whitham, 12th Battalion, told me when he had called on his men from his boat, but three had responded—the rest had been shot.

It is impossible to say which battalion landed first of the brigades. Generally it is conceded that the Queenslanders got ashore first, but only a few seconds later came the remainder of the troops from every State of the Commonwealth. The 1st and 2nd Brigades landed at six o'clock and were on shore by nine. The beach from a distance looked a surging mass of khaki figures, while the hillsides were covered with groups of men, who were working like fury, digging holes and tearing down the bushes. Pinnances, stranded and sunk, lay along the shore, barges, too, and boats.

Major Cass (now Colonel Cass, D.S.L.), Brigade-Major of the 2nd Brigade, commanded by Colonel M'Cay, described to me the landing of the Victorians, who now followed hard after the clearing party, together with the 1st Brigade, under Colonel M'Laurin. I will repeat it here as the testimony of a gallant soldier:

Transports moved into position, but they could not get forward, as warships and T.B.D.'s with the 3rd Brigade, still occupied the allotted places. In consequence, the 7th Battalion and portion of the 6th were embarking in boats before the 5th and 8th could get to their places. The enemy now had light enough to use his field guns from Gaba Tepe, and shelled the boats heavily. Gaba Tepe was at once engaged by the Triumph and Bacchante, but the guns were so well placed that they continued in action at intervals during the whole landing. This shell fire enfiladed the beach and caused many casualties in the boats. Those casualties caused further delay in the disembarkation, as wounded men were left in the boats, and even put in the boats from the beach. When the boats returned to the transports it was necessary to take the wounded on board, and, as provision had not been made for this, increasing delays took place with each tow or string of boats. It was interesting at this stage to watch the demeanour of the troops. At least 90 per cent of them had never been under fire before, and certainly 95 per cent had not been under shell fire. Yet they looked at the wounded, questioned them, and then went on with their disembarkation in a matter-of-fact way, as if they were used to this sort of thing all their lives. There seemed to be one desire—to get to grips with the enemy. Quickly and methodically the boats were loaded, tools handed down and stowed away, and all made ready, as had been practised at Mudros, and the tows started for the shore. On reaching the beach there was a certain amount of confusion. Men from all four battalions of the 2nd Brigade began landing at the one time, to find on the beach many men from the 3rd brigade who had gone forward. Because of the landing being made a little farther north than was anticipated or intended, the 3rd Brigade had gone to the left flank, and the 2nd Brigade, after a hurried consultation between the two brigades, moved to the right flank. The first ridge emphasised the necessity for discarding the packs, and thus free of their loads, the men moved on. But practically all semblance of company and battalion formation was lost.

And here let me write of the praise that all ranks have for the 26th Indian Mountain Battery that landed with the Victorians and pushed immediately into the heart of the position. The busy bang, bang of those terrible relentless little guns did much to stiffen and strengthen the next twenty-four hours' resistance of the army. 'Yes, there are the guns, men, just behind you,' and the officer saw on the face of the soldier a contented smile. 'We're all — well right now, let the — come!' and on the soldier went digging. I shall have more to say of these Indians later.

By midday the whole of the Victorians and the New South Wales Brigades were landed. Unavoidably, in the stress of battle they had mingled their battalions with the 3rd Brigade's, now forming a curved line on the edge of the plateau that lay on the far side of Shrapnel Gully, from a point about a mile from Gaba Tepe round on to the shoulder of the main ridge, thus forming an arc of which the beach made the cord. For, while the Australians had been holding the main ridge with a line running almost due north and south, the New Zealanders had landed, and had stormed and captured the ridge that lay almost at right angles (a last spur of Sari Bair) to the beach, advancing from the first ridge that had been stormed by the 3rd Brigade and making good the plateau called—after their leader, Colonel Plugge (Auckland Battalion)—Plugge's Plateau. Some of the landing parties, I have related, had got ashore at the point of Ari Burnu, or even farther north, and were enfiladed from machine guns placed in some fishermen's huts about

200 yards along the beach. With magnificent gallantry Captain Cribb, a New Zealand officer, led a party of men to the huts, which he captured at the point of the bayonet, killing or dispersing the Turks, who fled into the hills, leaving a quantity of ammunition and some stores to fall into our hands. Rid of this menace, the beach here suffered only from a frontal fire from the ridges, as it always did even in subsequent months.

Later in the afternoon and evening the 4th Infantry Brigade, under Colonel Monash, that came swiftly up, filled the gap at the head of Shrapnel Gully and united the Australians and New Zealanders at a point where the Turks might have easily come and severed our lines, at the head of what was subsequently called 'Monash Gully,' near Pope's Hill and Quinn's Post.

Now the fight for that main ridge was fierce in the extreme. While the beach and the landing waters were raked with shrapnel that caused hundreds of casualties, the gullies were also swept by fearful machine-gun fire. Overhead whizzed and burst the continuous pitiless shells. 'Don't come up here!' yelled an officer to Lieutenant Mangar as he attempted to lead a platoon of men over a small under feature that formed a way to the main ridge. 'This is riddled with machine-gun fire!' It was an exclamation often heard as parties of men strove to link up the firing-line. Early in the afternoon the Turkish first attack developed. At three o'clock they attempted to pierce our line in the centre along the main ridge. Already many of the most advanced parties, that had gone well forward, unsupported on either flank, for more than a mile farther (nearly three miles from the landing shore), led by corporals, sergeants, and what officers where available—alas, whose names must go unrecorded!—had driven back and back fighting, even cutting their way out. They saw that to remain would mean to be slaughtered. The Turks were hurrying up reinforcements. How many men fell in that retirement I would not like to estimate. Of the 5th Battalion alone, Major Fethers, Major Saker, Major Clements—all leading groups of men towards the heart of the Turkish position—each fell, mortally wounded—finest types of soldiers of the army. Hundreds of men sold their lives in reckless

114

valour, fighting forward, led by their officers, who believed that while they thus pressed on, the hills behind them were being made secure. This, indeed, was exactly what did happen, which always leaves in my mind the thought that it was the very bravery and zeal of those first lines of men—men from all battalions of various brigades, who pushed forward—that enabled the position in rear to be held and made good, though the pity was that sufficient reserves were not ready at had to make good the line, farther inland, on the last ridge that overlooked Boghali and the main Turkish camp— a ridge some men reached that day, but which Army Corps never afterwards gained.

On Lieut.-Colonel M'Nicol, commanding the magnificent 6th battalion and a portion of the 7th as well (Lieut.-Colonel Elliott, their leader, having been wounded), the main fighting fell in that first attack made on the right of the main ridge. Between him and the next battalion on his flank, the 8th, under Lieut.-Colonel Bolton, was a gap of some 400 yards. It was a desperate time holding these until the arrival of Lieut.-Colonel Thompson with the 4th Infantry, that effectively filled the gap, driving back the Turks, though losing their gallant leader in the charge. No time yet to dig in; the Turks' attack was pressed with fury. Hand-to-hand fighting resulted in the Turk going down as the Australian yelled defiance at him in his excitement and frantic despair at the terrible hail of shrapnel raining from above. There seemed to be constant streams of men making their way to the dressing-station. Major Cass told me 'four well-defined and partly sheltered tracks were followed, but even along these tracks men were being killed or wounded again by shrapnel coming over the firing-line on the ridge. This continual thinning of the already weakened line for a time seemed to imply disaster. The shrapnel of the Turks was doing its work with a deadly thoroughness. The enemy's guns could not be located by the ships' guns. We had only one mountain battery ashore, and it was seen and met by a storm of shrapnel, losing half its strength in casualties. Reinforcements were urgently needed, and so slowly did they come that they appeared to be drops in the bucket. But with dogged persistence our troops held the main ridge. In advance of this line were still to be seen a few small parties of men—the remains of platoons which had pushed forward and hung on.'

As night fell, the line, though not continuous, was linked in two sides of a triangle round the position, with the beach as a base. The 4th Brigade had, under Colonel Monash, been dashed up to the central portion of the line, where the Turks were massing in the greatest numbers. General Bridges had come ashore and so had Lieut.-General Birdwood, and sought to gain the true strength of the situation from the leaders. For a memorable conference had been held between the three Brigadiers earlier in the day, when roughly the line was divided up, the 2nd being to the south, then the 3rd, the 1st, and finally the 4th near the Sari Bair main ridge. It was not as the original plans had been conceived, but it served well. The line was now desperately in need, everywhere, of reinforcements.

On the beach the scenes were indescribable. The wounded were pouring into the temporary dressing station that Colonel Howse, V.C., had rapidly erected ashore; the boats that brought to the beach the living, went back to the ships with the wounded and dead. General Bridges would not permit the guns to be landed—thereby adding to the chaos on the beach, where stores, equipments, and ammunition came tumbling from the boats on to the narrow shore, not 10 yards wide—until after dusk, when the first gun was brought into action, a Victorian gun, under Colonel Johnston. Some guns of Colonel Rosenthal's Artillery Brigade had come ashore at noon, but Colonel Hobbs, under orders from the Army Corps, sent them back. It was, as yet, no place for guns, with the Turks massing for attack and the situation critical, but it was guns that were urgently needed.

The cry for reinforcements became more insistent as the night wore on. Lieut.-General Birdwood was recalled to the *Queen*. Orders were given to prepare for evacuation, and at midnight the boats were simply carrying off the wounded in tightly packed boat-loads. Delay was inevitable with such casualties—three or four thousand—yet it was this delay that made the situation desperate. Would the wounded have to be abandoned when the position was relinquished and another 3,000 men lost? Before night had deepened the Turks commenced to counter-attack again. Charge after charge they made, their shrapnel bursting in front of them over our lines; but they would never face the lines of bayonets that waited for them, and well directed volleys sent them back to their trenches and silenced their shrill cries of 'Allah, Allah Din!' Towards early morning the position became calmer, as the Turks were flung back. What troops could be spared dug and dug for their lives, exhorted by their officers. Orders, counter-orders, false commands, came through from front to rear, from rear to front, from flank to flank. Snipers fell to blows from the butt of a rifle, prisoners prayed for safety, never dreaming it would be granted them.

So the crisis came and passed. A determination, long fostered in the hearts of all, to 'stick for Australia,' to hang on or die in their trenches, won the day. Moral, if not very sanguinary support was given by two 18-pounder guns that opened fixe from our own trenches on the Turkish positions at dawn of the Monday morning. I doubt if more surprised men ever faced shells than the Turkish leaders when they realised that in the very firing-line, by the side of the landed infantry, were field guns, generally in rear of the battle line, and now firing at point-blank range at the enemy entrenched lines. It was a feat of no mean importance to drag by lines of men, as the Italian gunners later did at Gorizia, those great guns to the front of the battle; it required great grit to keep them there. How the 'feet' cheered the gunners on that morning as they plumped shell after shell into the disordered Turkish ranks. 'There they go! Give it them, the blighters!' yelled the excited infantrymen; and they poured their rifle fire into the bodies of Turks that could be seen moving or crawling in the green bushes which in those days covered the plateau.

So ended the most horrible night ever spent on Anzac, and thus began the dawn of that famous position.

CHAPTER XII
A TERRIBLE THREE DAYS

Dawn on the 26th came stealing over the hills beyond the Straits and snow-capped Mount Ida, showing her pink peak above the dark grim fortifications of Kelid Bahr, and along the Dardanelles Straits. Dawn awoke to hear the thundering boom of the guns from the fleet in amongst the valleys and gullies of Anzac, the rattle of muskets and the rip-rip-rip of machine guns. It spread with an echoing roar to the beach; it was taken up by the ships that lay one or two miles off the coast; it was intensified and flung back to shore again by the monster guns on the deck of the *Queen Elizabeth*. Down to the entrance of the Straits rolled the sound; and back from the Straits came the thundering roar as of a million kettledrums, while the fierce attacks and counter-attacks of the British pushed in on to the fortifications, and turned the Turks in terror to the foothills of Achi Baba. The enemy had abandoned their smashed guns; they had evacuated the fortifications and the village of Seddul Bahr, as the magnificent, imperishable 29th Division had managed to gain a foothold round the toe of the peninsula. Word had early been flashed up to Anzac that the landing had been a success, but had been resisted more fiercely, more terribly than even the most sanguinary expectations predicted.

It was the naval guns that took the place of the field guns, bursting shrapnel in the front of the Turkish lines, that held back the enemy charges, that decimated their men, that enabled the British and the Australian troops to effect the landing and hang on to the ridges until their trenches were deep enough, their guns landed, and the lines organised to withstand any attacks, however violent. It was artillery fire that the infantry (30,000 infantry) needed most at Anzac, and it was heavy artillery fire with a vengeance they got. As I watched the warships pumping in shells on to the hills, saw the Turks answering with the bluish white, curling clouds of shrapnel that burst over the sea and the gullies, it gave me an indication of the fury of the battle of which these were the only visible signs at long range. There was a balloon observing for the ships. The *Queen Elizabeth*, the *Triumph*, and the *Bacchante*, and five other warships lay off Anzac. There were three times as many off Cape Helles, with the French fleet steaming off Kum Kale. I watched the leaping tongues of fire from the warships' sides, and heard the muffled report as the smoke blew back over the decks in a yellow cloud; and before it had vanished (but many seconds later, as it had whirled miles in the air), the explosion of the shell bursting on the side of the hills and among the trenches. The wounded felt that shelling most, as they lay on the cliffs, on the shore, on the decks of the transports, with the ships firing point-blank at them. It shook them—it chilled their blood. But the men in the trenches knew that on the naval gunners depended their lives, depended their success; it was these protecting screens of fire, of huge shells, that gave them time to dig, and to settle down into what was fast becoming trench warfare. The Turks gathered battalions to battalions and flung them against the parts of our lines where the configuration of the country made them naturally weakest. The shells form the warships decimated them.

If Sunday had been the critical night for the Army Corps at Anzac, Monday and Tuesday were the critical days. Each party of men fought as a separate, desperate unit. The Turk might throw his complete reserve battalions against the right, the centre, or the left of our thinned ranks, but it was only the grit, the determination of the fighting spirit of the Australians and New Zealanders that enabled them to hold back the enemy or continue the attacks in small units led by a corporal or a junior subaltern. Reinforcements were hastily gathered, such parties as might be found in the valleys going to join the scattered regiments, or trying to find their comrades of a battalion. No counter-attack on a large scale could be ordered while such disorganisation prevailed; but each section of the line sought to advance, as it was found necessary to take and straighten and strengthen the position on the second ridge, so as to eventually link up the whole line.

In this way, then, the firing-line was roughly divided—on the first morning after landing—into four sections. On the extreme right was mostly the 2nd Brigade, under Colonel M'Cay, next to him the 3rd Brigade, under Colonel Maclagan, with battalions of the 1st Brigade, under Colonel M'Laurin, on his left. The 4th Brigade, under Colonel Monash, filled the apex of the position, and turning back the flank to the beach were the New Zealanders, under General Russell. A rough-and-ready division of the line it was, but it held, and, with little alteration, was kept as the sections of the position. Units were terribly mixed, and battalions, irrespective of brigades, were ordered to defend weakened positions or reinforce where the Turkish attacks grew most violent. Daylight found the troops still digging for their lives. Rain fell slightly. The men had some cover now, and found to their satisfaction and comfort that shrapnel no longer worried them so long as they kept in their trenches. How true in those days that the safest part of the position was the firing-line; for the tracks across the gullies were naked and open to the fire of the snipers' bullets that came even behind the line where the Turk had crept (for the gullies had not yet been searched and cleared). One party of Turks, indeed, endeavoured to get a machine gun through the lines on a stretcher, roughly covered by a greatcoat, as if they were carrying out a wounded man. They had not gone far before the trick was discovered, and these daring men were shot down. They were German non-commissioned officers in charge of machine guns. Lieutenant Mangar told me how he lay wounded behind a bush watching these German gunners, not 10 yards from him, pouring lead into our retreating parties of men. Finally, they, in turn, were forced to retire, and he crept in, under cover of darkness, to his own trenches.

The opening round of our guns was the signal for rejoicing, and five guns were firing throughout the day. A New Zealand battery first came into action with a roar, and some of Colonel Rosenthal's 3rd Brigade were landed later in the day. Artillery lanes had been cut round steeper slopes, over which the gunners and infantrymen dragged them, once they had been brought along the beach by the gun teams. Desperate efforts were made by artillery officers to silence the battery of guns that the Turks had skilfully concealed on Gaba Tepe, and though our field guns still continued to do terrible execution on the landing beach and amongst the troops entrenching on the right of the position. A landing party had been repulsed with heavy losses, finding the beach a mass of barbed-wire entanglements, and machine guns concealed in the cliffs. Hang on and dig, hang on to the edge of the second plateau, back on to which they had been, forced after the charge across the three ridges to the last lines of hills that looked down on the green, cultivated plains stretching almost to the Dardanelles, was all the Australians could do now. As far as possible the officers were endeavouring to reorganise their companies and battalions. Brigadiers have explained to me how for days, as they could, they gathered 50 or 60 men from this unit and that, and would communicate with the brigadier next along the line, and a transfer would be effected. It was not possible to let many men from the firing-line at one time, as the Turks were furiously making preparations for attack. Practically nothing could be accomplished on this Monday or Tuesday. In the still all too shallow trenches the 'spotters' for the warships (young lieutenants from Duntroon College, Australia, had been chosen) telephoned to the beach, from whence, by means of a wireless signal station, they directed the ships' fire with telling effect. Officers had but to find targets to be able to get any number of shells from the *Triumph* or *Bacchante*, or the destroyers that nosed close inshore, hurtling in the required direction.

Throughout the morning of Monday the Turks again began their counter-attacks, which with brief intervals, it seemed almost without ceasing, for two days they dashed first at one and then at another section of the line. A Turkish order may be quoted to show the manner in which the German leader, Liman von Sanders, endeavoured to inspire his troops, which now numbered probably 40,000 men, to further sacrifices. It ran:

> Attack the enemy with the bayonet and utterly destroy him. We shall not retrace one step, for if we do our religion, our country, and our nation will perish.
>
> Soldiers, the world is looking to you. Your only hope of salvation is to bring the battle to a successful issue, or gloriously to give up your life in the attempt.

It may be added here, too, that after two days' constant attack the Turkish leaders refused to ask their troops to face the ships' fire again during the day. For it was the ships' fire (with the *Queen Elizabeth*'s enormous 15-inch shrapnel pellets—a thousand in a case) as well as our machine guns and the rifles and the Indian Mountain Artillery (magnificently served were these guns) that the Turks faced as they charged.

First on the right of the line the attacks began. The Turks were hurled back by the 8th Battalion, under Lieut.-Colonel Bolton. The Australians stood steady, sweeping the enemy's lines, heaping up the dead. The Turks advanced in the favourite massed German formation. Grimly, with bayonets fixed, the Australians waited in their unfinished trenches. At the apex of the line, the head on Monash gully, the great Turkish attack of the day developed. Two ridges met here, and formed what was named at one the 'Nek.' The Sari Bair ridge ran at right angles to the beach, beginning with what had been named Walker's Ridge and Russell Top, and continuing on past Chunak Bair to Hill 971, or Koja Chemin Tepe. Just above Russell Top the broad plateau (on the edge of which most of the Australian army now clung desperately) joined the Sari Bair ridge at the Nek. This main Australian ridge ran in a bow round to Baba Tepe. So steep was the head of the gully and so cut up with hills (for a spur ran out from the very centre of it—Pope's Hill) that it was not possible to get a continuous line of trenches across to the Nek. There was no alternative but to dig in here from Russell Top, down across the gully, and up again on to the knob which struck out into the gully, dividing its head in two (called subsequently Pope's Hill), and from this point across to Quinn's Post, so linking up with the rest of the right of the line. The summit of the arc, as I have described our position—now for the first time more definitely defined—was the gully. On the left the New Zealanders held Walker's Ridge, Plugge's Plateau, and the section of Russell Top, and the trenches leading down on their left into the valley; with the result that the Turks chose this point as the best for breaking through our position and coming in behind our lines. Had they succeeded in their endeavours, which lasted till Wednesday, it would have meant the cutting of Anzac in two.

The 2nd Battalion, under Colonel Braund, had held the trenches nearest the Nek until relieved by the New Zealanders on Sunday night. Meanwhile the 4th brigade, less many companies, had been flung into the central position. All the hills were still at this time covered with thick scrub, and favoured the tactics of the Turks, who crept through it until they were near enough to make a rush at the trenches. But the men of the 2nd Battalion and the new Zealanders stood firm. From the Nek, and what afterwards became the Chessboard trenches, the Turkish snipers shot down into the gully, which was a veritable death-trap with this menace above it. No wonder to it clung the name of the 'Valley of the Shadow of Death.' It took many days for our sharp-shooters from the high positions we had won to compel the enemy to keep under cover, and eventually to withdraw their snipers—those who were not shot at their posts.

Farther along the line M'Cay's Hill and Braund's Hill, in the centre of the right of the position, were subjected to a furious bombardment by the Turkish artillery, and their machine guns were playing on these points until nearly three o'clock, when the attacks of the Turks began to increase in fury. They send wave after wave of men against our lines, and the 8th Battalion were forced to retire to the edge of the ridge. The enemy now came across from up Happy Valley and other gullies on the right, and were threatening to break through and get behind our lines round M'Cay's Hill. It was then that two battalions, the 9th, now under Major Robertson, and 10th, under Lieut.-Colonel Weir, which had already suffered under racking fire, and had had to retire from distant ridges to which they had penetrated in a counter-attack, were brought up from a gully where they had been held in reserve. They straightway commenced to retake the lost hill. Three times they charged before the Turks finally broke, unable to face the reckless bravery of the Australians, and the hill was finally in our possession. But our losses were again heavy. This finally settled the possession of the hill, which enabled the line to be drawn straighter along the right.

Meanwhile General Bridges had completed an inspection of the ground of the position, and determined that certain portions would have to be straightened out so that the best advantage might be taken of the country before them. For this duty the 4th Battalion, or rather remaining section of it, which had been kept in reserve, were ordered to advance some hundred yards and occupy the new line. Since the landing the enemy had crept into our lines as spies, dressed in the uniforms of fallen men, and had been successful by various ruses in trapping more than one officer. They had passed false messages down the line, and had caused men to cease fire for a time, before the fallacy of the orders had been discovered. On this occasion the 4th, led by Lieut.-Colonel Thompson, believing that the whole of the line was to charge, went forward, charging on and on through two valleys to a distant ridge—Pine Ridge. They passed a small Turkish camp, and were only stopped at length by a terrible machine-gun fire when still 1,000 yards from the mouth of the enemy's heavy artillery. They had then to retire, realising the hopelessness of their position. They fell back. As they reached what was intended for their objective they entrenched. But their gallant leader was killed in the charge.

Again and again during Monday night and Tuesday the Turks charged and counter-attacked along the whole front, but the Australians, confident of their prowess after twenty-four hours' continuous fighting, grimly held their ground. They had learned that trenches gave some protection from shrapnel, and those that were not fighting were burrowing like rabbits, digging in, while their comrades held the line. The Turks continued to direct their hardest blows against the centre, but as fast as they hurried up their reserves so did the Australians come hurrying up from the beach. The unloading of the shells and supplies had proceeded rapidly now that it had been determined to hold on. The Anzacs had come for good, they left no doubt about that, and, with the guns firing from the very trenches, it was with a cheer that the lads waited for the Turks. Never would the foe face the last 20 yards and the glistening line of bayonets. Sometimes a section of our men would leave the trenches, sufficient indication of what would follow, so sending the Turks shambling back. They feared the Australian in those days and the use he made of his bayonet. It even happened that the fixing of bayonets, the men stopping their digging, halted a Turkish charge. Not that I wish to suggest that the Turk was not brave, but he had been badly rattled and shattered with the ships' appalling fire. But our troops were getting sleepy and tired, for they had been fighting for three days continuously. They had plenty of munitions and rations, and with judicious use (a thing that the Australians taught the English Tommies later on) their water supply held out. But everything had to be laboriously carried up those hills from the beach.

The casualty lists show the high percentage of officers killed and wounded, due, I believe, not only to their heroism and example of leadership, but to the nature of the country. Brigadiers and battalion commanders exposed themselves, standing among the bushes and undergrowth, so as to find out where the attack might be coming from, while a tornado of lead swept past them. There was no cover other than very rough and very inadequate look outs. The snipers of the Turks were still playing havoc in our lines; many, indeed, were still behind the troops, dug into pits, with days' supplies of food and ammunition, concealed by bushes, and that was why the men as far as possible kept down in their trenches; it was that which made Shrapnel Valley the Valley of the Shadow of Death. It was while reconnoitring thus the Brigadier of the 1st Brigade—a soldier who could ill be spared at such a time or at any time, Colonel M'Laurin—fell, shot through the heart, and his Brigade-Major, Major Irvine, was killed standing alongside of him. This sad loss happened on Tuesday during the afternoon, when the Brigadier had come out from his dugout close to the firing-line (all quarters were in those early days, and were little better afterwards, so far as situation went). Some idea of the fierceness of the fighting may be gleaned from the casualties the 1st Division suffered. The 3rd Brigade in the first two days, Sunday and Monday, had 1,900 the 2nd Brigade 1,700, the 1st Brigade 900 killed and wounded. In the 2nd Brigade alone 11 officers were killed at the landing, 34 wounded, and 2 missing, afterwards discovered to be killed.

There but remains now to complete the story of this great landing battle by reference to the part that the 4th Brigade took during the days till Wednesday, some mention of which has already been made.

Two separate manoeuvres were tried by the Turks to break our line. They tried them both at once. One was an attempt to drive in our right flank and get round by the beach to the heart of the position. This they failed to do, as the knolls were so strongly held (the 2nd Battalion had been specially thrown on to the extreme right flank to guard against this); while the fire from the warships, especially the *Queen Elizabeth*, was far too accurate and bloody, so that the enemy dared not show themselves on those exposed slopes and in the gullies, easily raked either by direct or indirect fire from the warships, officers spotting, as I have said, from the trenches. The other attempt, a separate and even sterner battle, was the stabs that the Turks, made at the highest point of the arc of our semi-circular position—or at the apex, as it has been termed—near the head of Monash Gully. Our trenches were down in the gully. They were overlooked by the Turks. Shrapnel fell over them constantly and for long periods at a time. On the edges of the main ridge the position grew more and more perilous. Only for the gallant defence of Quinn's and Pope's Hills nothing could have stopped the wedge that the Turks sought to make being driven in. An officer of the 14th Battalion seized the pint known as Quinn's Post, a knoll on the side of the ridge, and held on like grim death with his gallant men. I venture to say that had the Turks, rallying their numbers, succeeded in dislodging this little band of heroes from their position on this knoll, who must then have been dashed to their doom in the Shrapnel Gully, they would have gained their purpose and that great and important artery would have been commanded by Turkish fire. On Wednesday Major Quinn took it over and held it, and the post from that time on bore his name.

Pope's Hill filled the gap between the heads of Monash Gully. It will easily be realised from a glance at a map (it was a thousand times more evident to see) that only for this post and this feature, the Turks would have wrought havoc in our position. An officer of the 1st Battalion took Pope's Hill with a body of about 100 men, composed of various units. In fact, he had under his command men from practically the whole of the 1st Division, whom he had gathered up as they wandered up the gullies looking for their units. He held on until the evening of Sunday, when he was relieved by a composite force, under Lieut.-Colonel Pope, with whose name this dangerous and vital hill has been ever since associated. Under his command Lieut.-Colonel Pope had about a battalion and a half, consisting of a company of the 15th, a company of the Auckland Battalion, and the 16th battalion, about 400 men in all. In this first conflict the 4th Brigade won its renown, and Colonel Pope his name. This gallant officer had been guided up from the beach by a Staff officer, but the force, small as it was, in the darkness got divided. Part debouched to the south flank and were absorbed in the trenches there; the remainder pushed on firmly and reached the spur, Pope's Hill, and relieved Captain Jacobs, who had all the day been clinging with his little band of 100 men to this desperate position.

It was shortly after these relieving troops arrived that a most curious incident occurred, which showed the cunning tactics of the Turks. Information, originating no one knew where, was passed along the short firing-line from the left that Indian troops were in possession of the ground immediately to the left of the hill at the very head of the gully. It was clearly advisable that the gap which existed between the Australian line and these Indian troops should be closed, as it gave the Turks a free passage-way down the gully, steep as it was, thereby cutting our position in two. Immediately on receipt of the verbal message Lieutenant Easton, 16 Battalion, and Private Lussington, who understood Hindustani, were dispatched, and they soon got in touch with a party of Indians that were entrenched on the side of the hill. The Indians stated that a senior office was required to discuss matters with their officer, and accordingly Captain R. T. A. M'Donald, the adjutant, was sent forward. He had not gone far—the whole of our line to the Turkish trenches at the very head of the gully where the parley took place was not more than 150 yards—when he called back out of the darkness that the O.C. alone would do to discuss the position with. Colonel Pope went at once, and reaching the northern edge of the gully, found his adjutant and the two men who had been first sent forward talking with a party of six Indians, who had stood with their bayonets fixed. One glance was sufficient to convince the O.C. that these men were not Indians at all. He had suspected that something was wrong when called, and no sooner had he joined the party than he called out a word of warning. The Turks—for such these Indians proved themselves to be in disguise—at once formed round the Australians. Colonel Pope, who was nearest the edge of the gully, with rare courage, broke through the ring and leaped down some 12 feet into the gully below. Shots were fired after him, but he escaped, and, with a severe shaking, reached his lines. The other three men were taken prisoners at once and sent to Constantinople. In the possession of the Adjutant were important documents, plans, and maps, which in this way early fell into the hands of the Turks.

Colonel Pope lost little time in extending his position across the hill that he held. His front covered about 300 yards. He had barely 400 men under his command. From this onward, through the night and succeeding days, every spare moment was spent in improving the trenches on the hill which sloped down into the gully.

It was almost a sheer drop at the head of it of 80 feet, and the hillside was covered with loose earth and dense bush. There were snipers on the hill still, in concealed pits, and snipers, too, firing from the opposite side of the gully, where there had been a small Turkish camp. At periods through Monday, on until Tuesday morning, fierce attacks were made against Pope's Hill, but the Turks were repulsed by the steady fire of the defenders of the post. Reinforcements had brought the garrison up to 450 men. But both machine guns of the 16th Battalion were put out of action during Monday, and it was not till Tuesday that these were replaced by guns from the Royal Marine Light Infantry, who were now hurried up as a reserve, as will be explained in a subsequent chapter. On the 30th the 16th Battalion was relieved by the 15th. So began in bloody battle the history of this famous post, some of the still bloodier onslaughts against it remaining to be described, as they occurred, later. The topography and defences of this post and this section of the line must form always a separate chapter in the history of Anzac.

The failure of the Turks to smash the resistance in the first days determined the success of the Australians. Fit as no troops have been, fit for fierce fights, from thence onward the invaders had a contempt for the Turks, and only were anxious that he should attack. In those few early days it is said that the Turks suffered nearly 50,000 casualties at Anzac and Cape Helles. Ours were over 8,000 and the British twice as many again. The enemy left thousands of dead on the battlefield before the trenches. But while they were reorganising their great attack on Wednesday there was a lull, a curious solemn quiet that spread all along the line, which had ceased to spit and splutter except in a spasmodic way. On Tuesday the commencement of the reorganisation of the Australian army was begun. It was completed by Friday. Anzac, after four days' fighting, was established. Australians had won their first battle, had gained, in that first desperate encounter, deathless fame by deeds that have no parallel in history (not even remembering the scaling of the heights of Abraham), and which rank in glory with the imperishable records of the gallant 29th Division and their attack and capture of the Turkish positions at Cape Helles.

CHAPTER XIII
A BATTLE PANORAMA
OF GALLIPOLI

This narrative is devoted to the deeds of the Australians, but on that account it must not be judged that the scanty reference to the part played by the British troops indicates that part was but of secondary importance to the Dardanelles operations and the Gallipoli campaign. On the contrary, the position may be best summed up by the words of General Sir Ian Hamilton, who said to me on Imbros one day: 'We [the British] have occupied the end of the peninsula, while the Australians are a thorn in the side of the Turks. When the time comes we will press that thorn a little deeper.'

Yes, the British had occupied about 4 miles of the toe of the peninsula in those early days, and were slowly pushing the Turkish line back into the Krithia village and on to the great Achi Baba Hill; but to do so the aid of the French had to be called up and the Asia Minor campaign had to be abandoned.

Now, I was fortunate to have been near enough to watch the French and British warships bombarding the Turkish position on Sunday morning, 25th April, on either side of the Straits, and to have seen the hosts of transports creeping from round the shores of the islands. It was only a little Greek trading steamer that I was on, and it impudently pushed its nose into the heart of these stupendous operations. I was on her by design; she was there by accident. The whole of the fleet had lain for days at their anchorage behind Tenedos. I had seen them there, their anchors down, on the very ocean bed where the Greek anchors had rested when they planned their descent on Troy to rescue the beautiful Helen. It was one of those radiant mornings that are so typical of the spring months of the Levant. The sea was almost without a ripple on it. A haze hid the distant headlands as in a shroud and cast a soft, flimsy mantle round the ships. The smoke of battle hung on the shores and round the battle-cruisers. Along the Asiatic coast, opposite the island of Tenedos, was steaming slowly a huge six-funnelled battleship of the French, its guns darting tongues of flame, three or four or six every minute. On shore the French troops were fighting their way inland and pushing back the Turkish field batteries that were answering the warships and shelling the invaders, then we went on up towards the entrance to the Straits amongst the great liners, on which was more than one high General directing the landing of the finest British troops that the Home-land had ever produced, the 29th Division. They had been the last regular Division available, and General Hamilton had in them the mainstay of his army, the tested stuff, for that difficult landing on four beaches at the Dardanelles entrance. I watched the cruisers come steaming by, and then, signalling, steer for the shore and commence the hurling of shells on the edge of the cliffs and farther inland, where the Turks were still clinging to the battlements round the shores of their peninsula. By dawn the British, as well as the Australian, landing had been effected—at fearful cost certainly, but nevertheless accomplished—and Fusilier regiments had pushed inshore and died on the beach in lines. Their comrades had scaled the cliffs, while the Turks inch by inch, one can write, were driven from their forts, their guns broken by the weeks of bombardment.

Round the toe of the peninsula the troops landed. All day the desperate fighters of the 29th Division clung to their terrible task, completing it under cover of darkness on the Sunday evening. From V beach to Morto Bay, 2 miles away, near which inlet, under the fortress of Seddul Bahr, the *River Clyde*, creamed with 2,500 men, had steamed in and been run ashore (or as near shore as reefs had permitted), the fighting continued. From the bows of this transport (an Iron Horse indeed!) a dozen machine guns were spitting darting tongues of red as still against her iron sides rattled the hail of Turkish bullets or burst the shells from the guns of the forts. It is not in my story to describe the landing from that ship—alas! now blown into fragments. It was not till some months after she had run aground that I was aboard her. In the last days of April she was the object to which all turned their eyes in recognition of a gallant undertaking, magnificently carried out by Captain Unwin, who was in charge of her. For his work this brave officer was awarded the V.C.

Now the Australians faced sheer cliffs; they rushed down into gullies and up on to farther ridges. The British troops scaled cliffs or found stretches of sandy beach, defended with almost impenetrable barbed-wire entanglements; but beyond was a garden of loveliness— almost level fields still bearing ripening crops, and trees laden with fruits; poppies, anemones, and the hundred smaller wild flowers of the Levant carpeted the soil. Those were the shores strewn with the bodies of the most gallant men that ever fought, who had never flinched as they faced murderous fire from far fiercer guns than any that opposed the first rush of the Australians up that narrow section of the Anzac hills. Yet the Turks fell back. The warships, with their protective armour, moved in and wrought havoc on the enemy as they were driven back and back. Behind steamed the transports. Amongst all this mixed fleet thickly dropped the shells, splashing the water in great fountains over the decks, casting it 50, 100 feet into the air.

Fifteen miles away Anzac was stormed and won. The Australians held with the same bulldog grit that gave the British their footing ashore. How did the French come to Helles? It was a few days afterwards, when the reinforcements for the British force were so urgently needed that it became necessary to evacuate the Kum

Kale position, on the southern entrance to the Straits, and transfer the entire French army to the right flank of the Cape Helles position. That was the way the French troops came with their wonderful '75's, that later in the week were so accurately finding out the Turkish trenches, throwing a curtain of fire before the Allied lines.

I do not believe in the history of any war (and one remembers particularly the storming of the heights of Quebec in this regard) has there been any battle panorama so truly magnificent, so amazingly impressive, as that 20 miles of beaches and the entrance to the Dardanelles as seen from the hilltops of the islands scattered round the entrance to the Straits. Rabbit Islands may not be marked on maps—they are only little dotted rocks on charts—but they have a light on them to guide the mariner to the entrance to the Dardanelles, which is about a mile and a half away. From them and the shelter of a single farmhouse you might look right up almost to the Chanak forts, certainly up to Kephez Bay, where the warships, screened by destroyers and minesweepers, were pressing their attack on the Narrows. They commanded a view of the beaches, round which transports had gathered with lighters, tugs, trawlers, pinnaces, and barges, disgorging materials and men for the great fight progressing now over the flowered fields above from the tops of the cliffs. The white hospital ships loomed like aluminium-painted craft in the fierce sun, and their yellow funnels seemed fairer still by the side of the darkened smoke-stacks of the panting destroyers, the smoke belching from their short stacks as they raced back and forth amidst them, dragging barges here, nosing in between warships there—warships from whose grim grey sides sprang red-tipped tongues and sheets of flame and rolled clouds of smoke. High into the air tore the screaming shells, which in their parabola passed over the defenceless shipping and the troops bayoneting the Turks on shore, to destroy the main Turkish position. Battleships, standing farther off still, sent shells 5, 6, 8 miles up on to the enemy forts that barked and snapped still in the Narrows.

That was one picture. Take, then, the broader view from the hills of Imbros, 9 miles away. The whole peninsula was sprawled out in all its irregularity, with its still green slopes ending abruptly at the dark cliffs. In the centre were the masses of gathered hills (Kelid Bahr position), crowned with forts, invisible even at the closest observation except from aeroplane above; and beyond, across the slender rim of blue of the Narrows, the towering white of Mount Ida. I remember looking right down into the Narrows from a certain hill on this salubrious island. How intensely blue its waters were, on which I saw quickly pass a transport and a cruiser. I wondered that the yellow balloon looking down on to the straits, signalling to the Allied warships, did not sink them with those shells which long-range guns dropped right across the 7,000 yards of the narrow neck on to the town of Maidos and Turkish transports lying at the wharves there. At Nagara there was a lighthouse that was an easy landmark to pick out, and not far distant white barracks and hospitals. Then, passing down towards the entrance, the huge citadel of the Straits, Kelid Bahr, blocked the view of the opposite shore and of the fortress Chanak, and yet lower down still, where the peninsula fell away, I could see across the narrow channel the white scarps of Dardanus and the town called Whitecliffs. These towns in the afternoon looked like miniature cities on the side of a vivid, wonderful landscape; they were a mass of white domes and towers. The sun glinted on the windows of the houses, and a thousand scintillating lights darted like the fire of rifles from the dwellings. Blue, beyond, the hills round Troy stood back from the raging battle being fought on the point of the peninsula. An aeroplane swung out of the distance and flew up and down the Straits, its observer prying into the secrets of the forts.

Achi Baba was the dominating feature of the lower end of the peninsula, yet it seemed very flat beside the greater feature of Kelid Bahr and the hills of Anzac. From the angle at which I was observing the village of Krithia was just visible, snuggling between two shoulders of low hills, tucked away, it seemed, from the guns. Yet I was destined to see that village reduced to crumbling ruins by the battering guns, and watch the burning fires covering the peninsula with grey smoke. At night how they glowed and smouldered dully!

Far more terrible was the fire that broke out at Maido on the afternoon of the 29th April, when the shells from the warships destroyed the barracks, the wharves, the granaries, the arsenal, and set fire to the town. The smoke rose in a huge black column, and then, reaching a higher current of air, was carried down to the very entrance to the Straits, until in the oblique rays of the setting sun it became a dirty brown smudge above the peninsula. Next day the fires were burning still; at night the reflection lit the sky and silhouetted the hills beyond. For days afterwards the smoke was shielding from view the waters of the Narrows.

I take the following extract from my diary, written at the time from the Imbros hills:

2 p.m.   Discovered four tents Cape Tekel. Balloon observing over Straits.

2.15   Turkish guns observed in wood on the left of Tree Hill (Achi Baba).

2.30   Smoke rising over Straits north of Kelid Bahr.

2.35   Aeroplane flying up the Dardanelles over Turkish forts.

2.40   Ships dropping shells on village of Everden (Turkish headquarters).

3.00   Smoke rising south of Maidos.

3.15   Considerable activity amongst warships.

3.20   Dense smoke 100 yards long, 400 feet high, believe to be Cham Kalesi

4.00   Certain smoke from village Maidos, rising now 2,000 feet high—still burning. Bombardment ceased for last ten minutes

4.30   Firing at Gaba Tepe, warships plastering cliffs.

4.45   Intense fire from the fleet.

4.50   Maidos still burning. Balloon observing north Tree Hill (Achi Baba).

6.30   *Queen Elizabeth* and balloon observing ship
Ark Royal going towards entrance to the Straits.
All quiet. Maidos burning fiercely. Turkish guns silent.

And so it was day after day.

What of Anzac! It was 9 miles away, but with powerful field-glasses the boats near to the beach could be seen. The glinting rays of heliographs shone from the cliffs. An aeroplane came rapidly from over the crests of the hills and dropped down beside the parent ship and was hauled on board. Four, five, or six times a day would the 'Baby' observation balloon ascend and remain with its line of flags below, motionless in the air for hours. The destroyers, those rats of the seas as they have been called, scampered over the blue water. Their guns thumped the flanks of the Australian position close to Gaba Tepe, near which point always there lay some battleship, generally the *Queen Elizabeth*, while at Suvla Bay, close inshore, the warships closed in to throw shells on to the Sari Bair ridge and Battleship Hill, a flat peak that just showed a bald top above the ridge. Anzac itself was wrapped in impenetrable mists for those first three days. From the gullies dated flashes of the guns—our own guns, almost in the infantry trenches—while the Turkish woolly balls of shrapnel came tumbling above the beaches, above the tops of the hills where the troops were digging— digging for their lives. Our own shrapnel I could see bursting far inland and on the point of Gaba Tepe, where hidden enemy guns were silenced. It was awe inspiring to watch the mass of earth thrown skyward by the striking of the *Queen Elizabeth*'s shells on Mai Tepe, a feature which dominated the alluring plain, crowned with olive groves and guarded solely by the batteries at Gaba Tepe. How entrancingly green those plains looked with their few scattered vineyards and olives! I remember wondering what would have been the result if the troops had been advancing across them just in the same way as I was watching the British advancing from the shores up the peninsula.

There came the morning—29th April—when on the end of the peninsula, near Cape Tekel, white-topped tents appeared, and horses could be seen in lines. They were hidden from the Turkish view by the cliffs, but none the less shells fell among them occasionally. It denoted the British were firmly established. The press of shipping had increased. At a hundred I lost count of the ships.

At Anzac there was not less than half that number, all transports, waiting—waiting as if to remove the landed army. I could find no other reason for their being there, idly changing position, while from their sides constant strings of boats came and went: but in them, I learned later, were the wounded. The transports became floating hospital wards. Up and down the shore from Anzac to Helles patrolled the cruisers, bombarding the red road open to view, where the Turkish columns were moving. From the very midst of the merchant fleet the warships' guns thundered with their 'b-brum-brum-m-m,' two guns together, and the faint, dull shell explosions sounded on land along the road to Krithia, where wide sheers of riven flame rolled along the ground, and a sickly yellow cloud enveloped horses, men, and guns in its toils as the Turks retreated.

Then there dawned the day when the Royal Naval Air Service armoured motor-cars dashed into action, grappling wire entanglements, and sped back, with the Turkish shells bursting after them from the guns on Achi Baba as the retired.

Unforgettable will remain the memory of the panorama: the calm of the sea, the havoc on shore, the placidness of the shipping, the activity of the fleet. Down below me in the mountain glens, where trickled sparkling brooks, patient Greek shepherds called on Pan pipes for their flocks, and took no more notice of the distant roar of battle—the crackle of rifles and machine guns could be heard—than of the murmuring of the sea on the seashore; and like it, unceasingly, day and night for weeks, was a horrible deadly accompaniment of one's dreams.

CHAPTER XIV
AN UNFULFILLED ARMY ORDER

It is impossible to contemplate the position at Anzac on Wednesday, 28th April, when the fighting for a foothold on the peninsula had finished and the Turks had been crushed back, without feeling that the battlefields of France and Flanders had not taught the lessons that were only too startlingly obvious—that success was only won by adequate reserves being ready to hurl against the enemy *in extremis*. Granted that two or three days—Tuesday, Wednesday, and Thursday—were necessary for the reorganisation of the Australian lines, bent but not broken, and full of fighting vigour, and eager to fulfil the task that was set them of breaking across the peninsula at this, almost its narrowest neck, there seems to be no explanation why there was such a miscalculation by experienced Generals of Turkish strength, and lack of reserves, which left the Turks the same three days to lick their wounds and bandage them, and return, greatly reinforced, to the fray. It becomes more inexplicable still when it is found that certain Army Corps orders were issued for a general advance, and that a chance word alone was the means of that advance being altered to a mere straightening of a portion of the strongly entrenched line. I do not think it was because we feared the Turks: that would be to pay him more credit than his actions warranted. It was, to put it quite plainly, faulty Staff work. Events are too near to attempt to place the blame; for assuredly there was some one blameable for the great wasted opportunity to crush the Turkish army of Liman von Sanders.

Behind the apparent chaos of Anzac Cove and the fighting force on the hills during the first three days there was, nevertheless, the great purpose that mattered. Every one was doing his utmost to reduce the lines of communication, the stores on the beach, and the army itself to their proper and normal state. Those days from Tuesday onward may be regarded as showing some of the finest Staff organising work that has been done in the campaign. By Friday the position was completely reorganised. Units had been rested and linked up; trenches had been straightened, strengthened, and defended against attack. Water, ammunition, food, were trickling in regular streams up the gullies; guns were in position, and fresh troops had been landed to relieve the strain and hurry matters forward. Unfortunately, it seems they were not in sufficient numbers apparently to justify a general offensive immediately. The 1st Light Horse Brigade, under Brigadier-General Chauvel, and the Royal Marine Light Infantry, those young troops that had seen their first service in the defence of Antwerp, were put into the trenches to relieve the men who had won their first fight and fame in a three days' battle. For seventy-two hours these heroes had been without sleep; they were dropping in their tracks from fatigue. They had had water and biscuits and bully beef, but until Wednesday nothing warm to eat or drink. All day and night small parties of perhaps as many as 50, perhaps only 10 men, were to be seen going from one section of the line to another; men who had been collected a mile away from their original unit, who had got separated in the wild rushes over the hills, who had gone into the firing-line at the nearest point at which they found themselves to it. It was essential that commanders should have their own men before any move forward could be attempted on a large scale. In digging alone, the men suffered terrible hardships after their advances, strategical retreats, and the endless fatigues for water, food, and munitions.

In order, therefore, that the battalions could be reformed and rearrangements made in the commands of the companies, units were withdrawn at various points from the firing-line, as they could be spared, and placed in reserve gullies, where the men obtained good sleep and rest, a hot meal, and, generally, a swim down on the beach.

Now, in this 1st Division reorganisation work no officer took a greater or finer part than. Colonel C. B. B. White, the Chief of General staff to General Bridges, ably supported by Major Glasfurd. He seemed indefatigable, never perturbed, always ready to remedy a defect. Major Blamey, who was Intelligence Officer, carried out daring reconnaissance work towards Maidos, leaving our lines under cover of darkness and penetrating to a distant ridge and determining much of the enemy's position on the right. Meanwhile, complete field telephone communication had been established under most awful conditions, directed by Major Mackworth, D.S.CO., whose gravest difficulty was the constant breaking of the lines, through men stumbling over them in the saps and shrapnel fire, that led to the beach and the Army Corps headquarters, not usually a matter for much worry, as being distant many miles from the firing-line, in an ordinary battlefield.

On 28th and 29th April a comparative calm stole over Anzac. Gradually the Turks had ceased their intense bombardments of the gullies. Their waste of ammunition had been enormous, 600 shells falling often in the course of a few hours in one small gully; yet the damage on the beach was almost negligible. Their shelling of the cove was now regulated to odd times, and never lasted for more than half an hour of an hour. The Australians had orders not to waste their rifle fire in blazing away into the darkness to no purpose, and scarcely fired a shot except at periods throughout the night when fierce bursts foreshadowed an enemy counterattack. Anzac of the first days and Anzac of this second period was a contrast as of a raging ocean to a placid sea.

By 30th April all initial difficulties had been overcome. It was on that day occurred the incident, already briefly mentioned, that had such far-reaching effects on the destinies of the Australians, and I venture to say, on the whole of the Gallipoli operations. I refer to the formulation of an order for a general advance that was never executed. Many officers will recall that the leaders of the armies were, on the evening of the 30th April, summoned to conferences, the 1st Division under Major-General Bridges, and the 2nd Division under Major-General Godley. Now, Major-General Godley had already been informed of the serious and vital nature of the centre of the line, the apex, of the position, which was blunted, for the Turks still held trenches at the head of Monash Gully which commanded portions of it. He had not visited General Monash's positions and had hinted that there would be a forward movement when all units would be 'out of it,' and meanwhile 'Cling on' was the order the 4th Brigade received.

It is with this latter conference we are mostly concerned. General Godley was very seriously talking with Generals Russell and Johnston (New Zealand officers) when Brigadier-General Monash, commanding the 4th Infantry Brigade, arrived from the firing-line. Outside the dugouts there were many Staff officers. The 'pow-wow' was held to disclose the plans for a general attack, ordered from Army Corps headquarters, to take place on the following evening. It was to commence at 7 o'clock.

The plan disclosed that the 1st Australian Division (now roughly holding the main ridge that ran in a south-easterly direction) was to advance due east—that was, across Mule gully on to Pine Ridge and towards the villages of Kojadere and Bogali, lying beyond; while the 2nd Australian and New Zealand Division was to advance due north beyond Chanak Bair up the back of the great Sari Bair ridge, of which we already held the spur, known as 'Russell's Top.' This position lay just south of the point where the ridge occupied by the Australasian division at Pope's Hill and Quinn's Post joined the Sari Bair crest.

General Monash, on hearing General Birdwood's orders, immediately pointed out that if such an advance were made the gap that already existed in the line at the head of Monash Gully, between the left flank of the 4th Brigade and the right of the New Zealand troops, would be widened. Now a very unfortunate circumstance prevented this discussion being continued to its conclusion, for a telephone message had come from that section of the line held by General Monash's troops that the R.M.L.I. (who had been holding the trenches) had been driven out by the Turks, who were pouring in at the head of the gully. There was no alternative under the circumstances but for the General to return to his headquarters, situated in Shrapnel Valley, more than a mile away, to supervise the regaining of the lost trenches. But before he hurried away General Monash was told by General Godley that the gap would be remembered when making out the divisional order that night. At any rate, it was the business of General Monash to see that touch was maintained with the New Zealanders in the coming fight. The divisional orders duly arrived next morning, in which the 4th Brigade was ordered to keep touch with the New Zealanders on the left. It was very apparent to General Monash that if the advance was persisted in, the centre, which he was responsible for, would he the weakest section of the whole line, and would, as the advance continued, grow weaker and weaker as the armies advanced to their separate objective, the gap widening all the time. It would fall to the already much reduced 4th Brigade alone to extend its flanks and to keep in. touch. Two new battalions would be needed to make good the gap.

Consequently, on Monday morning General Monash met Brigadier-General Walker, who was commanding the 1st Infantry Brigade (Colonel M'Laurin having been killed in the circumstances related), and very forcible pointed out, not on the map, but on the actual ground itself from an overlooking point, what exactly would be the result of the execution of the new plan. General Walker agreed. 'It cannot be done,' he said. Soon afterwards General Walker arrived, and, after a conference, strode over to the telephone without comment—in his usual silent way. It could be seen he was convinced, and in the next few minutes the statements he made while waiting at the telephone left no doubt about the matter. He called up General Birdwood, who was reported to be on the battleship *Queen*, then lying off the position. General Bridges turned and said: 'I take it on myself; the Australian Division will not attack. You [addressing General Monash] may tell General Godley so from me.'

General Godley, on being informed of this message by telephone a little later by General Monash himself, announced his determination of carrying out the attack. 'Very well,' he said, 'the New Zealand Division will carry out orders and attack.' General Monash then asked that a Staff officer should be sent up to reconnoitre the position. This was done, and he, after visiting Quinn's Post and the position in the vicinity, reported that the manoeuvre was highly impracticable, with the troops detailed, with the result that General Godley too cancelled his section of the orders.

Yet the Army Corps order remained uncancelled, as it remained unfulfilled. One can only conclude that it was drawn up without a proper reconnaissance of the country having been made. That there should have been a general advance is recognised on all hands, and there is no doubt in the minds of many Generals with whom I have spoken that it would have been possible that day, had proper provision been made in the original orders for the filling of the very vital gap in the centre of our line. The whole lamentable incident must be put down as indicative of bad Staff work—for thus it was that the whole future of Anzac was changed by a chance meeting of three senior officers on the main ridge and General Bridges' firm decision.

Two days later an attempt, that may only be termed half-successful, was made to effectively seal the head of Monash Gully against Turkish advance. The attack was begun with great gallantry, some of the Naval Brigade penetrating through many Turkish lines, but the increasing battle-front as the plateau of the ridge broadened out, and the strength of the Turks (left unchallenged from the right of the line opposite the Australian position) enabled them to concentrate their attention on the centre. The troops were compelled bit by bit to withdraw to the edge of the plateau, where they clung on and remained clinging on for the rest of the period that Anzac was held.

On 2nd May, exactly a week after the landing, the Australian and New Zealanders were charged with the task of capturing the head of Shrapnel Gully and the plateau beyond that led up to the Baby 700, a rounded feature, the first step in the ridge, of which Chunak Bair was the second, and highest point. The

Australian line stretched across the gully, with Pope's Hill held in the centre. On the right were Quinn's and Courtney's Posts, with the Bloody Angle, one head of the gully between, held by the enemy. On the left from Pope's Hill the line went down into the main head of the gully, up the eastern slope of the hill on to the summit, where the New Zealanders were holding on Russell Top. Practically the whole of the 2nd New Zealand and Australian Brigade were to take part in the operations, supported by Royal Marine Light Infantry troops.

Lieut.-Colonel Pope was to advance up the head of Monash Gully and then storm the heights on the right of the gully, while the Otago Battalion, under Lieut.-Colonel McDonald, was to advance up the gully and take the left slopes, which was the sector after-wards called the Turkish Chessboard trenches. The 13th Battalion was to support the 16th, and was, on reaching the high ground, to link up the two battalions by turning to the left. This manoeuvre meant that a line was to be drawn in front of Pope's Hill and that the 15th Battalion, which held that post, was to make a sortie. The attack was timed for seven o'clock.

An intense bombardment opened the battle. Warships and the guns available on shore commenced to prepare the position by blowing up the Turks. The battalions were moving up the gullies and were waiting for the ceasing of the firing to attack. At 7.15 the bombardment ceased as suddenly as it began, and the men, cheering and singing snatches of 'Tipperary' and their new Australian song, 'Australia will be there,' commenced to charge. Against them came a torrent of lead from rifles and machine guns, for the Turks had occupied the week in fortifying the plateau, of which we only yet held just small pieces of the outer edge.

A reconnaissance had been made during the day and the leaders knew just where their objectives lay. By 8 a.m. a ridge—a sort of false crest immediately in front of Pope's hill and to the left of Quinn's Post and covering the south-easterly front of the general position—had been captured at the point of the bayonet. Fierce hand-to-hand fighting had occurred in places before the troops got a footing and routed the Turks from the line of trenches. The enemy counter-attacked almost as soon as we had gained their position, but they failed to dislodge the Australians.

Meanwhile, on the left flank the Otago Battalion, who had had to make a detour round the mountain ridge from their position, had arrived late for the battle, having found the communication-ways blocked with wounded. They did not reach their point of concentration till a quarter to eight, and it was only an hour later that they charged the position, which had been partially held for them by an extension of the 13th Battalion's line. This Australian battalion, led by Lieut.-Colonel Burnage, had stormed the ridge on which the Turkish entrenchments had been dug, just immediately in front of Pope's Hill, and the Turks, though they counterattacked, were unable her also to regain possession of those trenches.

The Nelson Battalion of the Naval Brigade now sent up a company under Major Primrose, and, with a company of the 14th Battalion, the position of the 16th was rendered a little more secure. In the darkness touch had not been kept on the left, their flank was in the air, and the 13th battalion had not linked up as it should. The Turkish fire was smashing down the resistance of the men on the left, and the position was fast becoming untenable as the dawn broke. At 4 a.m. the Portsmouth Battalion was ordered up to support the 16th and to strengthen its left flank. Through some misunderstanding of orders valuable time was lost by the leader of the Marine battalion, who was unwilling to enter the firing-line when orders had only been given him to form a support. The Commanding Officer would take no responsibility for going into the firing-line. While the position was still in doubt, the situation became utterly untenable owing to shells that commenced to burst in the 16th Battalion trenches, which subsequently it was found came from the destroyers, who mistook the target—so close were the trenches—and before this ghastly error could be rectified, the battalion was forced to retire on this left flank.

To make matters worse a stampede ensued in the rank and file of the Portsmouth Battalion, who were congregated in the gully below. It was only by the presence of mind and great personal effort of Major Tilney, second in command of the 16th Battalion, and Major Festian, Brigade-Major of the R.M.L.I., that the stampede was checked. Efforts were made to direct gun fire on what at first were believed to be the Turkish artillery. Horrible confusion prevailed. Daylight was breaking. Some of the Portsmouth Battalion occupied a ridge on the left of the gully, on to which the Turks were firing a deadly enfilade and almost rear fire from their centre position. Until ten o'clock in the morning the 13th and 16th clung to the trenches (some of their trenches were blown away into the gully by gun fire), but, exposed to a withering fire, had at length to withdraw. At one o'clock the gully and captured trenches were abandoned.

The Otago Battalion meanwhile, on the extreme left, joining with the 13th battalion, had faced a terrible fire, but reached almost to the point of its objective in line with the remainder of the line there, well in advance of Pope's Hill. There they stuck desperately, waiting for reinforcements, which were to come under cover of darkness from the Canterbury battalion. This succour was found impracticable, as it had been found on the right that an advance was not possible. Shells began to destroy the trenches dug overnight, with the result that the left flank of the New Zealanders was driven back. There remained but the 13th Battalion and a party from the Otago Battalion clinging on to the sharp ridge in front of Pope's Hill. They were digging hard throughout the day, while the Turks, too, were digging so close to them that it was almost impossible to say which trenches belonged to which. But the Turks, also, were working round behind the position, and at dusk there was nothing for it but that the gallant 13th should retire from their position, now being enfiladed from both flanks. The Otago Battalion, which was more or less isolated, clung on desperately to the position it had won until two days later, when it had to cut its way out.

The one object accomplished by the attack was the checking of any enemy offensive against the posts which were undoubtedly the weakest portion of the whole line. But the main objective, to straighten out the line, or rather to bring the line to a culminating point at the head of the gully, and gain a footing on the plateau where the main ridge linked up with the ridge running away to the south-east, was not accomplished. It was the greatest of the many attacks about this time planned for this purpose. All along this section of the ridge fierce fighting went on during the next weeks, sorties being made from various posts to prevent the Turk pushing our line from the edge of the ridge which they had so desperately won, until in the great May attack the Australians gained the upper hand and the mastery of the Turkish fire. Always a dangerous and nervy part of the line, it was only declared 'safe' after the Turkish offensive on 19th May.

CHAPTER XV
VICTORIANS' CHARGE AT KRITHIA

While the Australians' position at Anzac was being made secure, preparations were pushed forward at Cape Helles for the storming of the loaf-shaped hill of Achi Baba, on which the Turks had, after the fortnight's fighting, been forced to take up a defensive position. There they had strongly entrenched themselves behind line after line of trenches. Their actual first resisting line, however, was by this about 3 miles from the toe of the peninsula on the right, at a point near De Tots battery, the taking of which the French eventually accomplished with great gallantry. Later the Gurkhas on the opposite (the left) flank performed a magnificent feat in reaching a point south-west of Krithia village by storming and obtaining a footing on the slopes of the Great Dere, while the British line swung round before the southern angle of the Krithia village. The fresh 'shove' was meant to take the village at the point of the bayonet and capture the slopes of Achi Baba. Whatever that fortress position may have become later (and the German officers captured boasted that it was a position that would never be taken by frontal assault), at that time there seemed every prospect of it falling into the hands of bold, determined troops. It was for this reason, to give impetus to the attack, to strengthen the British troops that held the central portion of the line, that the 2nd Australian Brigade, under Colonel (later Brigadier-General) M'Cay, were, on the night of 5th. Many, silently removed from the beach at Anzac, and, 3,000 strong, were landed at Cape Helles at six o'clock in the morning. Though this brigade had been through the thick of the landing and attack on Anzac, it had, perhaps, suffered least of all the brigades, and was now chosen suddenly for this fresh assault. The New Zealand Infantry Brigade, under Colonel F. E. Johnston, was also landed, and took up a position of the left flank of the Australians; their left flank in turn in touch with troops on the coast.

So much for the general situation. The embarkation orders for the brigade came suddenly, while the troops were resting after a week's fight. At 9 p.m. the brigade was assembled on the beach. Here the men suffered a bitter experience, exposed to considerable fire, for insufficient transports had been provided. Eventually they embarked from six wharves and slipped silently away. Twenty casualties had been suffered from what were called spent bullets, the Anzac firing-line being over 1,000 yards away. The men left the shore in rowing-boats and went out to the trawlers, and then to the destroyers and on to transports. They knew naught of their destination. A very few hours' steaming and they arrived off the British position. All disembarked at 6 a.m. at Seddul Bahr (near the *River Clyde*) under a heavy shell fire from the Asiatic batteries, where the wandering, disappearing gun, 'Asiatic Algy,' began to pour shells on the brigade. The jetties at this time were only of the roughest wood, joining barges moored alongside one another.

One is never likely to forget one's sensations upon landing on the end of the peninsula in the track of the victorious British armies. Thick masses of tangled Turkish barbed wire (wire so thick that ordinary shears would not sever it) were rolled round deserted trenches, guns lay dismounted from their concrete bases, houses had been torn down and lay shattered, with hardly a wall standing. There were 30,000 French troops now on the British right flank. All manner of stores, including great casks of their ration wine, had been landed, and lay piled in the sandy cove that stretched between two headlands, Seddul Bahr on the right, Helles fort on the left. The menacing walls of Seddul Bahr rose above it round the cliff, but no longer a fortress of the Turks. The village, in ruins, was buried behind.

After a steep pull up a ridge (on which stood two haystacks) from this beach, the brigade advanced across country to the Krithia road. What country it was to look down on, after the bushy hills and gullies of Anzac! Here was a flowering heath and meadows of corn and poppies and wild flowers. There were orchards and aged olive-trees and some farmers' huts and houses in the distance; while cattle grazed in sheltered hollows. It was undulating country, resembling a hollow plain, of miles in extent, and especially flat-looking to the Australians, fresh from Anzac's rugged hills. Grim, but not very forbidding, stood the smoothly rounded hill of Achi Baba—Tree Hill—barring the advance up the peninsula, a long arm stretching down to each shore. Shells from the warships were plastering the face of it as the brigade advanced. Dense clouds of white shrapnel were bursting over the Turkish trenches which lay round the long, rolling slopes that ended at the village of Krithia on the left (the west), and which ran out to the Dardanelles on the east, falling away into steep gullies on the seashore.

The bivouac chosen for the brigade was about a mile from the landing and on the west of the road that led direct into the distant village. Here, as in every line, the troops might rest in some comfort, though not safety; for besides the shells from Achi Baba batteries there were guns firing from the Asiatic shore. Nothing remained but to dig and dig in for one's life. However, here a new difficulty was encountered, for water was struck when the trenches were sunk about 18 inches, and that is why in so many trenches there were such high parapets, it was the only means of getting sufficient protection. If one thing at this time and under the particularly trying conditions heartened the troops more than another, it was to hear, and watch, the French '75' batteries sending fourteen shells to the minute to the Turkish trenches. Moreover, Australian batteries—a whole brigade, in fact, under Colonel Christian—were discovered entrenched beside the French guns in the very centre of the peninsula, and the troops knew that, in any attack, they would have their own guns to support them. No sooner had they halted than they started to prepare their meal, and were laughing, singing, and joking. They felt a certain security even in the face of the foe.

That afternoon, the 6th May, the Brigadier (Colonel M'Cay) and his Brigade Staff (Major Cass and Captain Walstab) moved forward to a stony rise, occupied by the gunners as an observation station, and from there they looked down over the whole of the ground undulating away to Achi Baba, 4 miles distant. The country was, I have said, flat. It was not a plain, strictly speaking, for there were small depressions and dry creek beds that would be sufficient to protect a great number of troops when the time came for advance. The southern slopes of the big hill were intersected by many ravines, which in wet weather formed the head-water of the three *deres* or gullies that flowed south down the peninsula— the KerevesDere (the great gully) and Maltepedera and KanliDere. This divided the peninsula into three ridges, which ran parallel with one another in a northerly and southerly direction. On the eastern slopes, facing the Straits, these *deres* were particularly rugged and often precipitous. There still remained portions of a telegraph line across a ridge on the right going north-east from Seddul Bahr; it had been the scene of heavy fighting, in which the French made many gallant charges to take what has been called the 'Haricot,' a formidable redoubt placed on the crest of a hill, and which had held up the French advance for many previous days and cost many lives to finally capture.

To realise how any advance across such open country could be accomplished, it is necessary to explain that the guns on the peninsula were placed in a great semi-circle, starting from the northern slopes of Morto Bay, where the French guns, hidden behind the grape-vines and clustered corn and hedges, lay. In the valley between the low hills through which the Krithia road runs, were some British 60-pounders, and on the southern slopes of a hill in the centre of the peninsula British and Australian 18-pounders were firing. Hidden amongst some trees was a heavy British battery, and in the Kanli Valley were other guns.

The French firing-line extended along in front of their batteries for about 1,000 yards, and adjoining them on the left was the Naval Division. Next to their left flank was the 29th Division. It was the New Zealand and Australian Brigade and General Cox's Indian Brigade that formed a composite Division held in reserve to the 29th.

It must be here explained of this composite Division that in the first day's fighting the Australians took no part. The New Zealanders were called into action to support the 29th Division, and suffered heavy casualties. But to give the true significance to the share of the Australians in the grand offensive during the early days in May, the early stages of the battle that began on the morning of the 6th at eleven o'clock and continued for three days, need describing. The artillery duels of those days were terrific in the extreme, and the whole of the battle lines were violently swept with shell. The configuration of the country was such that the hills on the extreme end of the peninsula gave a grand-stand view, and the Staffs of the Army Corps operating could be seen on these points watching the armies moving forward into action. It has been described as 'a Melton Prior battlefield,' where you saw each unit going into action. Such an offensive was only possible on account of the comparative weakness of the Turkish trenches, a defect which they lost no time in rectifying later on, when a period of sullenness set in. For the Turk has, in this campaign at least, proved himself to be a most industrious, even colossal, digger of trenches and a fine trench fighter, however poor he shows himself to be in open combat.

A general advance was the order on the 6th. The French '75' batteries, with their sharp bark, began fiercely to smash the enemy trenches, concentrating fire on the 'Haricot' and KerevesDere, and the valleys beyond that contained Turkish supports. The Krithia village was shelled by the heavy British guns, aeroplanes spotting. French and British battleships had moved up on the flanks and were pouring a terrible enfilade fire on the Turks and covering the slopes of Achi Baba with sheets of flame as the shells burst along the position. It was in vain that the Turkish batteries, prodigal with their ammunition, tried to silence our guns, carefully concealed, and in the absence of aeroplanes, which the Turks did not seem to possess at that time or were afraid to send into the air, the British and French gunners went on without interruption, except for chance disabling shots which put a gun or two out of action.

As the French and British lines advanced there came the roar of musketry and the rattle of machine guns to add to the already terrific din. The British maintained their advance, though the machine guns in the thick scrub could not be located, while the French swept on, gaining the 'Haricot,' then losing it. All this battle panorama was rapidly passing before the eyes of the leaders of the Australian troops, who were waiting their turn to charge and take their part in the battle. Soon the French were forced to retire to the trenches they had lately left, much to the chagrin of all, though the British troops held their gain of about 1,000 yards, while the Naval Division had gone forward about 700 yards in the centre. The 29th also advanced nearly 1,000 yards on the left, near the Ægean shore. This line they entrenched during the night. It was a very bent line, with the French farthest in the rear. The Turks were too exhausted to attempt any counter-attack, and so the line stood till the morning of the 7th. Then a further advance was made at 10.30, the guns blazing the way and plastering the slopes of Achi Baba for the infantry to advance. As on the previous day, the Australian officers watched the fighting from a position which overlooked the battle-front of 4 miles, subjected only to an occasional whizzing bullet and a stray shell.

This was a curious battlefield for modern warfare, where most of the fighting is underground. Imagine an area of about 5 square miles. The valley road was the main transport route, despite the fact that the enemy overlooked and commanded it. On the west side were the red and pink farms, hidden by a copse of fir-trees. The French at this time had placed their headquarters in one of these houses. With a start of surprise one saw their Staff moving along, with orderlies, mounted messengers, and signallers, all beautifully mounted, riding right up to within half a mile of the firing-line down this valley, through the shot and shell. Along the road rumbled the French ammunition-wagons, the caissons, turning east to Morto

Bay, bearing supplies to the batteries there. The French gunners got their supplies by day and the British, who were more exposed, by night; and so the traffic on the roads was regulated, otherwise the congestion, would have been terrible. A motor-cyclist, with the latest word from the battlefield, would ride at breakneck speed through the traffic, and, once past the mules, plodding stolidly along, would travel at 50 or 60 miles an hour for the short stretch until he dipped out of sight behind the last ridge of the peninsula. Dust rose constantly in dense clouds. I remember looking at these clouds as the armoured cars on another occasion swept forward, and wondered that the Turks did not shell them, which eventually they did; but during these days they directed all their energies to searching for the guns and plastering the slopes of the Seddul Bahr ridges and the clumps of trees scattered over the peninsula, where it seemed obvious our artillery might be concealed.

It was not till the third day that the Australians went into the fight. This Saturday, 8th, had opened much as the other two days had done with intense bombardments, and then an advance by the infantry in short rushes, always driving the Turks before them, pressing them back to the village of Krithia and the foot slopes of Achi Baba. But by this time on the flanks the Turks had concealed a great many machine guns in the fir woods, and built redoubts, and such advances became terribly expensive. On the 7th the New Zealanders had moved away to the support of the 29th Division, and they lost heavily from these guns. At 10.30 on this morning they were ordered to go through the British lines and try to take the trenches on the left front of Krithia—now a village wrecked and shattered by the shells that burst in it and smouldering with fires that the artillery had started. Once I had seen it, a pretty little hamlet with white and red-roofed dwellings snuggling down in the hollow of a hill, with the stern, flat-topped Achi Baba mound lying just to the east. On a ridge stood sentinel windmills, their long arms stark and bare, waving from the side of a curious round stone store, like a silo. They were the Turkish granaries, and made fine observation posts. The Wellington Battalion, under Lieut.-Colonel W. G. Malone, was on the left, the Auckland, under Lieut.-Colonel A. Plugge, in the centre, and Canterbury, under Lieut.-Colonel D. M. Stewart, on the right. The Otago, under Lieut.-Colonel T. W. McDonald, was in reserve. On the flanks the battalions, facing an awful fire, slowly moved up about 300 yards, but the centre battalion, a dense copse in front concealing a strong force of the enemy, were unable to go ahead. By 2.30 there was nothing left for the gallant New Zealand battalions to do but to dig in. The Otagos had been called to support and repair the fearful losses, but the advance was checked. However, it was determined that the New Zealanders should again attack just at dusk. Later on this order was changed to a general attack by the whole line. With but a few minutes' notice the Australians, till then in reserve, were ordered to prepare to form the front, or rather centre front, of the advancing line.

It had been bright and crisp all the morning, and the troops were in high fettle. At midday, General Paris, commanding the composite Division, had ordered the Australians to move up in support of the British centre, which they did, advancing due north about a mile. Their new position was in a broad *dere* (fully), and as fairly a protected and comfortable spot as such places go so near the firing-line. Colonel M'Cay, to reach it, had deployed his troops on lines best calculated to avoid searching shrapnel fire, moving them up in platoon columns, that is, in small bodies placed some 200 yards' distance from, one another, which had the effect of almost neutralising the shelling of the Turks. The 6th Battalion was in the lead, followed by the 7th, 5th, and 8th. The Turks, for some reason, did not open fire as the troops moved across the valley, though it was fully expected they would, and so they arrived at a position where there were trenches—some British, some Turkish—already dug, while the *dere* itself offered further cover. The men began to deepen and widen these trenches for their comfort. The 6th, under Lieut.-Colonel M'Nicol, was bivouacked on the steep sides of the stream; and opposite them on the left was the 8th, under Lieut.-Colonel Bolton. About 30 yards in rear of the 6th was brigade headquarters, just in line with Colonel Cox's Indian Brigade. Lieut.-Colonel Garside, commanding the 7th, was behind the 8th, and headquarters and the 5th, under Lieut.-Colonel Wanliss, behind the 8th. In the midst of taking in reinforcements and entrenching, the plan for the general attack was communicated to the Australian leaders.

Just a few minutes after five o'clock Colonel M'Cay received by telephone from General Paris orders to advance without delay. It was now definitely known that the French had been held up at the 'Haricot' for two days, and that they had now been ordered to make a general advance (which they did with colours flying and bands playing, an extraordinary and inspiring sight, white and black troops fighting side by side). At all costs the Turks had to go. So sudden had been the decision for the general advance that there was no time to issue written orders, a dilemma in which the Brigadier (Colonel M'Cay) found himself. However, by 5.15 the troops were on the move, the Brigade Staff giving the directions and the orders verbally. So, one may write, there began an offensive which in detail and execution was like the battles of half a century ago, when generals, calling on their men, dashed into the thick of the fray.

No man will ever be able to do justice to the events of the next half hour or fifty minutes. As might have the finest regulars in the world, those Victorians moved from their bivouac, into which they had yet scarcely settled. The 7th were to occupy about 500 yards of front on the right, and the 6th Battalion on the left with a similar frontage. The general direction of the attack was the north-east, and striking point just on the east of the village of Krithia. The flanks rested, therefore, on two valleys: on the right Mai TepeDere, and KanliDere on the left. The 5th Battalion was supporting the right flank, and the 8th the left. Seeing the preparations for the new attack, the Turkish guns turned from the first line of British troops, already in position some 500 yards away ahead, and directed a veritable hell-fire of shrapnel and bullets against the supports, which they rightly judged must be moving up about this time.

The whole Allied front was barely 4 miles, swept by a terrible inferno of shells. The air was filled with the white, woolly clouds that the Anzac men—old soldiers now—knew meant a hail of lead.

The ground was torn and ripped up as the shells fell; little parties of men were swept away, killed outright. Overhead whined and whistled the shells; ours on their way to the Turkish trenches, theirs coming on to our advancing line. Overhead might have been a whirling shield of armour.

Rapidly the Australians scrambled over the Indian trenches which were in their path, the 7th doubling forward so as to continue the line of the 6th, and together with the other two regiments (in support), the whole mass of 3,000 men started to move forward rapidly towards the front trenches occupied by the Naval Division. Pictures of the ground will show its openness; they do not show the first slight slope up which the Australians charged in a 1,000 yards advance, of which that was the first sector. At the top of the slope—it was hardly appreciable to the casual glance—were the Naval Division trenches. Beyond these the ground sloped away down into a broad depression, that only began to rise again a little to the south of the Krithia village and Achi Baba. Once it had been cultivated ground. Over this the Australians charged. The right flank was resting now on the Krithia road. The troops were heavily laden; for besides their packs, many carried shovels, entrenching tools, and picks; they had to dig in when they had advanced. They stumbled or fell into the British trenches, where they lay for a while panting. Many lads were unable to reach the security of the trenches (for they were strongly held and crowded), and so they lay in whatever depressions were available behind the parados, while the lead streamed over them—whizz—swing—whizz—swing—little singing messages of death. You heard them close to your ear even above the din of the booming shells.

With bayonets fixed the Australians left the trenches. Colonel M'Cay—surely his life was charmed that day—walked along the parapet swinging his stick, as was his custom, and looking down into the trenches, called: 'Come on, Australians!' The Brigade-Major, Major Cass, was in another sector doing the same. No second call was needed to rouse the troops. They would follow those brave officers to the very jaws of death. They scrambled to the parapets, and crouching low, began to advance, 50, 60, 70 yards at a rush, and then, as exhaustion overcame them, a short respite lying flattened to the ground. But the line never wavered, though thinned at every step, going on and on with the officers rallying the men as they panted forward.

God! The marvel of it! The ground was quite bare, except for isolated bushes of green shrub, through which the bullets sang and tore. Intense masses of rifles and machine guns poured down lead on to the advancing Australian lines. The British had cheered these heroes as they left the trenches—now they stood watching and wondering. Rushing downhill, the troops were in a regular shallow basin, like a huge plate. The Turkish trenches lay scarcely 800 yards ahead. That was the only information that the Australians got as to their objective: that was all they wanted; anyway, no enemy could be seen now in the battle smoke and dust. No reconnaissance had been possible, except in a general sort of way, and it was for this reason that Colonel M'Cay led his men and allotted sections of the line to the rest of his Brigade Staff. For the rest he trusted to the spirit of his men.

The Turks, well entrenched and concealed, waited for the Australian charge. No use for the attackers to fling themselves down and fire; they had no target. On again they went, panting, lying down, advancing in short rushes of 50 yards, or less, as the men grew more and more tired. The line thinned. The slopes were covered with dead and wounded. Darkness was falling. A constant stream of disabled men were toiling slowly back to the shelter of the gullies. Stretcher-bearers, regardless of the stream of lead, were going forward and dragging back to the naval trenches those men whom they found badly wounded. Sometimes a British soldier leaped out to help in a comrade.

Then, after a charge of 400 yards, across the Krithia road was seen the low parapet of a Turkish trench, and the 7th Battalion opened fire as the Turks commenced to fly before the unbroken Australian line; but it was only a short halt, for the 6th Battalion was still advancing so as to get to close quarters with the bayonet. 'Bayonet them' had been the orders, and the steel the Turks were to get if they waited. On went the 7th, the reserve battalions now coming up into the firing-line. Losses got more and more terrible. They reached the parapet of a now deserted enemy trench, yet still the Turkish fire came in a steady stream from the front and the left, where machines guns were rattling from a copse that had before broken the New Zealand ranks. On the right it had become silent. Major Cass, leading there, found it strangely so, and for the moment, could not account for the pause, as according to the plan the French were to have charged and advanced. What had happened he learned very shortly. Again the French had been checked. But 400 yards' advance had been made by the Australians and New Zealanders. The extreme left of the line was brought to a standstill, the British Indian force unable to press farther on. Australians, and alongside them New Zealanders, were entrenching for their lives. The Turkish trenches had been stormed, and the first objective taken, though Krithia was still unstormed, 800 yards away. But, in this moment of success, a horrible fresh danger made itself manifest.

The French had not taken the 'Haricot.' While the Australians' right still pushed on the Frenchmen were not advancing. A gap of many hundred yards yawned between the right of the Australian line and the left of the French. Into this breach the Turks were not slow to hurl their men. They began working down a gully. The manner in which the discovery of this attempt to pierce the line was made is dramatic in the extreme. Major Cass, who had been leading the right of the Australian line, had fallen wounded, shot through the shoulder (it broke his collar-bone), and as he lay behind a slight mound that had been dug for him by some of his devoted men, there came from the left, almost at right angles to him, a bullet that smashed his other shoulder. Although suffering from shock, his arms helplessly hanging by his side, he managed, nevertheless to get his pocket-book out, and began to write. As a soldier the truth had quickly flashed in his mind: the Turks were between the Allied lines, and very soon they would be in the rear as well. The peril of the situation demanded instant action. Hastily he scribbled a note in triplicate, explaining the position to the Commander of the Naval Brigade, holding the trenches in the rear, through which the Australians in their charge had advanced. Major Cass sent these notes back by Private H. Wilson, Headquarters Staff, who returned with an answer after what, to the wounded man, seemed an interminable time. The shrapnel still screamed overhead and the bushes were cut by the descending bullets, that made a spluttering sound as they swept the valley. Another verbal message was sent by Lieutenant Stewart to the Brigadier. At last the reassuring reply came back from the Naval Brigade that the breach would be filled. The Drake Battalion advanced with the 5th Australian Battalion, under Colonel Wanliss, until the distance between— some 300 yards—was filled. So was the Turkish flanking movement hindered and pressed back. Five hours later Major Cass, in the early hours of the morning, reached the beach and a hospital ship. The devotion of the messenger who carried the message and then wished to take his officer from the firing-line was duly rewarded, while Major Cass received the D.S.O.

Meanwhile it happened that the reserve battalions had come up into the firing-line almost at the same moment as that line came to a halt, exhausted. Entrenching tools and sandbags were carried, and at once the whole line commenced to dig in. It was dusk. During the whole of that night the Turks kept up a continuous fire, with the idea, no doubt, of preventing reinforcements being brought up by us under cover of darkness. Nevertheless, further drafts of reinforcements were hurried into the firing-line, and the new trenches were secured. Not a single yard of trench was retaken by the Turks. From that day on till the final evacuation of the peninsula was accomplished, visiting officers would be shown the 'Australian' trenches, which marked the point of their magnificent charge of 1,000 yards—a sheer gain of some 400 yards, made in a few minutes. The brigade held the trenches until the following Tuesday morning, when they were relieved by the 29th Division.

The Australian losses had been appallingly heavy, partly on account of the open ground over which the advance was made, and partly from the fact that the Turks had a concealed and well fortified position. The whole of the Brigade Staff was wounded, and the casualties amongst the officers were very severe indeed. The Brigadier, Colonel M'Cay, was wounded about nine o'clock as he was returning from the trenches, having lived a charmed life for many hours as he superintended the men digging the new trenches. Lieut.-Colonel Garside, who was commanding the 7th Battalion, was killed almost at the side of Major Wells, both fine soldiers, who had showed magnificent courage. It was in this charge, too, that Lieut.-Colonel M'Nicol, of the 6th, received machine-gun wounds which nearly cost him his life. For his magnificent work he received the D.S.O. Probably half the brigade was either killed or wounded, and the Brigadier estimated his loss at 1,800, thereby reducing his command by half.

Till Monday night the removal of the wounded proceeded. Progress to the beach, 2 miles away, was painfully slow. Never, so a wounded officer told me, shall he forget the calls of the men for 'water,' for 'help' as the stretcher-bearers and doctors, working with unsurpassed heroism, passed to and from the first dressing-station, 2 miles in the rear. Here the wounded could be placed on rough general service wagons and taken over the fearful rutted roads to the beach. Two further transfers had to take place before the men reached the hospital ship. The bitter cold of the night added to the intensity of the suffering of the men. Yet so long as they knew that they would be found the men bore their wounds and pain patiently and stoically, content in the news from the front that they had won and the Turks had fled.

On the 12th, the brigade—all that was left of it—was withdrawn from the firing line, and on the 15th reached Anzac again, to the tired troops almost like a homecoming. They came back to a new fight, but one in which the Turks attacked, were broken, and repulsed.

CHAPTER XVI
TURKISH MAY ATTACK
AND ARMISTICE

The Turks' strongest attack of the campaign was made in the middle of May, when they attempted an assault all along the Anzac line. Both sides had had time to reorganise, and both had received reinforcements. The Turks probably had 35,000 men in their trenches at this time, while the Australians had 30,000. During the first fortnight of the month the enemy had brought up guns of bigger calibre, and had placed in the Olive Grove, from which they could enfilade the beach from the east, a six-gun battery which even the warships and the Australian gunners were unable to completely silence. The Allies had aeroplanes and captive balloons spotting for them, and yet the Turkish batteries, skilfully concealed, managed to continue shelling the beach and the incoming barges. Very little notice was taken by the Navy of this shelling, and very soon, too, the troops regarded it as the natural thing. What they would have felt like, these Australians, had they been fighting in France, where, for certain periods, they would be relieved and taken from under constant shell fire, it is not easy to say. The strain wore them down certainly, but it never affected the army nerves or its heart or its determination.

Nevertheless, May was a sad month for the troops, though it also brought later a chance of the Turks being taught a lesson. On Saturday, 15th May, Major-General Bridges, the leader of the 1st Division, fell mortally wounded. It had often been remarked by the troops at Anzac that their General was absolutely careless of his own safety. He was daily round the trenches, a rather glum, silent man, but keenly observant, and quickly able to draw from his officers all the points of information he required. Often he recklessly exposed himself to gain a view of the Turkish positions, despite the remonstrances of his Staff. As time wore on he took heed, and on the morning when he fell had been more than usually careful. General Bridges had left Anzac Headquarters, near the beach, at about 9.30, and was going up Shrapnel Gully, and at this time that terrible gully had no secret sap through which one might pass with comparative safety from snipers' bullets coming from the head of the gully. It was a matter of running, from sandbag traverse to sandbag traverse, a gauntlet of lead, up the bed of the dry gully.

General Bridges had just passed a dressing-station dug into the side of the hill, and had received a warning from the stretcher-bearers standing round the entrance. 'You had better run across here, sir,' they told him, 'as the Turks are pretty lively to-day.' He did, and reached a further traverse, where he stood near another dressing-station smoking a cigarette. 'Well,' he said to his Staff officer, after a few minutes, 'we must make another run for it.' He ran round the corner of the traverse and through the thick scrub. Before he could reach the next cover, not many yards away, he was struck by a bullet and lay prone. It is believed that the sniper at the head of the gully was waiting and watching that morning, and had already inflicted a number of casualties. Medical attention was immediately available. A doctor at the adjacent dressing-station found that the femoral artery in the thigh had been severed. The bullet, instead of merely piercing the leg, had entered sideways and torn a way through. Only for the fact that skilled attention was so prompt, General Bridges must have died within a few minutes. The wound was plugged. Taken to the dressing-station, the General's first words were, 'Don't carry me down; I don't want any of your fellows to run into danger.' Seeing the stretcher case, the Turks did not fire on the party that now made its way to the beach, all traffic being stopped along the track. The dying leader was immediately taken off to a hospital ship, but his condition was critical. Before the ship left his beloved Anzac, his last words to an officer, who had been with him from the first, were, 'Anyhow, I have commanded an Australian Division, for nine months.'

General Bridges died four days later on his way to Alexandria. It was very typical, that last sentence of the man. His whole heart and soul and energies had been devoted to planning the efficiency of the 1st Division. A born organiser, a fine tactician, he was a lone, stern figure that inspired a great confidence in his men. His judgment in the field had proved almost unfailing. Unsparing to himself, he demanded, and obtained, the best in those he commanded. He was one of the finest leaders on Gallipoli, and in him General Hamilton and Lieut.-General Birdwood reposed the highest confidence.

General Birdwood, cabling from Army Corps headquarters to the Governor-General of Australia, said:

> It is with the deepest regret that I have to announce the death on 19th May of General Bridges, who has proved himself the most gallant of soldiers and best of commanders. I am quite unable to express what his loss means to the Australian Division, which can never pay the debt it owes him for his untiring and unselfish labours, which are responsible for the high state of organisation to which the Division has been brought in every detail. The high ideals placed before the boys trained at Duntroon, and which he succeeded in attaining as far as my knowledge of those now serving with the Australian forces in the field is concerned, will, I hope, go down to the honour of his name as long as the military history of Australia lasts.

The Commander-in-Chief, General Sir Ian Hamilton, cabled on 20th May:

General Bridges died on the passage to Alexandria. The whole force mourns his irreparable loss, which was avenged yesterday in a brilliant action by his own troops, who inflicted a loss of 7,000 on the enemy at a cost of less than 500 to themselves.

It is this Turkish attack that I now shall describe, and the nature of the revenge. Brigadier-General Walker, who had been commanding the 1st Infantry Brigade since the death of Colonel McLaurin, succeeded to the immediate command of the Division.

The new Turkish batteries employed at this time contained some 6-inch guns, and it is believed that the *Goeben* or one of the cruisers belonging to the Turks had come down from Constantinople and was stationed, just parallel to Bogali, in the Straits. Enemy warships, it is believed, were able to throw shells accurately into the heart of our position, searching for the guns. By the 18th May the Turks had an 11-in. gun, some 8-in., and a number of 4'7-in. guns trained on Anzac. With the support of these, and with the small mountain and field pieces that they had been using before, it has been since learned, they felt that they could safely attack. Their offensive was fixed for the 19th May. Preliminary bombardments began on the evening before, 18th, and were the fiercest that had yet been experienced. The hills echoed with the chaotic explosions of the bursting of heavy shells. One of the Australian 18 pounders was knocked out completely, and other shells reached the gun-pits; but the gunners stuck to their posts and replied effectively to this Turkish bombardment. It was reported that evening from aeroplane reconnaissances that the Turks had been seen landing a new Division at the Straits, and that they were marching to the support of the Anzac troops. Headquarters were located at Bogali. At once the warships commenced a bombardment of the main road leading along the side of the hills to Krithia village, where troops could be seen moving. They followed them up and shelled the general Turkish Staff out of a village midway between Kelid Bahr and Krithia.

Attacks at Anzac were always determined by the time at which the moon sank. I can remember on one occasion waiting night after night in the trenches, when the Turks were supposed to be about to attack, until the moon would sink. We would rouse up and watch its departing sickly yellow circle dip behind the hills of Troy, and then turn towards the Turkish trenches, which we could see occasionally spitting fire, and wait for the general fusillade to open. Now, on the 18th the moon dipped down at a little before midnight, and just as the midnight hours passed, from the centre of the line round Quinn's Post arose the clatter of Turkish bombs. In the closely wedged trenches the Australians answered this attack with similar missiles, and for a while a little 'bomb party,' as it was called by the troops, began. From an intermittent rifle fire the sound of the sharp crackle of rifles intensified and extended from end to end of the Turkish lines. It was as if thousands of typewriters, the noise of their working increased a thousandfold, had begun to work. Every second the racket grew; in less than two minutes the gullies were torrents of singing lead, while the bullets could be heard everywhere whizzing through the bushes. The rapid beat of the machine guns began, their pellets thudding against the sandbag parapets. Bombs, bursting like the roar of water that had broken the banks of dams, drowned the general clatter. Immense 'football bombs' (as the troops termed them) they were, that wrought awful havoc and formed huge craters. For halt an hour the fury lasted. Then it died down, much as violent storms do, arising suddenly, and departing by fading away in a curiously short, sharp burst of firing. Again the sudden rapid fire arose and then again the splutter of ceasing shots. Bombing had stopped.

It is hard to know what the reason of the Turk was for this 'bluff,' for it was such, for no attack followed. It was not exactly an unusual incident in itself, but, nevertheless, always had the effect of rousing up the line and the troops manning the trenches. Probably the Turks calculated that we would be led to believe that the whole show was over for that night, and consequently without further bombardment they began a few hours later their extended attack.

Just in the hour preceding dawn—about 3.30 the time is given—the Turks began silently and stealthily to approach the trenches. Without a sound they came, in large and small bodies, up the gullies, working by the help of a marching tape that would keep them together. They approached to within, in some cases, 30 or 40 yards of our trenches. At that time coloured rocket shells were not so much used as they were later; no coloured green and red lights that would burn for some minutes, lit up any section of the line. But the sentries on the parapets suddenly began to detect, even in the blackness of the night preceding dawn, crawling figures. The Turk was always a good scout, and would get right under the parapets of our trenches almost undetected. But when he came to facing the Australian bayonet and jumping down into the trenches it was a different matter altogether. Now, it was just at the centre of the right of the position, at the point where the 1st Brigade and the 1st Battalion of that brigade held the line, that the alarm first was given. The sentries shot down the advancing figures. Immediately others rose up quickly and rushed silently at the trenches. A few managed to jump across the parapets and down into the trenches. It is a brave man indeed who will do such an act.

The attack was launched. Right down the Australian line now spread the order for rapid fire, for the Turks could be seen and heard calling 'Allah! Allah!' They came in great numbers, dashing forward in the already coming dawn, for in the sky behind them the sun would rise, and now already its faintest streaks were appearing, casting an opaque tinge in the heavens. Gallantly as the Turks charged, the Australians stood magnificently steady, and fired steadily into the masses of moving silhouetted figures. It was 'terrible, cold-blooded murder,' as one of the defenders described it to me later. 'They were plucky enough, but they never had a dog's chance.'

Now in a few places the Turks did reach our trenches, but they found themselves trapped, and the few who escaped with their lives, surrendered. Across the poppy-field the Turks had pressed hardest, but they were thrust back and back. Next morning, when the dawn came, their bodies could be seen lying in heaps on the slopes. It was as if the men had been mown down in lines.

While the attacks were developing against the centre of the right of the line—company after company and battalion after battalion were sent on by the Turks in their endeavours to push the Australians off the peninsula—there began fierce fighting on the extreme right, on the left, and at the apex of the position at the head of Monash Gully. It was a desperate enough position, for the Turks were not more than 10 or 20 yards away in places. Our machine guns ripped along their parapets; when one gun ceased, to fix in its jaws a new belt, another took on the fire; so the noise was insistent, and the Turks, yelling 'Allah! Allah!' stumbled forward a few paces and were mown down, but never were able to advance to the trenches. Far into the morning the attacks continued. Mostly they were short rushes, opposed by terrific bursts of fire, bombs hurled into the advancing mass; a check and then a pause. As the enemy were still advancing, only at isolated points could their machine guns reply or rifles be fired. That there were some enemy bullets did not affect the troops, who regarded it as too good an opportunity to miss. The Australians' sporting instincts were roused, and at many points the men could be seen sitting on the parapets of the trenches, calmly picking off the Turks as they came up, working their bolts, loading, furiously. This was the way in which the few casualties that did occur (100 killed and 500 wounded) were sustained. It was a bloodless victory, if ever there has been one.

Once a German Albatross aeroplane had come sailing over the position at a very high altitude, the Turks must have known that their chances of success were gone. They commenced to shell the shipping off the beaches, in the hope that any reinforcements that might be arriving might be sunk, but they were not even successful in this. Our artillery had the range to a few yards, and as the Turks left their trenches (though only so short a distance away) the shrapnel swept along their parapets, and they were shot down in rows. It is calculated that 3,000 Turks perished in that attack. Some make the estimate higher, and there is reason to believe that they may be right. The wounded numbered nearly 15,000. It was their one and only general attack. It failed hopelessly. It was never repeated.

So horrible had the battlefield become, strewn with Turkish dead, that the enemy sued for an armistice. On the day succeeding the engagement and the repulse of the Turks, towards dusk white flags and the red crescents began to be hoisted all along the line. Now of the Turks and their flags of truce something had already been learned down on the banks of the Canal. On the other hand, in the evacuation of wounded from Gaba Tepe, when the attacking parties had failed to get a foothold on the narrow beach, and had been forced to retire leaving their wounded still on the shore, those soldiers were tended by the Turkish doctors. Their subsequent evacuation by the Navy under the Red Cross flag was accurately observed by the enemy. But that did not prevent this 'new move' being regarded with some caution. It was between five and six o'clock that in the centre of the right of the line a Turkish Staff officer, two medical officers, and a company commander came out of their trenches—all firing having ceased, and by arrangement through an interpreter who had called across from our own to the enemy trenches during the day—and met Major-General H. B. Walker, who was commanding the 1st Division, on the neutral ground between the trenches. It was stated by the Staff officer that he had been instructed to arrange a suspension of arms in order that the dead between the lines might be buried and the wounded tended and removed. The position was, to say the least, a delicate one. The officer carried no written credentials. General Hamilton's dispatches convey the subsequent proceedings as they were viewed at the time by most of the leaders at Anzac:

He [the Turkish Staff officer] was informed (writes the Commander-in-Chief) that neither he nor the General Officer Commanding Australian Division had the power to arrange such a suspension of arms, but that at 8 p.m. an opportunity would be given of exchanging letters on the subject, and that meanwhile hostilities would recommence after ten minutes' grace. At this time some stretcher parties on both sides were collecting wounded, and the Turkish trenches opposite ours were packed with men standing shoulder to shoulder two deep. Matters were less regular in front of other sections, where men with white flags came out to collect wounded (some attempted to dig trenches that were not meant for graves). Meanwhile it was observed that columns were on the march in the valley up which the Turks were accustomed to bring their reinforcements (Legge and Mule Valleys).

On hearing of these movements, General Sir W. R. Birdwood, commanding Australian and New Zealand Army Corps, ordered his trenches to be manned against a possible attack. As the evening drew in the enemy's concentration continued, and everything pointed to their intention of making use of the last of the daylight to get their troops into position without being shelled by our artillery. A message was therefore sent across to say that no clearing of dead or wounded could be allowed during the night, and that any negotiations for such purpose should be opened up through the proper channel and initiated before noon on the following day.

Stretcher parties and others fell back, and immediately fire broke out. In front of our right section masses of men advanced behind lines of unarmed men holding up their hands. Firing became general all along the line, accompanied by a heavy bombardment of the whole position, so that evidently this attack must have been pre-arranged. Musketry and machine gun fire continued without interruption till after dark, and from then up till about 4 a.m. the next day.

Except for a half-hearted attack in front of the Courtney's Post, no assault was made until 1.20 a.m., when the enemy left their trenches and advanced on Quinn's Post. Our guns drove the Turks back to their trenches and beat back all other attempts at assault. By 4.30 a.m. on 21st May musketry fire had died down to normal dimensions.

Negotiations were again opened up by the Turks during the morning of the 22nd. It must be recollected that by now the battle-fields had been, three weeks fought over, and many Australians as well as Turks who had perished in those first awful days, still lay unburied where they had fallen. The stench of decaying flesh threatened terrible calamity to both armies. For two days the Turkish dead in thousands lay rotting in the sun, their swollen corpses in some places on our very parapets. General Hamilton accordingly dispatched his Chief of Staff, Major-General W. P. Braithwaite, during the morning of the 22nd, to assist General Birdwood in coming to terms with an envoy that was to be sent by Essad Pasha, commanding at that time a section of the Turkish forces. Accordingly, on the afternoon of the 22nd an officer rode in from the extreme right of their line, across the plain that dipped down to the sea between the headland of Gaba Tepe and the last knoll of our position. He carried a white flag of truce. It was an impressive moment. He was beautifully mounted, and his uniform was a mass of gold lace. He was met by Staff officers from the Australian Army Corps. Now, coming to the wire entanglements that had been, made across the beach—the visiting officer had already been blindfolded—it was a matter of doubt for a moment how he was to be taken across within the Anzac lines. A solution was gained when four Australians stripped off their uniforms and, placing the officer on a stretcher, bore the Turk round through the water to the other side. There he remounted his horse, and was escorted along the beach to the prepared dugout, where he met in consultation General Braithwaite and representatives of the Australian and New Zealand Corps, with interpreters. It took two days to arrange the details of the armistice, and eventually the terms were satisfactorily agreed on, written, and signed in duplicate by both army leaders.

On the 24th May—Empire Day, as Australians know it—the armistice was begun at eight o'clock, and lasted till five o'clock in the evening. Some of its features are interesting, gruesome as the object was. Burial parties were selected from each side. Groups of selected officers left the trenches and started to define with white flags the lines of demarcation. It had been decided there should be a central zone where the men from the two sides might work together— a narrow strip it was, too. The Turks were not to venture into what might be termed 'our territory,' that varied in width according to the distances the trenches were apart, and the Australians were not to venture into the enemy's. Orders were issued that there was to be no firing anywhere along the line. Arms were to be collected and handed over to the respective armies to which they belonged, minus the rifle bolts. No field-glasses were to be used, and the men were to keep down in the trenches and not look over the parapets.

Now one of the disadvantages of the armistice, from the Australians' point of view, was that the topographical features of the position enabled any of the Turks who might approach within a certain distance to look down into the heart of the Anzac position (that was, into their own gullies), but also into gullies that now contained the Australians' reserve trenches and bivouacs, and where the troops were sheltered and stores placed. It seems very probable that the enemy realised this advantage, however slight. I do not think they were able to gain much. Nevertheless, in the interests of the health of all at Anzac, it was essential that the armistice should be arranged. So the party of the armistice went carefully round the 2-mile front of the position, moving the flags a little nearer the Turkish lines here, there, nearer the Australian. Following these slowly worked the burial parties, all wearing white armlets—doctors and padres.

Under guise of a sergeant of the Red Crescent walked General Liman von Sanders, the German leader against Anzac, and he mixed with the burial parties. It was a misty and wet morning, and every one wore greatcoats and helmets that were sufficient cloak to any identity. All day the parties worked, collecting the identity discs of many gallant lads whose fate had been uncertain, men whose mouldering bodies had been seen lying between the trenches. They were buried in huge open trenches, often alongside their fallen foe, as often it was impossible, owing to the condition of the bodies, to remove them to the Turkish burial-grounds. Once some firing began on the right, where it was alleged some parties were digging firing trenches, but it was hushed, and I have never been able to find an exact and official statement of this.

Some of the Turks who were directing operations mingled with our men; they spoke perfect English. By judicious handing out of cigarettes they sought to discover as much as they dared or as much as they might be told. Brigadier-General G. J. Johnston (Artillery officer) told me an interview he had with a Turkish officer who asked him about the number of men Australia was sending to the war. The Gunner replied, 'Five times as many thousands as had been already landed, while hundreds of thousands more were ready.' Another conversation shows very clearly the absence of bitterness on one side or the other. It concerned the meeting of two men who exchanged cards, while the Turk told (one suspects with a cynical smile) of many haunts of pleasure and amusement in Constantinople where the Australian could amuse himself when he came. I do not wish to convey that the Turks believed that they would be beaten, but they were not hated enemies of the Australians, and on this, as on other occasions, they played the game. Over 3,000 of their dead were buried that day. They lay in heaps; they sprawled, swelled and stark, in rows, linked together by the guiding ropes which they had clung to. Many were lying just above the Turkish parapets, where our machine guns had mowed them down as they left their trenches. And these the Turks themselves just barely covered, as was their custom in burying their dead.

Chaplains Merrington and Dexter both held short services over the graves of the fallen in the few hollows near Quinn's Post and other points farther south. A cairn of stones was left to mark the spot on which some day a greater memorial may be raised; down in the gullies rough wooden crosses mark other graves.

Gradually, after 3 p.m., the parties withdrew from their solemn task, and as the last white flag was struck and the parties retreated into their own trenches, the snip, snip, zip, zip, and crack of the bullets and boom of the bombs began again, and never ceased till the last shot was fired on the peninsula.

CHAPTER XVII
ANZAC COVE

The evolution of Anzac was as the growth of a mining settlement. Little had been done by the Turks in their defensive preparations to disturb the natural growth that spread from the crest of Maclagan's Ridge almost down to the water's edge—a growth of holly bush, a kind of furze, and an abundant carpet of grasses, wild flowers, poppies, and anemones. Round Ari Burnu their line of shallow trenches had run along to the Fishermen's Huts, but there were no tracks, other than the sheep or goat track round the base of the cliffs that the farmers might have used coming from Anafarta on to the plains below Kelid Bair and across to the olive groves, on the way to Maidos and the villages along the peninsula road to Cape Helles. Anzac Beach—'Z' Beach in the scheme of operations—was covered with coarse pebbles, occasionally a patch of sand. Barely 20 yards wide, and 600 yards long, the hills and cliffs began to rise steeply from it. The shore was cleft in the centre by a gully—Bully Beef Gully—which opened into the Cove. It was no more than a sharp ravine, very narrow, and in the days of April and in November very moist, and wet, and sticky. It took very little time after the dawn of day on that April Sunday morning for the point of concentration to be fixed on in this Cove. The whole of the stores, equipment, as well as the troops, were landed from end to end of the beach. Somehow there was a feeling of greater security in this Cove, but in fact it was so shallow, so accurately plotted in the enemy's maps, that the Turks had little difficulty in bursting the shells from one end of it to the other at their will. Luckily, the water was fairly deep almost up to the shore. Twenty yards out one found 15 feet of water and a stony bottom, which enabled the picket boats and pinnaces to come close in, as it allowed barges to be drawn well up to the beach, so that the stores could be tumbled out. Photographs, better than word pictures, describe that beach in those first days and weeks. Ordnance officers of both Divisions, as well as of the Army Corps, wrestled with the problem of making order out of chaos. Once the army was to stick, it had to stick 'By God!' and not be allowed to starve, or want for ammunition or entrenching tools.

A small stone jetty was the first work of the Engineers, and this was rapidly followed by a jetty that the signallers, under Captain Watson (for the Engineers had vastly more important duties that called them away up to the gullies and the firing-line), constructed. But that was done after the second week. The Army Medical Corps worked in a dressing-station, just a tent with a Red Cross flying overhead. Yet it could not be said that the Turks wilfully shelled this station, though necessarily they must have dropped their shells round its canvas doors, while inside it came the bullets, because of the stores that lay about, blocking, choking the beach. Many were the experiments that were made to distribute the supplies. Colonel Austin, Ordnance officer, 1st Division, with his staff-sergeant, Tuckett, had attempted to erect the piles of boxes of biscuits, as well as picks and shovels and ammunition around Hell Spit. Promptly the Turks dropped shells right into the middle of them, scattering the whole and killing several men. There was nothing for it but to move back along the Cove, dig into the sides of the cliffs, and pile the reserve stores up the main gully. On the beach cases were stacked in the form of traverses, round which the men might take such shelter as was afforded when the guns—Beachy Bill, from Olive Grove, and Anafarta, from the village near Suvla—commenced their 'hates.'

This beach and the cliffs overlooking it might be best described as 'The Heart of Anzac.' At the foot of the gully was camped General Sir William Birdwood—the 'Soul of Anzac'—and his whole Staff in dugouts no different from the holes the men built in the hills. A hundred feet up the slopes on the south side was General Bridges and his Staff, and on the other hand General Godley with the 2nd A. and N.Z. Division. Those first quarters were only slightly varied in after-months. General Birdwood remained always on the beach, almost at the foot of the jetty. Here it was that one found the living pulse of the position—the throb of life that meant the successful holding of the acres so gallantly won, the strength that held back the Turks, while road arteries cut into the hillsides and formed the channels down which the best blood of the Australians and New Zealanders flowed. One cannot help recording that constantly shells burst round the leader's dugout. Thus it happened that his Staff officer, Captain Onslow, met his death under tragic circumstances in July. It was a particularly hot night, and this popular officer said he would sleep on the top of his dugout as being cooler. The Turks commenced to shell the beach (probably in the belief that we were that night landing men and stores, which we were not). Captain Onslow retired within the poor and partial shelter, emerging again after about a quarter of an hour, when he fancied the guns had stopped. Unfortunately, it was only a lull, and the next shell burst right on the dugout, killing him instantly.

'It is only a question of time,' was a phrase current on the beach amongst the working parties. It meant one had only to be there long enough and the inevitable shell-burst would find its victims. Yet considering the traffic—that the whole army of 30,000, increasing to 50,000 in July and August, as the zealous Australian Light Horsemen (dismounted) came into action, where fed from that 600 yards strip of beach—it was astonishing that the casualties were as low as they were. Twenty men were killed at a shell-burst once—that was the most horrible incident. Thousands of the heaviest shells fell harmlessly into the water. Six hundred shells a day, at one period, fell along the shore and around the pinnaces and lighters or amongst the slowly moving transports. No large ships were sunk. 'The Beach'—and those two words were used to include the thousands that inhabited it and the adjacent hillsides—watched the vessels chased from anchorage to anchorage. The army blessed their lives they were ashore; while those afloat wondered how any were left alive after the 'hottings' the beach got. But the casualties from both Turkish enfilading batteries were never reckoned in all at 2,000—big enough, but very little result for the molestation that the Turks hoped to throw down on the heroes who toiled there day and night. For most of the work was done at night, in the small hours of the morning, when the transports under a darkened sky—the moon had to be studied studiously on Gallipoli—could come close inshore with 100-gallon tanks, thousands of Egyptian water-tins, millions of rounds of ammunition, and thousands of rounds of shells, scores of tons of beef and biscuits. Bread and the little fresh meat that came ashore were landed from the regular trawler service that arrived from Imbros by day, via Helles.

Once a great steam pumping engine was landed. One heard it afterwards puffing away on the beach, sending the water from the barges (filled with water from the Nile and anchored by the pier) up to the tank reservoirs on the side of the ridge, where began a reticulation scheme all over Anzac to the foot of the hills, thereby certainly saving the energy of the army expended on fatigues. How the troops blessed it! None of that 'luxury,' however, in the early days; only the monotonous grind up and down the slopes with water-cans.

You come on the Telephone Exchange of Anzac (to which led what appeared an impossible tangle of wires) and the Post Office, on either side of the entrance to Bully Beef Gully, opposite Watson's Landing. It is possible to talk all over the position from here. Three or four men are working constantly at the switches. Farther along the beach on the right and you find the clearing stations, under Colonel Howse, V.C., wedged in between the hillside and the screen of boxes on the beach. You come to Hell Spit, round which you might be chased by a machine gun from Gaba Tepe; and beyond, the graveyard, open to shell fire. Burials mostly have to be carried out at night, when the shelling is not so dangerous. There was a chaplain who, with his little band of devoted stretcher-bearers and the comrades of the fallen, was performing the last rites at this spot, when, to his dismay, the Turks commenced the shelling again. 'Dust unto dust,' repeated the chaplain, and the bursting shell flung the newly exposed earth over the party. 'Oh, hell!' said the padre. 'This is too ho-at for me! I'm aff!' And he went. So was the spirit of war bred in the souls of the men. It was sheer madness, the risks the troops would take on the beach when the Turks had fired old Beachy Bill from the Olive Grove—bathing under shell fire. But if needs must they always faced those shellings, anxious to get back to their job—to get supplies ashore before they were sunk, to get comrades away to comfort on the hospital ships. No amount of shelling interrupted the daily swim for long.

So you walk north back along the beach, pondering, looking up at the heights above Ari Burnu Point. You wonder at the men of the 3rd Brigade who stormed it and the ridge on your right. The idealness of the Point for machine guns to repel any landing, seems only too evident. You pass the Army Corps headquarters—a line of dugouts, well shielded from the sun with canvas and blankets. Above is the wireless station, with its widespread aerials on a bare hill—deserted except for a few casual men who had burrowed deep and took their chance—and immense searchlights for signalling in a cavern in the hill. Near at hand, too, is the Army Post Office, in a low wooden building, one of the few at Anzac. Tinkerings and hammerings arise from the bomb factory, next door almost, where the finishing touches are put to the jam-tin bombs, originally constructed in Egypt, and to the Turkish shell cases, converted into 'surprise packets' by diligent sappers, who work day and night to keep pace with the demand for twice any number that the Turks might throw. Up farther on this bared hill is the corral built for the reception of Turkish prisoners, You meet them, tired-looking, sullen men, being marched down through the gully to the pier. Hereabouts is an incinerator, always smoking and exploding cartridges that have fallen into it.

You come to two more gullies before you reach the northern point of the Cove. Up one is the New Zealand Headquarters, bunched—huddled, in fact—on the side of the ravine, with the terrace in front, on which the leaders sit and yarn in the spare moments, watching the shells burst on the beach, the warships racing about from harbour to harbour, destroyers nosing slowly into the flanks of the position, aeroplanes skimming away to the Turkish lines. In the next and last gully there are many scores of placid mules, munching away, waiting for their work at sunset. You reach the Point (Ari Burnu), a flat, rounded, rather sharp bend, and you find yourself amongst a great many mule-wagons, standing in the sand, and before you a 2-mile sweep of yellow beach (Ocean Beach) that bends round to Suvla Bay. There rises up from the shore a mass of knolls and hills, the under features of the Sari Bair ridge, with the Salt Lake (the salt sparkles in the sun) drying at their base. Immediately in the foreground, and to the left, are the abrupt terminations of the Sari Bair ridge: Sphinx Rock and the brown, clayey, bare slopes of Plugge's Plateau, the whole hillside so mouldered away with the lashing of the Mediterranean storms, that the shells which burst on it bring tumbling to the gullies below vast falls of earth, until it appears that the whole hill could easily be blown away. Away up higher, beyond, is the battle-line; its spent bullets come flopping about you, splashing up the water, flicking up the sand. They are never so spent that they won't penetrate your flesh or bones and stick.

Hastily you turn into a sap, and all that wonderful broad expanse of beach and hills is lost. For by day the Ocean Beach is impracticable, and at night, only by taking a risk, which the Indian muleteers do, can the nearest portion of it be used, thus relieving the pressure of traffic in the great communication-way. What a task to dig this sap miles out into the enemy's territory, the only link with the strong, but isolated, posts (beyond Fishermen's Huts) held in turn by parties of New Zealanders, Maoris, and Light Horsemen, under Lieut.-Colonel Bauchop! It is deep, broad—7 feet broad—hot, dusty, but safe. You may leave it just as you reach the Ari Burnu Point, and, passing through a gap in the hills and down a gully, regain the Cove. Just round the Point you may look in at the Ordnance Stores, indicated by a dirty blue-and-white flag, ragged and torn with shot and shell. That flag was brought ashore by Colonel Austin, and was the only army flag ever flown at Anzac.

Surely there is a smithy? A clanging sound of blows on an anvil makes cheerful noise after the frenzied burst of shells. The workshops are protected with huge thicknesses of stores; guns of all descriptions are being made and remade here. Farther along are the medical stores, and you find a spacious dugout, lined with lints and ointments, bandages, splints, stretchers, and disinfectants. Hospital supplies were never short at Anzac. Gurkha, Maori, Englishman, Australian, New Zealander passes you on the beach. You may meet them all together, talking. You may see them only in their respective groups with their own kin. It all reminds you of an anthill. There are men—not hurrying, but going in all directions—stopping to talk every dozen paces, and then going on or turning back, apparently without motive, without reason. There are some that march alone and never halt. But the whole trend of traffic is from the hills and to the hills. Outward they go loaded, and return empty-handed for more.

There came a time, not infrequent, when placid twilights fell on Anzac, when even the intermittent crack of rifles or the occasional burst of a bomb passed almost unnoticed. The wicked 'psing' of bullets passing overhead on their way to the water went unheeded. A solemn stillness filled the air. Yes, quiet as a mining camp on the seashore, far away from war's turmoil, the beach nearly always rested with the sinking of the sun behind the massed hills of Samothrace—the island refuge of ancient oracles; its departing rays lit the sky in golden shadows, that mingled with blue the orange and green tints in the sky. Deeper shades darkened the island of Imbros and cast into silhouette the warships, waiting and watching till the aeroplanes sailing overhead should transmit their observations, which meant targets, for the bombardment of new enemy positions. The warships lay, like inert monsters, on a shimmering sea. Sunsets on Gallipoli took away the sting of battle. The shore parties, their most arduous labours still to come, watched the twilight in a state of suspended animation. Five o'clock was the house for the commencement of bathing. It usually was, too, the signal for a Turkish 'hate' of ten minutes or more, to banish the bathers. Any who could be spared stripped off their remaining few clothes, clambered aboard barges, or dived from the end of the pier, and washed off the sweat of a sweltering day in the clear waters; for Anzac was for five months as warm a corner as any in the Ægean. Generals, orderlies, intelligence officers, men who had been toiling round the firing-line from dewy dawn, plunged in, spluttering an interchange of scraps of gossip of this position and that, and news from the outside world that seemed almost lost to those on this battlefield. You carefully placed your clothes, ready to dodge along the pier back to comparative safety, behind high stacks of stores, as the first shrieking shell came hurtling over from Olive Grove. 'Old Beachy Bill snarling again,' was the only comment, and once the little 'hate' had ceased, back again for the last dive.

Then sometimes out of the stillness would sound a gong— a beaten shell-case—bidding the officers to an evening meal; or the high-pitched voice of Captain Chaytor, the naval officer in command on the beach—as brave a fellow as ever stepped. The Navy took no more notice of shells than they did of Army orders— they were under 'the Admiral.' Still the co-operation between the two services was never marred by serious obstructions.

'Last boat for Imbros,' announced the naval officer. He might have said 'Last boat for the shore.' Gripping handbags or kitbags, there was usually a party waiting, and they dodged out now from behind shelters or from dugouts. They were off to one or other of the bases on duty, and the trawler or destroyer was waiting offshore for the pinnace to come alongside.

'Picket boat ahoy! Where are you from?' Again the naval officer is speaking.

The voice of a midshipman, suitably pitched and full-throated, replies, '*London*, sir.'

'I did not ask where you were born. Where are you from?'

'*London*, sir.'

Then the naval officer remembers his evening aboard the battleship *London*, and orders the panting craft alongside. The shells begin to fall. He gives sharp orders through his megaphone, and pinnaces begin backing out from the shore, scattering in all directions till they are half a mile from the beach, and have become almost impossible targets for any gunners. The Turks desist. On the beach bathing is promptly resumed.

General Birdwood rarely ever missed his evening dip. He bathed amongst his men, shedding off rank with his uniform, which led more than once to amusing incidents. One day the canvas pipe of the water-barge fell from the pier into the sea, and an irate man on the barge, seeing someone near it, cursed him, and asked him if he could '— well lend a fellow a — hand to get the — thing up.' General Birdwood—for it was he—delights to relate the story himself, and how he hastily commenced to pull the pipe into place, when a sergeant dashed up and offered to relieve him, in the midst of abusive directions from the bargee, who, unconscious of the signals from the sergeant and of the vacant staring of all around, urged on his General to more strenuous and more successful efforts. Did it endear the General less to the men? Rather not. A quiet, very firm, but very friendly man was this leader of the Australians, who understood their character admirably.

On another occasion, when returning to his dugout over the top of the hill where rested the bomb factory, he accidentally stood on the roof of a dugout, and stones and earth began to fall on the occupant beneath. 'Quick, quick!' said General Birdwood, knowing his men; 'let me get away from this! I would rather face half a dozen Turks than that Australian when it comes out!'

There is a 'beach' story, too—all stories originated on the beach—far too characteristic to go unrecorded, of any Australian 'pinching' extra water from the water barge one very still evening, when he was caught by the naval officer on duty, who, in the pure English of the Navy, demanded, 'What are you doing that, sir?' and up to the dugouts on the hillside floated the prompt reply, 'Getting some — wart-ar, sir.'

But night has fallen and the beach wakens to its greatest degree of activity. Long since have efforts to load and land stores, to take ammunition to the firing-line, been abandoned by day. The Turkish observation at Gaba Tepe stopped that. All the hillside glows with twinkling lights; the sound of laughter or stern commands floats down from the higher steppes of the hills on to the beach. There is a fine dust rising from the strand as the traffic increases and becomes an endless stream of men, of mules, of wagons. Somewhere offshore—you know that it must be about 400 yards—there come voices across the waters as the barges are loaded and the steam pinnaces tug them to the shore. They are lashed to the narrow piers, where the waves lap their sides. Parties quickly board them to unload the food that is the life of the army, and the munitions which are its strength. There are heavier goods, too, to bring ashore, some-times needing large parties to handle. There are rifles and machine guns, there are picks and shovels, iron plates for loopholes. Wood, too, forms not the least strain placed on the transport.

So it goes on night after night, this constant stream of mate-rial to keep the army efficient, ready for any attack, ready, too, for any offensive. The trawlers have sneaked close into the Cove. The Turkish gunners, as if seeing this, begin to shell the beach. The work in the Cove stops abruptly. Men come scrambling from the pier and the boats to seek the shelter of dugouts and the great piles of stores. The shells fall harmlessly in the water (unless they destroy a barge of flour). When the bombardment ceases the routine is resumed. From Gaba Tepe the Turks could not see into the heart of Anzac, but their guns easily reached the distance, measured exactly. Opposite the pier-heads the men congregate. You find it difficult to push your way amongst the Indian mule-carts, to reach the canvas water-sheet and the tanks from which the men are getting supplies. The traffic divides. One section goes north to the No. 2 and No. 3 outposts, 2 miles away, out through the long sap: the dust from the shore is almost choking as you reach the sap, for the strings of mules pass and repass almost endlessly. The other branch of the traffic goes south (along the beach too) in front of the hospitals round Hell Spit, and then, striking one of many paths, is diverted along the right flank of the firing-line. No long line of sap to protect you here, and always a chance of a dropping bullet.

Only when the moon rises above the horizon and the pine ridges and then above the battle front is it time for the beach to rest. Higher and higher it mounts, until at midnight it is slanting towards the entrance to the Dardanelles. One by one the lights have gone out and cooks' fires have ceased to flicker. On either flank two long arms of light, that broaden as they reach the hill, start from the sides of the destroyers. They were staring into the Turkish hills and gullies. Behind them the gunners watch all night for movements in the enemy's ranks, and the guns boom at the slightest stir. After the alarms of the night and the bursts of rapid fire, the dawn brings another lull over Anzac, when the constant rattle of muskets in the firing-line a mile away over the ridges and the swish and t-tzing of the little messengers of death as they pass out to sea, are like to be forgotten or accepted as part of the curious life of Anzac. But the work never quite ceases, and morning finds tired officers giving the last directions before they turn into their dugouts and escape the morning 'hate' that the Turks with the first flush of dawn begin to throw over the beach and amongst the lingering, dawdling trawlers and transports that have drifted inshore. The shells follow the ships till they regain the circle of safety, some 2 miles from land. 'Keep your distance, and we won't worry you,' say the Turks.

It is exciting to watch the steamers dodging the shells just as the sun first casts a glitter on the blue Ægean. But they have accomplished all they need, and till the arrival of the daily trawlers from Imbros, Mudros, and Cape Helles, there is no need for worry. So the workers take a morning dip and turn in, while the men on the pinnaces are rocked to sleep as they lie wallowing offshore, and the pump begins its monotonous clanking.

On rugged cliffs and amongst bristling bush the heart of Anzac began to palpitate with power and life. With roads and terraces was the hillside cut in May and stripped of its bush. The throb of the heart was the pulse of the army, its storehouse, and its life; but the shore of the Cove was dyed to the murmuring waters' edge with the blood of the men that made it.

Anzac was divided into two parts by Shrapnel Gully, which ran from Hell Spit right up to the very apex of the position, at the junction of the ridge that the army held and the main ridge of Sari Bair. Thousands of men lost their lives in this great broad valley during the early days of the fighting, when the Turkish artillery burst shrapnel over it. That was how it got its name. It was there that General Bridges met his death, in this Valley of the Shadow of Death. In its upper course it merged into Monash Gully called after the Brigadier of the 4th Brigade, that had held its steep sides at Pope's Hill—which was a knuckle—at Quinn's Post, and between the two the sharp depression on the edge of the ridge—'The Bloody Angle.' A daring sniper might always reach the very head of the gully and shoot down the long valley. Only, in time, the superiority and alertness of our sharpshooters overcame that menace. Few Turkish snipers that played that game returned alive.

I went without a guide round Anzac, because the paths were well worn when I trod them, though there were many twisted roads, but all leading upwards to the trenches winding round the edge of the ridge. One could not miss one's way very well by keeping on the path that led southward from the heart of Anzac round to the first point—Hell Spit (beyond, a machine gun played and chased any who approached, unless the Turks happened to be off duty, as they sometimes were), and there you found the broad, open mouth of the gully. Usually a party of men were coming up from bathing. They were sun-burned right down to their waists (for they never wore shirts if they could possibly avoid it, and looked more like Turks than the Turks themselves), and you found them squatting in a sap, the mouth of which gaped on to the beach, secure behind the angle of a hill. By their side were large Egyptian water-tins. The 'coves' up above in the trenches were drinking this ration of water for their evening meal, but there was always time to have a chat with a comrade or mate from the northern side of Anzac, or with men who lived in the heart of the position. For the troops knew only their own section of the line, and had seen nothing of famed posts and positions captured and held. In fact, it was a sort of mutual understanding that these fatigue parties always stopped for the purpose of swapping stories about adventures with Turks.

'Had much fighting, Fred, down your way?' one would drawl.

'Bit of an attack, but the blighters would not face the — bayonet.'

'Was out doing a bit of scouting the other night from Russell Top,' spoke another fine-featured man, 'and only for a thunderstorm would have captured a bit of a ridge, but a blooming interpreter chap got the shivers, and we just got back without being nabbed.'

It would make a book in itself to record all the conversations one dropped amongst, of scraps of fighting, of one section of the line and another. The men flattened themselves against the side of the sap to let a stretcher case pass, always asking, if the wounded man showed any signs of life, about the wound and his regiment. About July, in the saps one met men carrying large quantities of sheet-iron and beams of wood to form the terraces up along the sides of the hills. One sheet of iron could make a dugout magnificent, even luxurious; two was a home fit for a general. This sap wound backwards and forwards up the gully, just giving glimpses of the tops of the ridge, over which bullets came whizzing and embedding themselves against the hillside. That was the reason of the sap. The little graveyard you passed was full of these spent bullets: shells whined away over it to the beach.

You came out into the open again where the gully broadened out. Looking round, there were three or four wells visible, where the engineers were busily erecting pumps. Iron tanks, too, were being brought into use, part of the great reticulation scheme of Anzac, and round them were grouped the men who had come down from the hilltops. That water, blessed though it was, was thrice blessed by the men who once carried it on their shoulders, grown sore under the weight. Some men with 18-pounder shells tucked under their arms passed. 'Heavy, lads?' 'Too blooming heavy altogether; one's about enough up them hills!' Thus, by a stream of munition-carriers, was the artillery kept supplied with its ammunition. Shells were not too plentiful in those days, but the gunners were busy laying in supplies for the great artillery duel that all knew one day would be fought. Ammunition, it may be recorded, went by the beach at night, and so up to the very highest point of the gullies possible, on mules.

Just at this broadening of Shrapnel Gully on the right (south) was the Indian encampment. A mass of rags and tatters it looked, for it was exposed to the fierce sun, and when gay coloured blankets were not shielding the inmates of the dugouts, the newly washed turbans of the Sikhs and Mohamedans were always floating in the idle breeze. Their camp was always busy. They never ceased to cook. Though the wiry Indians could speak little English, they got on well with the Australians, who loved poking about amongst their camps hunting for curios, while the Indians collected what trophies they could from the Australians.

If you looked intently hereabouts, you might make out, smothered away in the shadow of a hill, the dark muzzle of a gun in a pit, with the gunners' camp beside it. He would have been a keen observer in an aeroplane who could have detected those guns and marked them on his maps. Sufficient proof of this might be found in the fact that nearly all these guns were brought away at the evacuation. One or two that I saw in the firing-line, or just behind it, had been battered.

187

Three ways lay open to you, now that you had crossed the broad bottom of the gully. You might turn to the right and continue on up the main gully till it joined with Monash Gully, and so go on a visit to the apex of the position. You might turn off slightly to the left and reach, by a rather tortuous track, the centre of the left flank (or by this route travel behind the firing-line along the western slopes of the hills to Lone Pine, and then reach the extreme left). A far shorter, and the third way, was to go round the Indian encampment, and either up White Gully or through a gap in another spur of the main ridge, and come out on to Shell Green. This patch of once cultivated land was a small plateau—the only cleared space on Anzac. The Turkish shells passed over it on their way to the beach from the olive-grove guns concealed 2 miles away. Sometimes, also, they dropped on it. You crossed at the northern end of it, and reached the artillery headquarters of Colonel Rosenthal's 3rd Brigade dug into the side of the hill. It was across the gully facing the southern edge of this green that the big 6-in. field gun, fired for the first time in August, was placed. I remember watching the huge pit that was dug for it, and the widening of the artillery roads that enabled it to be dragged into position. Directly above Shell Green—a very dirty patch of earth after very few weeks—was Artillery Lane, which was a track that had been cut in the side of the hill, and which also served as a terrace. Dugouts were easily accessible along this road, though it was subject to some shell fire, so lower down the hillside was preferable, even if the climb was steeper and the promenade more restricted. Brigadier-General Ryrie, commanding 2nd Light Horse Brigade, had his headquarters at this spot, and also the 3rd Infantry Brigade, under Brigadier-General Maclagan. Lieut.-Colonel Long too, with the Divisional Light Horsemen, also made his camp there. All of which troops were holding, in July the section of the line that reached down to the sea on the extreme left.

It was a complicated position, for a series of small crests had had to be won before Chatham's Post was established and an uninterrupted view obtained of the Turkish huts along Pine Ridge and the plain where the olive-groves were. Down on the beach that led round from Gaba Tepe—the beach where the troops should have landed—were barbed-wire entanglements and a series of posts manned only at night. Along that beach a little way, the commander of the post, a Light Horseman, pointed out to me a broken boat. It was a snipers' nest, he explained, where the Turks sometimes lurked and waited. We now stood out in a cutting looking down on Gaba Tepe at the Turkish trenches that ran in parallel lines along the hills, till a bracket of bullets suggested the wisdom of drawing back to cover. Along a very deep sap (so narrow that in some places one had to squeeze one's way through) and down a hill brought one up to Chatham's Post, called so after a Queenslander, who captured it, of that name. Right on the crown of this knoll and along its western slope were a series of machine-gun positions, striking at the heart of the left of the Turkish lines.

I was asked, 'Like to see an old Turk we have been laying for, for some time?—a sergeant he is. The beggar doesn't care a jot for our shooting.' Several rifles cracked as the observer made way for me to put my eye to a telescope. Very clearly I saw a fine big Turk moving along one of the enemy's communication-ways: it was apparent he was supervising and directing. He bore a sort of charmed life, that man. Eventually (some days later) he was shot. His name? Why, Abdul, of course—they all were. Our telescope was withdrawn just in time, and the iron flap dropped over the loophole as bullets splashed against it and the sandbag parapets above.

'Damn them and their snipers!' said a young bushman, and began again his observation from another point. Up and down and through a long tunnel and we came back again to the rear of the main hill. When I saw where I had walked, set out on a map, it seemed very short after the miles of winding trenches that disappeared in all directions over and through the hill. Yet the troopers were still digging. Their troubles!

Brigadier-General Maclagan had a birthday—or he said it was about time he had—one day when I came in, and he celebrated it by cutting a new cake which his Brigade-Major, Major Ross, had obtained through the post.

'Luxury,' began the Brigadier, with his mouth full of currants, 'is only a matter of comparison. Look at my couch and my pigeon-holes, my secret earthen safes, and—bring another pannikin of tea.'

Yes, it was comparison. 'Ross, you will show the trenches—fine fellow, Ross,' and the Brigadier cut another piece of cake.

Other officers dropped in and the cake slowly vanished. I wondered what Ross thought. 'No use,' he said to me later. 'Better eat it now. Might not be here to eat it tonight. What about these trenches, now? You have a periscope? Right.' As we started I felt his position was like that of the officer who, having received a hamper with some fine old whisky, found himself suddenly grown popular and received a great many visitors in one night. News spread quickly at Anzac!

It was the middle section of the right of the line that I was visiting, adjacent to the Light Horse position, just described. The Turks started shelling before we had fairly started, and I watched the shells bursting on Shell Green—harmlessly enough, but very thick. The Brigade-Major left word at the telephone switchboard where he was going, and, choosing one of three ways, dived into a sap on the hillside that was reached by a flight of steps. One had not gone far to be struck by the scrupulous cleanliness of this under-ground line. No tins, papers, or broken earthworks: everything spick and span. I was being told how the wheatfield had been taken at the time just as we were passing across it—through a sap and working up under cover on to the outer ridge. That day I seemed to do nothing else but grip hard brown hands and meet new faces. That splendid Staff officer had a word for all his men.

'Wish the beggars would only attack. We have everything nicely prepared for them,' he began to explain as we walked through a tunnel and halted on the side of a hill. We stood behind some bushes in a machine-gun pit. 'Never been fired,' said the officers, and then smiled in a curious way. 'Got four more all along the top of the gully in two tiers. We expect—that is our hope—the Turks will come up here to try and cut off that hill which we have taken. Let 'em.'

It was the first time that I had seen a real trap. God help any foe that entered that valley!

Did I want to see all the position? I did. It took two hours—two of the shortest, most amazing hours I spent at Anzac.

'We are going now to see the gallery trenches. Always believe in making things roomy below ground,' the Major explained, 'so that the men do not get any suggestion of being cramped.' So we entered a find, high, and broad gallery, lit by the holes that were opened at intervals along it and used as firing-steps. My guide chuckled as he came to a point where it was rather dark. He stopped before more manholes filled with barbed wire. On the firing-step a soldier was carefully handling his tin of stew. This was a mantrap—a small hole and a thin crush of earth and wide pit—prepared against the rushing of the position, one of the dozens that were all round the front as a protecting screen.

It was rather a difficult matter getting round the galleries as the afternoon wore on, for the men had commenced their meals. They gathered in small groups, someone always on guard for his comrades. Rifles were ready, standing by the wall. It was not exactly a solemn meal, for plenty of curses accompanied the passing of some 'clumsy devil' that knocked down earth into a tin of tea. The trenches were remarkably sweet. The Major drew one's attention to the fact with justifiable pride.

Of the Turks that were entrenched on the other side of the ridge one saw nothing. Through a periscope you could make out their earthworks. One stumbles on adventure in the firing-line. I was without my guide, proceeding along a trench, when I was advised it was not worth while. Quite recently it cut a Turkish trench, and now only a sandbag parapet divided the two lines. It really was not worth occupying, except when there was a fight on. It was too deadly a position for either side to remain long in!

How the line twisted! Turning back along an angle, I found we had got back again into the gully—the Valley of Despair I have heard it called—only much higher up. There was an interesting little group of men round a shaft. Major Ross explained: 'Trying to get their own water supply. Down about 80 feet. Yes, all old miners. The Tasmanians have done most of this tunnelling work: must have dug out thousands of tons of earth. Perfectly wonderful chaps they are. Dug themselves to a shadow, and still fought like hell. Me thin? Oh, it does me good walking out these hills; I can't sit in a dugout.' A messenger came up from the signal office. 'You must excuse me. I have to go back to B. II' (a junction of a trench and sap), and he dived into the trenches again.

Imagine, now, you have begun walking back along the firing-line, going from the extreme right to the left. Already two sections have been passed. Had you continued along from the last gallery trenches, you would have come out into the section opposite the Lone Pine trenches of the Turks. The enemy here was a more discreet distance of 80 to 200 yards away across a broad plateau. The ridge was higher at this point, and one might look back through a periscope (with great care) from certain sharp-angled look-out posts; raised slightly, according to the conformation of the ground, above the level of the ordinary trenches, down the back of the ridge, and on to the positions one had just left. They call this spot 'The Pimple.' Some of the posts were the observation posts for artillery, others for special sentry posts. As Lone Pine will form the subject of a separate chapter, the trenches will not be elaborated here. Sufficient to say that here, too, were gallery trenches, but lower and darker and less roomy; but, nevertheless, absolutely effective either for defensive or offensive purposes. You reached them by climbing to the end of Artillery Lane up through Browne's Dip.

It was on the second day that along this roadway the guns were dragged into the firing-line, when Major Bessell-Browne had a battery right on the crest of the ridge almost in the firing-line (the guns were actually in the infantry trenches for a time), until the Turks made it too warm for them. Now, this hilltop, which lay just behind the position held by the 1st Infantry Brigade and to the south-east of White Gully, was bare of any infantry trenches. It was, moreover, covered with furze and holly bushes. The trenches had been advanced to the edge of the plateau, on the other side of which the Turkish lines ran. With Colonel Johnston, Brigadier of the Victoria Artillery Brigade, I had climbed up here one morning to see the gun positions. One passed from Artillery Lane into an extremely narrow trench right amongst some bushes, and found oneself in a snug little position, completely concealed from observation. Out of the midst of these earthworks a gun pointed to the Turkish positions on Pine Ridge, Battleship Hill, and Scrubby Knoll. There was a telescope carefully laid through a loophole, the iron flap of which was discreetly dropped. It swept the Turkish ridges closely. A sergeant was in a 'possy' (the soldier's term for his position in the firing-line and dugout) watching a party of Turks digging. He could just see their spades come up in the air. It was believed that they were making emplacements for new guns. Colonel Johnston let the enemy nearly finish and then blew them and their earthworks to pieces. It was what he called 'stirring up a stunt,' for not long after, sure enough, as he anticipated, the Turks commenced to reply, and shells began dropping in front of and over this post as the Turks searched for our guns. These little artillery duels lasted about half an hour, and when ammunition was plentiful (the daily limit was fixed for many weeks at two shells a day unless anything special occurred) two or three 'stunts' might occur during a day. Sometimes word would come down from the infantry trenches that Turks were passing in certain gullies or could be seen working up on to Battleship Hill or up the side of Baby 700, and the guns would be laid accordingly. It would be difficult to estimate the number of targets that had been registered by the active artillerymen. They had them all tabulated, and could train their guns on to any spot during a night alarm in a moment. For from some point or other good views could be obtained of the Turkish positions: not in detail, of course, but sufficient, with the knowledge that aeroplane sketches and reconnaissance provided (Major Myles was one of the most successful of the artillery officers who went observing from the hangars at Tenedos), to cause great havoc amongst the Turkish supports and reserves.

But such shelling, whatever damage was done, never prevented the Turks from digging new firing-lines and communication and reserve trenches. Their industry in this respect was even greater than the Australians', who moved whole hills or honeycombed them with galleries until you might expect that a real heavy burst of shells or a downpour of rain would cause them to collapse. The Turks had mobilised digging battalions, units in which men who had conscientious objections to bear arms (many of them farmers) used to work. This is how Pine Ridge became such a huge mass of enemy trenches. Why, there were secret saps and ways all along from Kojadere right to Gaba Tepe Point. But sometimes the Turks were caught napping, as when the Australians captured an advanced spur or knoll or the plateau that gave a glimpse down a gully (for the other side of the plateau that sloped away down to Kojadere was just as cut by ravines as was the Anzac side), and after a few days' quiet preparations—the Turks being ignorant of our new advantage—our machine guns swept backwards and forwards along it, while the artillery drove the Turks into this hail of lead with shrapnel and high explosives.

With Colonel Johnston I went farther back towards the seashore along the back of one of the spurs, and round Majors Phillips', Caddy's, Burgess's guns, well dug into deep pits protected by solid banks of earth, covered with natural growth of bushes. It seemed to me unless a direct hit was obtained there was little chance of their being destroyed. Space was conserved in every way so as to leave as little opening as possible; magazines were dug into the cliff and dugouts as well. Yet several guns were knocked out. There was one gun crew amongst whom a shell had burst. Two men had been killed outright, and others badly wounded. When the stretcher-bearers rushed into the gun-pit they found a dying man trying to open the breech of the gun to load. His strength failed, and he fell back dead in a comrade's arms. Those men thought only of the gun and their mates after that explosion.

Little gaps occurred in the Anzac front where two gullies met on the razor-back crest of the hill. One was at the head of Wanliss Gully, between the 4th Battalion of the 1st Brigade and the 5th Battalion, holding the section opposite the German Officers' Trench. Here the crest of the hill had been so worn away, and the head of the gully was so steep, that no trenches could be connected. As a result, all the protection that could be given was to bend back the trenches on either side down the hill, and establish strong posts and make entanglements from side to side of the gully. It was a source of intense anxiety to Colonel Wanliss (commanding 5th Battalion), who was early responsible for its protection.

The 2nd Infantry Brigade held the section of trenches going to Quinn's Post during the greater part of four months: held them sometimes lightly, sometimes in great strength. Opposite were the Turks' most elaborate works, designated 'German Officers' Trench' and 'Johnston's Jolly.' These series of Turkish trenches varied from 20 to 80 yards from the Australian lines. The origin of their names is interesting. German officers had been seen in the trench that bears their name, which offered sufficient reason, as there were not a great number of Hun officers on the peninsula. The other series of trenches had presented to Colonel Johnston's mind a good target, on which he always said he would have a 'jolly good time' if his guns had only been howitzers and able to reach them, which, with his 18-pounders, he could not. The Turks had used huge beams many feet in thickness to fortify these trenches along this sector of the line. Probably it was because it led directly to the heart of the enemy's position (Mule Gully was beyond and Kojadere) that such measures were taken. No artillery bombardment had had much effect on these trenches. One day—it illustrates the spirit of the Turkish army—a Turkish officer was seen directing the erection of some overhead cover down a communication trench behind this position. A burst of shell had warned him that he was observed, and bullets from machine guns played round him. He paid little attention, and went on with the directing of his job. When complete it was blown down, and continued to be blown down as fast as it was constructed, until the Turks had to give it up in despair. That brave officer directing the operations, was killed.

Opposite the left front of 'German Officers' Trench' came Steel's Post, and next to Steel's, Courtney's Post, both called after officers of the 4th Infantry Brigade, whose regiments had held the positions in the first awful fortnight's fighting. Really they might be more aptly termed by the number of the regiment—14th Battalion— and the fine men who composed it. The Turks' line drew very close at this point. A gully cut into the plateau from the Anzac side and formed the 'Bloody Angle.' On the north of it was Pope's Hill, and on the south was Quinn's—the famous post cleft in the hillside—a concave position, at the heart of which the Turkish rifles pointed from the north and south, for it was from the night of the landing a savage thorn pressed in their side. But the history of these posts needs a special chapter. By them Anzac held or fell.

Early I said Anzac was divided into two halves by Shrapnel Gully—the southern has just been travelled over. There remains to describe only those trenches that lay north of Shrapnel and Monash Gully, on the Nek, and back along Russell Top, the northern section of the famous position. It was mostly a New Zealand position; for New Zealanders and Maoris were largely responsible for its defence till the 3rd Light Horse Brigade, under General Hughes, took it over. Approached from the beach, the cliffs of Russell Top rise almost precipitously. The New Zealanders, mounted and dismounted troops, had had to set to work to cut a road up the face of this cliff to the top of the ridge It was the isolated nature of the position—until a way was cut down the slopes into Monash Gully to the very foot of the hill—that caused so much difficulty in moving troops, and was responsible for more than one delay in getting men to required posts at given times. Russell's Top might be best described as the end of the main Sari Bair ridge. Southward from the ridge, and almost at right angles to it, ran the spur commencing with Plugge's Plateau, that formed the first ridge (MacLagan's Ridge) stormed by the Australians. It overhung Anzac Cove. Incidentally it was the second line of our defence, the triangle within the triangle, and on it were the hastily formed trenches that the Australians had dug during the 25th, 26th, and 27th April, lest the Turkish attempts to 'drive them into the sea' proved successful. Guns were hauled up these ridges by hundreds of men, just as the Italians were doing on the Gorizia front. Had this last position been carried the guns could never have been got away. They might certainly have been tumbled down into the gullies below and spiked.

Russell Top itself was a short section or series of trenches grouped on either side of the ridge, and ending at the Nek. They faced roughly north and south. They commanded Anzac position to the south, and all the series of our works described in the early part of the chapter. On the north they dominated (the impossibility of getting very heavy artillery right along the ridge, owing to its precipitous and exposed nature, limited severely that command) all the series of foothills that led up to Chunak Bair and Koja Chemin Tepe. In this direction short, sharp spurs, covered with dense bushes and undergrowth, branched out from the Sari Bair ridge. To name them, starting from the beach: The first in our possession was Walker's Ridge, and then Happy Valley, then Turks' Point, then Snipers' Nest, where the Turks had command of the beach to good effect, and from which it was found impossible, though many stealthy attacks were made and the destroyers plastered the spur with shell, to dislodge them. Beyond, stern above all these crooked steep hilltops, was Rhododendron Ridge. Now, just after Turks' Point the ridge narrowed and formed the Nek. I do not think it was more than 160 yards wide at the utmost, just a thin strip of land, with sheer gullies protecting it on either flank. From here, too, the Sari Bair ridge began to slope up, rising rapidly to Baby 700, Battleship Hill, Chunak Bair. Immediately in front of the Nek, adjacent to the head of Monash Gully, were the terrible Chessboard Trenches, so named because the newly dug exposed earth where the trenches ran, lay in almost exact squares across the ridge from one side to the other, like a chessboard.

The New Zealand trenches (afterwards manned by Australian Light Horse) were about 80 yards from the enemy's lines, though the Turks occupied somewhat higher ground, and consequently looked down on to our trenches. But such was the superiority of fire that our troops had obtained, that the enemy were never able to take full advantage of this position. To hold these few acres of ground against fearful attacks cost hundreds of lives. The trenches were mostly sandbagged, the earth being too crumbling to hold against the searching fire of '75's' which the Turks (they had captured them in the Balkan War from the Serbians) had, together with Krupp artillery. Our machine guns commanded Snipers' Nest and the angle of Rhododendron Ridge where it joined the main ridge.

Traverses, therefore, became nothing but huge pillars of sand. The work entailed in keeping them clear and intact was very heavy indeed. A number of trench mortars concealed round the crown of Russell Top strengthened our position; while on the north flank many trenches existed amongst the undergrowth which the Turks were ignorant of. Still, through the possession of this ridge we had been able to fling out outpost stations along the beach towards Suvla Bay, and dig the sap which eventually was the connecting link with Anzac in the great operations at Suvla Bay on 7th August. But the Nek itself the Turks had mined and we had countermined, till beneath the narrow space between the trenches, was a series of mine tunnels with gaping craters above.

Only once had the Turks attempted to attack across this Nek, as I have described, but they so strengthened their position (and it was comparatively easy, owing to the configuration of the ground) that they were here probably more, what the Australians called 'uppish and cheeky' than in any other part of the line. One day, while I was standing talking with General Hughes, a message weighted with a stone was flung at our feet from the enemy's line. It looked like a pamphlet. It was written in Turkish, and then taken to the interpreter's quarters and transcribed, proved to be Turkish boasts published in Constantinople.

Round the flank of our trenches was a favourite way for deserters to come in, which they did on many occasions. Once on a dark night the sentries were startled to hear a voice speaking even more perfect English, and certainly more correct, then one was accustomed to hear in the trenches, saying: 'Will you please tell your men to cease firing, as I want to surrender?' Of course, the situation was rather difficult, as the Turks were fond of ruses, but eventually an Armenian officer jumped over the parapet and gave himself up. And very useful he proved, with the information he brought and gave during subsequent operations. But most difficult problem of all on this high plateau-top was the maintenance of supplies; not only of food and water, but of munitions. It was forty minutes' terrible climb to the top from the beach—a climb that needed every muscle strong to accomplish, even lightly laden.

To fortify the position as it had been, was a magnificent achievement, and could only have been done by troops with the hearts of lions and the spirit of the Norsemen of old.

It might have been thought in the face of such difficulties, with the fevers of the Mediterranean eating into their bodies, that the spirit of the army would have failed. On the contrary, the Australasians accepted the position just as it was, bad as it was: the sweltering heat and the short rations of water; the terrible fatigues, absent from campaigns in other theatres of the war zone; and, above all, the constant exposure to shell fire and rifle fire week after week and month after month. But the spirit of the trenches was buoyant and reflective without becoming pessimistic. The men were heartily sick of inaction. They rejoiced in the prospects of a battle. It was the inertia that killed.

CHAPTER XIX
LIFE AT QUINN'S AND POPE'S

It is doubtful if the true history of Quinn's and Pope's positions will ever be collated. But any soldier will tell you that these two posts made Anzac, for it was on the holding of these precarious and well-nigh impossible positions in the early days of occupation that the whole Australian line depended. The names will be forever bound up with the gallant officers who defended them, though it will be only meet that their subsequent commanders should have their names inscribed on the roll of the bravest of brave men that clung to the edges of the hillsides at the head of Monash Gully. There was, till the last days, always some fighting going on round Quinn's and Pope's, where the Turkish trenches approached to within a few yards of ours. Sorties by one side or the other were frequently made there; always bombing, alarms, mines, and countermines. I would never have been surprised if at any time the whole of Pope's and Quinn's had collapsed, blown to atoms by some vast network of mines, or wrecked by shell fire. The two places were a mass of trenches, burrows, secret tunnels, and deep shafts. They bristled with machine guns. My greatest difficulty is to adequately convey some detailed idea of the positions as I saw them—a few of the desperate conflicts have been already recorded, and I hope that what will follow will enable the nature of the fighting to be better realised.

Quinn's! The famous post was soon after the landing known throughout the Eastern Mediterranean, and its history, or a portion of it, reached England and Australia early in the accounts of Anzac. That it 'held,' the Turk found to his cost. He tried to overwhelm it; he was driven back into his trenches, not once, but scores and scores of times.

In the first weeks of the fighting, the Turk came on against Quinn's with cries of 'Allah! Allah!' and retired amidst weepings and moanings, leaving men dead and dying before the Post. From that day it became a desperate position, but when I examined it the men (they were Canterbury men from New Zealand and some of our own lads) under Lieut.-Colonel Malone, a magnificent stamp of leader, were quite cheery, and the whole tone of the Post was one of confidence, notwithstanding any attack the enemy might make. 'We are waiting for him, and wish he would come,' were the words of the commanding officer. 'Brother Turk has learnt his lesson; so he sits still and flings bombs—he gets two back for every one he throws.' That was the spirit which enabled Quinn's to be successfully held.

Once, in the early days, the way to Quinn's was through a hail of bullets up Shrapnel Gully, dodging from traverse to traverse, till you came to the foot of a ridge that ran almost perpendicularly up 200 feet. On the top and sides clung Quinn's. The ridge was bent here, where one of the heads of the great gully had eaten into the plateau. That was what made the hillside so steep. Quinn's helped to form one side of the ravine called the 'Bloody Angle.' Yes, in the early history of Quinn's and Pope's, just across the gully, not 100 yards away, had flowed down those hillsides the best blood of the Australian army. For the enemy peered down, into the hollow— then not afraid, as he was later, to expose his head and shoulders to take deliberate aim. The moral ascendancy of our sharpshooters was the first step in the victory of Quinn's.

After June it was no longer a matter of the same extreme peril coming up the broad valley, for there was a secret sap most of the way along Shrapnel Gully. Once you turned north, half way up the gully, you lost the view of the sea behind the hills, and you found yourself among a variety of Army Service Corpse units—among water-tanks and water-carriers. You heard the clatter of pumps and the rattle of mess-tins as the men stood out in long lines from the cooks' fires that gleamed, at half a dozen points. There was only a space of a few feet on either side of the path that contained the dugouts; the rest of the hillside was still covered with prickly undergrowth and shooting grasses. The sound of a mouth-organ resounded up the valley; bullets sped past very high overhead, and shells dropped very occasionally at this point among the inner hills behind the ridge. From the gully I turned on my left into a sap that wound about and shut off all views except that of Quinn's and Pope's. I came out of the sap again into the gully to a place where sandbags were piled thick and high to stop the bullets, for here it was not so comfortable, as far as the enemy's rifles were concerned. You went into a perfect fortress of low-flying squat huts, to which you found an entrance after some difficulty. I had to squeeze through a narrow, deep trench to reach it.

That was the headquarters of Brigadier-General Chauvel, who commanded the central section of the line that I could see all along the edge of the ridge about 150 yards away—almost on top of us—Pope's on the left, the isolated hilltop; then Quinn's, Courtney's, and Steel's. They were a group of danger points— a constant source of anxiety and despair to the General who commanded them. It was delightfully cool inside those caves in the gully after the heat of the sap. I was told by Major Farr and Major Williams, who were talking to the commanders of the posts by telephone, that I could not lose my way. 'Keep on following the narrow path, and if you are lucky you will be in time for a battle.' Each hung up the receiver and gave a curt order for some further boxes of bombs to be dispatched.

Battles on Quinn's were no mild engagements, for usually the hillside was covered with bursting shells and bombs that the Turks hurled over in amazing numbers. Fortunately, these 'stab' attacks were brief. As I pushed on towards the narrow sap that ran into the side of the hill, I could see by the excavated earth how it zigzagged up the side of the ridge.

I passed great quantities of stores, and, under the lee of a small knoll, cooks' lines for the men holding the Post above, which was still obscured from view. All one could see was a section of the Turkish trench just where it ended 20 yards from our lines, and the barbed-wire entanglements that had been thrown out as a screen. The air was filled with the appetising odour of sizzling bacon, onions, and potatoes, while shells whizzed across the valley. I was glad to be safely walking between high sandbag parapets.

Soon the path became so steep that steps had been made in the hill—steps made by branches interlaced and pegged to the ground. It was a climb, one ascending several feet in every stride. Sandbags were propped up here and there in pillars to protect us from the sight of the enemy on our left. One's view was confined to the wire entanglements on the skyline and the steep, exposed slope of the hill on the right. Behind lay the valley, full of shadows and points of light from dugouts and fires. They were quite safe down there, but you were almost on the edge of a volcano that might break out above you at any moment. You passed various sandbagged huts, until quite near the crest of the hill trenches began to run in various directions, and you saw the rounded top of the hill chipped away and bared under the constant rifle and bomb attacks. What had appeared ledges in the distance resolved themselves into a series of terraces, where the men found protection and, as busy as bees, were preparing for tea.

Lieut.-Colonel Malone was my guide. He was an Irishman, and keen about the Post and just the man to hold it. His great motto was 'that war in the first place meant the cultivation of domestic virtues,' and he practised it. He brought me up a gently inclined track towards a point at which barbed wire could be seen across a gully which ended in a sharp fork. That was the 'Bloody Angle.' Then we turned around and looked back down the gully. In the distance, 100 yards away on the right, along the top of the ridge, were two distinct lines of trenches, with ground between which you at once knew was 'dead' ground. The hill doubled back, which almost left Quinn's open to fire from the rear. 'That is our position—Courtney's Post and Steel's to the east,' said my guide, 'and those opposite are the Turkish trenches. We call them the 'German Officers' Trenches,' because we suspect that German officers were there at one time. Now we have given them a sporting chance to snipe us; let us retire. I always give a visitor that thrill.' It was only the first of several such episodes which vividly brought home to one's mind the desperate encounters that had been waged around this famous station. The men who held on here had a disregard of death. They were faced with it constantly, continuously.

There were four rows of terraces up the side of the hill. Once the men had just lived in holes, dug as best they could, with a maze of irregular paths. That was in the period when the fighting was so fierce that no time could be spared to elaborate the trenches not actually in the firing-line. Afterwards, when the garrison was increased to 800 and material came ashore—wooden beams and sheet-iron—conditions underwent a change. Four of five terraces were built and long sheds constructed along the ledges and into the side of the hill. These had sandbag cover which bullets and bombs could not penetrate. Just over the edge of the hill, not 30 yards away, were our own lines, and the Turkish trenches 4 to 25 yards beyond again. When the shells came tearing overhead from our guns down in the gully the whole hillside shook with the concussion of the burst. No wonder the terraces collapsed one day! I was standing talking to Lieut.-Colonel Malone and saw about 100 of the men who were in reserve leaning against the back of the shed that belonged to a terrace lower down. They were all looking up at an aeroplane, a German Taube, skimming overhead. A huge bomb burst in the trenches on the top of the hill, and the men, involuntarily, swayed back. That extra weight broke away the terrace, and it collapsed with a roar. Fortunately, the damage done was small, though about eight men were injured.

To go through Quinn's was like visiting a miniature fortress. The whole extent of the front was not more than 200 yards. One dived down innumerable tunnels that ran 10 or 20 feet in the clay under the enemy trenches, and contained mines, ready set, to be blown up at the first sign of an enemy attack in mass. A certain amount of protection had been gained at Quinn's from the deluge of bombs that the enemy accurately threw, by a screen of wire-netting that caught the bombs so they burst on the parapets. But such protection was no use against the heavy football bomb. Loopholes were all of iron plating, and in most cases of double thickness, and even thus they were almost pierced by the hail of bullets from the Turkish machine guns. The Turks did not occupy their forward trenches by day. Only at night they crept up into them in large numbers. Several craters formed a sort of danger-point between the lines where mines had been exploded, and into these it was the endeavour of some Turks to steal at night on their way to an attack.

Now, one of the stories about Quinn's—alas! how many tales of gallantry must go unrecorded—is that the enemy's troops became so demoralised by the nearness of the trenches and the constant vigilance of our men that, in order to properly man their trenches in this sector, the Turks had to give non-commissioned rank to all the men there posted. Our own garrison in June and July were changed every eight days. Lieut.-Colonel Malone, however, remained in charge, having under him mixed forces of New Zealanders and Australians. One day I went with him into one series of tunnel trenches that wound back and forth and that opened up unexpectedly into a strongly fortified emplacement either for a machine gun or an observation post. Lying all along the tunnels, either on the ground, pressed close to the walls, or in a niche, or ledge, were the garrison. It was difficult not to tread on them. We came to a point where, pegged to the earthen walls, were any number of pictures—of Sydney beach, of St Kilda foreshore, of bush homes and haunts, of the latest beauty actresses, and—most treasured possession—some of Kirchner's drawings and coloured work from French papers.

They were a happy family at Quinn's. Once orders had been given that conversations could be carried on only in whispers, so close was the enemy. For the most part, however, that was not necessary, but there were certain places where we had machine-gun emplacements—traps they were really, and the guns had never been fired. They were to be surprises for 'Johnny Turk' when he should attack again in force. Here certainly it would not have been wise to discuss the position, for the enemy, some few yards distant, might have heard and understood. One had only to show a periscope above the trenches at Quinn's to bring down a hail of bullets, and three periscopes was the signal for the turning of a machine gun on the sandbag parapets, with a broken glass in the periscope the only result.

The shells from our guns in the valley just skimmed the tops of the trenches, clearing them about 12 feet and bursting in the enemy's lines. it was a very sensational experience until one got used to the sound and could detect which way the shells were travelling. It is told of this Post that two men were sitting in the trench talking in whispers when a shell came whining and roaring towards them. It burst. They did not rise to see where, but it was near. Said the new arrival to his mate, 'Is that ours?'

'No,' came the hissed reply, 'theirs!'

'The —!' was the only vouchsafed and typically Anzac comment.

Yes, the Post was undoubtedly strong, for it could enfilade any attack from German Officers' Trench on the right, and the Turks knew that and attempted none. What was most amazing about the position were the series of gun-pits, dug out of the centre of a shoulder of the hill which ran down the right side of the position on the flank of the gully nearest to Courtney's. I went up through a winding passage-way, where blue-bottle flies kept up a drowsy humming. Every half-dozen yards there were small concealed openings in the side of the tunnel, through which I looked out on to the terraces and towards Pope's. When I reached the summit and found a series of three chambers each with ledges ready for machine guns, Lieut.-Colonel Malone explained. 'This,' he said, 'is the place to which we might retire if the Turks did break through the Post and come down the gully side. We would catch them here. They cannot detect the guns, for they are hidden by this thick scrub. We are now on the side of that hill you saw on to which the Turks, from in front of Pope's and the Bloody Angle, can fire. We could reach them, but the Staff will not give me the machine guns. The reason is we have not enough, as it is, on the Post—not as many as I would like. I would like a dozen—we have seven. The enemy would never get us out of here till we starved.' I no longer ceased to wonder why Quinn's was declared 'perfectly safe.'

To get across to Pope's you had to go down into the gully again by the steep way you had come, and travel another 200 yards up towards its head until you came to an almost bare and precipitous hillside, which you climbed the best way you could, picking a path in and out amongst the dugouts. If you had a load of stores, you could go to a part where a rope hung down from the crown of the hill, about 100 feet up, and by it you might haul yourself to the top. Pope's was even more exposed than Quinn's when you entered it. The Commander's dugouts were perched on the back of the hill, facing the gully, and bullets and shells burst round his cave entrances. Lieut.-Colonel Rowell, of the 3rd Regiment of Light Horse, was in charge the day I went over every section of it. The Light Horsemen were desperately proud of their holding this dangerous and all-important knoll that blocked the entrance to the gully.

Here, again, there were tunnels connecting up the front and support trenches. They twisted about and wound in and out, conforming to the shape of the top of the hill. But they were not connected on either flank. It was just an isolated post. There were positions for machine guns that by a device were made disappearing guns. They were hauled up rapidly by a pulley and rope and then lowered out of sight again. It was a rough-and-ready makeshift, but the only means of keeping secret positions (on a hill that did not offer much scene for selection) for the guns. Iron loopholes were absolutely essential; an iron flap fell across them as soon as the rifle had been withdrawn. I remember standing opposite one of these till I was warned to move, and, sure enough, just afterwards some bullets went clean through and thumped against the back of the trench. Many men had been shot through the loopholes, so close were the enemy's snipers.

Down on the right flank of the post, just facing the head of Monash Gully and the Nek and Chessboard Trenches, was a remarkable series of sharpshooters' posts. They were reached through a tunnel which had been bored into the side of the hill. The bushes that grew on the edge had not been disturbed, and the Turks could know nothing of them. It was through these our crack rifle-shots fired on the Turks when they attempted, on various occasions, to come down through the head of Monash Gully from their trenches on the Chessboard and round the flank of Pope's Hill. Maps show the nearness of the Turks' line to ours, scarcely more than 15 yards away in places: what they do not show is the mining and countermining beneath the surface. Constantly sections of trenches were being blown up by the diligent sappers, and in July, Pope's Hill had become almost an artificial hill, held together, one might say, by the sandbags that kept the saps and trenches intact. Words fail to convey the heartbreaking work of keeping the communications free and the trenches complete, for every Turkish shell that burst did damage of some sort, and nearly every morning early some portion of the post had to he rebuilt. Looking here across the intervening space—it was very narrow—to the right and left I could see the Turkish strong over-head cover on their trenches, made of wooden beams and pine logs. Between was no man's land.

What tragedy lay in this fearful neutral zone! The immediate foreground was littered with old jam-tins, some of which were unexploded 'bombs.' There was a rifle, covered with dust, and a heap of rags. My attention was called to the red collar of the upper portion of what had been a Turkish jacket, and gradually I made out of the frame of the soldier, who had mouldered away, inside it. It was a pitiful sight. There were four other unburied men from the enemy's ranks. Nearer still was a boot and the skeleton leg of a Turk, lying as he had fallen in a crumpled heap. I gathered all this from the peeps I had through the periscope.

Such is an outline of what the posts that Lieut.-Colonel Pope and Major Quinn won and established, had developed into after months of fighting. Something has already been told of the early battles round them. It is impossible to chronicle all the attacks and counterattacks. It must here suffice to continue the history already begun in other chapters by referring briefly to the sortie on 9th May, the third Sunday after landing.

Quinn's was still a precarious position. On both sides the engineers had been sapping forward, and the trenches were so close that the men shouted across to one another. Near midnight on the 9th, the 15th Battalion, under Lieut.-Colonel Cannan, with two companies of the 16th in support, about 900 men in all, attacked the Turkish trenches in front of Quinn's. They issued forth in three separate bodies, and after a fierce struggle routed the Turks. Rapidly communication trenches were dug connecting up the forward with the rear trenches, which meant that two island patches of ground were formed. Then it was found that all three parties had not linked up, and the Turks held an intervening section of the line. An attempt, by companies of the 15th and 16th Battalions failed to gain the Turkish parapets in the face of a terrible fire. When dawn broke the whole of the captured trenches became the centre of concentrated Turkish fire from two flanks, and our gallant men were compelled to make their way back along their new communication trenches to their own lines again. This, therefore, left the Turkish trenches and our own connected by three saps. It was an amazing position. Sandbag parapets had been hastily erected, and on either side of these the troops stood and bombed one another. The infantry called in Arabic they had learnt in Egypt, believing that the Turks would understand, 'Saida' (which is 'Good day') and other phrases. They threw across bully-beef tins or bombs, indiscriminately. It was what the troops called 'good sport.'

So the positions remained for five days until Friday, 14th May, when a Light Horse squadron of the 2nd Light Horse—C Squadron, under Major D. P. Graham—was chosen to attack the Turks and rout them from this unpleasantly close proximity to our line. The communication sap had first to be cleared. Two parties of men, 30 in each, with bayonets fixed, dashed from the trenches at 1.45 a.m. In the face of a tremendous machine-gun and musketry fire from the enemy they charged for the parapets, so short a distance away. The troops dropped rapidly. Major Graham, seeing his men melt away, endeavoured to rally those that remained. But the Turkish fire was too fierce, and the few that survived were compelled to jump into the communication sap, and thus make their way back to their lines. Major Graham himself, with the utmost coolness, brought in some of the wounded after the attack had failed, but at length he fell, mortally wounded. So ended the first May attack.

Desperate endeavours were made by the Turks, in their grand attack on 19th May, to enter our trenches, but the line was held safely under Major Quinn's command until Saturday, 29th May, when, after exploding a mine under part of our forward position, a strong body of Turks managed to penetrate, during the early morning, to our second line. The Post was at that moment in a desperate position. Major Quinn himself, at the head of the gallant 15th Battalion, commenced to lead a counter-attack. The din of battle was terrific. Few fiercer conflicts had raged round the famous posts than on this cool, clear morning. The Turks were routed and driven back to their lines, but the brave leader, Major Quinn, fell, riddled with bullets, across the very trenches which his men had dug. So fierce had been the charge that a certain, section of trench held by the enemy had been, run over by our troops. In that the Turks clung. They were caught in between cross-fires, but held desperately the communication trenches. After various attempts to dislodge them it was suddenly thought that they might surrender, which solution, on being signalled to them, they willingly agreed to. The post was immediately strengthened, and the dangerous communication trenches were effectively blocked and held by machine guns.

Lieut.-Colonel Pope, after desperate fighting on the hill that bore his name, still survived to lead his battalion in the great August attacks. The brigade, and, indeed, the whole Division, mourned the loss of so gallant an officer and so fearless a leader as Major Quinn. They honour his name no less than that of the dauntless Pope.

CHAPTER XX
JUNE AND JULY PREPARATIONS

There is no doubt that operations in May convinced General Sir Ian Hamilton that neither at the southern nor in the northern positions on the peninsula was his force strong enough to push back the Turks, though he held what he had won strongly enough. Consequently he cabled to the War Office, urging that reinforcements should be sent. But in the middle of May the withdrawal of the Russians from the Gallipoli campaign was declared from Petrograd, and the Commander-in-Chief found it necessary to increase his estimate of the force he would require to force his way across to the Narrows. His new demand was two additional army corps. Already the Lowland Division (52nd) had been dispatched, but this was but 20,000 men; four times as many were required to press home the offensive. The abatement of the Russian attacks had released about 100,000 of the finest Turkish troops, and these reinforcements began to arrive on the peninsula in June. General Hamilton writes in his last dispatch: 'During June your Lordship became persuaded of the bearing of these facts, and I was promised three regular Divisions, plus the infantry of two Territorial Divisions. The advance guard of these troops was due to reach

Mudros by 10th July; by 10th August their concentration was to be complete.'

So thus before the end of May the Commander-in-Chief had in mind the larger plan, beginning a new phase of the campaign, to be carried out in July, or at the latest August. Therefore, it may be truly said, the June–July Anzac battles were fought as preparatory actions (in the absence of sufficiently strong forces) to clear and pave the way for the great August offensive. The grip on the Turks was tightened.

Fighting round Quinn's Post, as already related, had been taking place during the greater part of May. Sometimes the Australians attacked, and, more seldom, the Turks counter-attacked. It was at any time a desperately held position. It continued so till the end of the chapter.

Now, while the Anzac troops could not yet advance, they could help any direct assault on Achi Baba, such as had been once tried in May with but partial success. So it happened on the 28th June the Anzac troops were ordered to make demonstrations to allow the pushing home by the English and French of attacks that had commenced on 8th May, when the Australians had taken so prominent a part in the advance on Krithia village. In this 28th June action the Gurkhas were ordered, and did advance, up the Great Dere, and flung the British flank round the west of that village. It was a fine gain of some 800 yards. However, the Turks had plenty of troops available, and they lost no time in organising terrific counter-attacks. Owing to the offensive taken at Anzac the Australians were able to draw off a portion from this attack, which tactics at the same time both puzzled and harassed the Turks. The details I will briefly relate.

In June the 2nd Light Horse Brigade, under Brigadier-General Ryrie, held the southerly portion of the line at Tasman's Post, that overlooked Blamey's Meadow. Next them, holding the line, were the 3rd Infantry Brigade, under Brigadier-General Maclagan, reinforced now with new troops, though with still a proportion of the men that had taken part in the landing. Except for patrol work and various small excursions and alarms against the Turks, there had been no big attack made yet. They were keen for battle.

All the night of the 27th–28th and during the morning masses of shells could be seen bursting on the hills round Krithia, and sheets of flame rolled along the slopes of the hills as the warships and the guns ashore bombarded the Turkish trenches. Early on the 28th news had been received that all efforts of the Turks to drive back the British had failed. The troops at Anzac revelled in that great artillery struggle. At midday their turn came.

For the first time, a day attack was planned. The Light Horse were to leave their trenches at one o'clock. Destroyers moved close in to Gaba Tepe and to the north of the Australian position, and began an intense shelling of the exposed Turkish trenches, that in some places were open to enfilade fire. Soon the artillery ashore began, and added further havoc. In front of the southern part of our line, near Harris Ridge, about 600 yards away, was a strong Turkish position on a rise—one of the many spurs of the main ridge. This was the objective of the attacking troops. All Queenslanders, Light Horse, and infantry, had been selected—a squadron and two companies, about 500 men, who were to lead the charge. They were to be led by Lieut.-Colonel H. Harris. The Western Australian Infantry, about 300 in all, were chosen to support the Queensland (9th) Infantry, led by Major Walsh; and New South Wales (7th) Light Horse Regiment, to support the Queensland (5th) dismounted squadron.

Just after one o'clock the guns creased, and the storming parties of Queenslanders dashed forward from their trenches, and, with comparatively few casualties, gained a footing on the nearest slope of the ridge, that was covered with thick brush. They found certain protection, and there they commenced to entrench. Just over the ridge was a plateau of cultivated ground, called 'The Wheatfield,' and across this the Turks had dug trenches at right angles to the ridge. From the trenches that the Light Horsemen had left, rifle fire could be kept up on these trenches. Beyond, the strong Turkish positions on Wineglass Ridge and Pine Ridge were being shelled by the destroyers and the New Zealand artillery. However, it did not take the Turks long to bring gun fire on these advanced troops, and high-explosive shell burst in the shallow trenches. The brown and red earth was flung up in dense clouds, but the troops held to their position. They went on digging. It was as fine an example of courage as one might wish to see—these splendid men calmly entrenching amidst the craters the shells left round them. Soon, however, the very object of the offensive was disclosed to the Australians themselves, for they could see Turkish reinforcements being hurried up in the distant gullies (they had come from the village of Eski Keui, half-way down the peninsula to Krithia). Turkish leaders could be seen in the fierce sunlight signalling to their troops to keep low, as they could be observed by our forces; and no doubt the Turks with their white fezzes and skull-caps made excellent targets, as they soon found, to their consternation and cost, by the accuracy of our gun fire. These enemy reinforcements were scattered, and, in disorder, sought what shelter they could in the gullies.

Having held the ridge and accomplished the diversion, the Light Horse gradually retired and regained their own trenches. By 4.30 in the afternoon the infantry too had been withdrawn from the advanced position. So not only had the attack been successful in drawing up Turks who would otherwise have gone to the assistance of their comrades hard pressed around Krithia, but they were, through bad leadership, brought up into positions in gullies which our guns had registered, and terrible casualties resulted. Both the Queensland units—Light Horse as well as infrantry—had shown fine gallantry, and they were dashingly led by Lieut.-Colonel Harris.

Once having stirred the Turk, it behoved the Australians to be ready for a counter-attack. But Tuesday, 29th, remained still and quiet; only the occasional bursting of a bomb round Quinn's and Pope's Posts and the intermittent crack of rifles, broke the calm of a perfect summer day. To the enemy there had been every indication that a serious advance was contemplated from Anzac. During the afternoon, growing nervous of the close approach of some of our mine tunnels under their trenches, the Turks exploded their countermines, which would effectively seal any advance from underground and through craters. Just afterwards a summer storm arose, which enveloped the Turkish lines in clouds of dust. What better opportunity could have presented itself for our attack? No sooner had the wind driven the dust over the trenches than the enemy commenced a fierce fire, which they maintained without ceasing for two hours. The stream of lead that passed over our trenches was terrific. Only when the storm abated did the Turkish rifle and machine gun fire die away. All of this the enemy did to check an anticipated advance which we had no intention of making. Millions of rounds of Turkish ammunition had been wasted.

But the Turks now determined to turn the situation to their own purposes, which apparently was to draw attention to their lines in this southern section, while they prepared to launch, unexpectedly, an attack from another quarter. The Australian leaders were already aware of this method of surprise, and had come to look on it as part of the Turkish 'bluff' for the enemy had tried it before, when they had blown bugles and shouted orders and given loud commands in their trenches, and nothing had happened—not at that spot. Now the firing ceased just before midnight.

An hour and a half later the enemy began a violent attack on the Nek, with new troops belonging to the 18th Regiment of the enemy's 6th Division. They had come recently from Asia Minor, and were some of the best troops of the Turkish Regular Army. Enver Pasha himself, the Commander-in-Chief of the Turkish forces, had ordered the attack so that the Australians might, once and for all, be 'pushed into the sea.' In this way began an attempt to rush our trenches at the head of Monash Gully. The line was here held by New Zealanders and Light Horse. On this left flank considerable rearrangement from the earlier days had taken place. The Maories held the extreme left down to the shore. On Russell Top were the New Zealand Mounted Rifles, under Brigadier-General Russell, and the 3rd Light Horse, under Brigadier-General Hughes. These fine men held the trenches opposite the mass of Turkish lines, the Chessboard Trenches. Brigadier General Chauvel's Light Horse Brigade was in the trenches at Quinn's and Pope's, together with some New Zealand infantry regiments. Thus was the gap at the head of Monash Gully up as far as Steel's Post, held.

From midnight till 1.30 an intense fire of musketry and guns was poured on to our trenches on Russell's Top. It was still bright moonlight when, in a series of lines, the Turks commenced to attack at 1.30. They came shambling on, shouting 'Allah! Allah!' towards the parapets of our trenches, less than 100 yards across the Nek. At this spot the Light Horsemen had been digging out two saps towards the enemy, and it was into these some of the enemy charged, our troops dividing to allow them to enter. Then the Australians fell on them from either side with bombs, and none escaped. For it was the habit of the Turk when he attacked, not to jump into the trench and come to hand-to-hand encounters if he could help it, but to lie on top of the parapet and fire down into the trench. Very few of the enemy, in these three charges that came and faded away, reached our lines. When the first charge had been so blankly stopped not many yards after it began, the Turks tried to work along the northern edge of the ridge, where the ground fell away steeply into the gullies below, and on the southern side of the Nek, where the ground was no less difficult, but not as deep, sloping down to the head of Monash Gully. Our machine guns wrought fearful havoc, and 400 Turks at least perished in the charges. Then the destroyers sent the rays of the searchlights farther up the hill towards the rounded top of Baby 700, and revealed the enemy reserves advancing. Gun fire destroyed these.

Meanwhile, a further attack was developing down the heads of the gullies on either side of Pope's Hill, the hill that guarded the entrance to the gully, and the centre of the position. I have already told how from the sides of this hill machine guns were trained down into the gully; and how the line of concealed sharpshooters' posts we had established, gave absolute command, and at the same time protection, to the holders of the gully. The bright rays of the moon aided the defenders, and they could easily detect the stealthily moving figures. Towards one o'clock the Turks commenced to work down this gully. It is related of that fight—an incident typical, no doubt, of many—that a Light Horseman, seeing a Turk silhouetted on the edge of the ridge, rushed at him with his bayonet, and the two men slipped over the edge of the cliff, down through the hush and loose earth, till they both were brought up almost face to face on a ledge. They crossed bayonets—one pictures the two figures in the indefinite light of the moon standing there motionless for a fraction of a minute—till the Australian, realising that he had in his magazine a cartridge, pulled the trigger. When his comrades came to his assistance, dashing through the undergrowth, they found him with the dead Turk, smiling.

Now, it was evident the Turks had meant to stay in that attack. The few men that did reach the trenches on Russell's Top, and were killed there, must have been men of the second or third lines. They carried large numbers of bombs and digging implements. They had quantities of provisions—figs, dates, and olives—and water-bottles filled. They were evidently intended to be the holding party. As daylight came, some of the enemy still lurked in the head of the gully on either flank of Pope's Hill, just before dawn a further line of 300 men attempted to rush the head of the gully. They reached the edge of the cliff, and then broke into small parties running this way and that, under the fire of our machine guns, which played on them from the Light Horse lines on Russell's Top (the main charge by this having faded away) and from the side of Pope's Hill. At the same time a few of the enemy left their trenches at Quinn's to rush our post on the side of the hill. None got more than a few yards. All the men of that last desperate attack were killed or wounded, A few were taken prisoners.

The scene next morning was ghastly. In the saps on the Nek twenty and thirty dead Turks lay piled in a row. Before Pope's Hill, never very strongly threatened that night, there were scores of dead. The total loss must have been nearly 600 killed and 2,000 casualties. It is historically important as the last Turkish attack against Anzac proper. The Turks showed a desperate courage; for this attack on the Nek was but sending troops to certain destruction; yet the men never flinched, and they were soon to show the same valour again, in attacks on the higher slopes of the Sari Bair ridge.

Throughout July it was always expected that the enemy's superstition would lead him to make a bold effort in the season of Ramazan—the end of July. Warnings had reached Anzac to this effect. Prisoners had anticipated it, probably due to the orders of Enver Pasha to dislodge at all costs the Australian forces. The enemy had been bringing up new regiments. All through July the Turks showed a nervous disposition to burst out into heavy fusillades all along the line. At night they sent coloured lights over the gullies and our position. Our gunners did the same, at the time when the moon dropped behind the hills of Troy, between midnight and 3 a.m. The troops stood to arms at moonset. Our trenches were then always fully manned. The reserves slept in the saps.

Ramazan passed; and still the Turks clung to the protection of their trenches. The June battles had completely disheartened them. Their ammunition was running short. Certainly ours had been none too plentiful, and orders had been given since May to conserve it as far as possible. Two rounds per gun a day was the limit, except under special circumstances. As General Hamilton himself admitted, 'Working out my ammunition allowance, I found I would accumulate just enough high-explosive shell to enable me to deliver one serious attack each period of three weeks.' It was exceedingly exasperating to the gunners, this shortage. There came times when, owing to the necessity of getting permission from headquarters, the gunners grew impatient, as they saw targets escaping into the folds of the hills. A General told me on one occasion how a column could be seen, moving about 4 miles away, but owing to the delay of hours in getting the necessary permission to loose off some twenty rounds of shell, the column, escaped. He had fired his allowance per gun, as was his invariable custom, just to remind 'Abdul' he was awake, early in the morning.

It was not, however, Sir Ian Hamilton's plan to draw much attention to Anzac just at present. He wanted the Turkish mind focused on Cape Helles, which was one reason for the period of quiet that occurred in July at Anzac, though care was taken that the moral ascendancy that had been gained over the Turks by the Australians was never lost, and not one whit less was given to the Turks now than had been given before in vigilant sniping and bombing. But the effect on the spirits of the Turks was noticeable, and at the end of July, long before the official information leaked out to the troops, there appeared in the trenches opposite Quinn's Post at notice-board, on which was printed in irregular letters,

'Warsaw is fallen.' The result of which little enemy joke was that thousands of rifle bullets shattered the notice. Notes began to be thrown over stating that the Australians would be well treated if they surrendered. In spite of which, Turkish deserters still continued to come into our lines, all of whom told of the growing fear of the Turks at the length of the campaign, and the disheartening of their troops. Incidentally, I may say, prisoners all believed they were going to be killed. I remember Major Martyn telling me how one party, on coming through a communication trench to our lines, had tried to kiss his hands in gratitude at being spared.

So, chafing under the delayed advance, the Australians waited for their chance to teach 'Abdul' a lasting lesson.

PART III

THE GREAT ADVENTURE

CHAPTER XXI
THE AUGUST PHASE AND
NEW LANDING

It will have been gathered from the fighting that followed the terrible May attack of the Turks, when they lost so heavily in trying to dislodge the Australians from Anzac and British from Helles, that nothing would have satisfied our commanders better than for a Turkish attack to develop during the end of July. This, I feel certain in saying, would have been repulsed, as others had been repulsed, and would have left the Turkish army weak, just at the moment when General Sir Ian Hamilton had completed all his plans for the continuing of the Great Adventure begun in April. The rumours of a projected Turkish attack at Anzac proved groundless. The Australians were left unmolested, while the Turks, conceiving that the British still intended to attempt the assault of Achi Baba, had gathered on the end of the peninsula great reserve forces. General Hamilton's strategy had had much to do with this (the great sacrifices of the attacks on Krithia would not then have seemed so vain had the full plan succeeded), for in his mind was just the reverse idea—that Anzac should be the turning-point, the pivot of all operations, as it had been intended from the first. It was to become the centre of an unlinked battle front, of which Cape Helles was the right flank and Suvla Bay was to be the left. An attack launched from this left—a new and an entirely unexpected left—would leave a way for the centre to push forward. Then automatically would the right have advanced.

This strategy was really an elaboration of the early plan of the Commander-in-Chief, aimed at the cutting of the Turkish communications to the great dominating fortress of Kelid Bahr, which afterwards could be reduced at leisure with the co-operation of the Navy. It has been often asked what advantage would have accrued from the Australians and the new British troops reaching Maidos and holding the heights of Koja Chemen Tepe. None less than the forcing of the Turkish communication from Europe into Asia, and that they should be compelled to undertake the very hazardous and doubtful operation of keeping intact the Gibraltar of the peninsula—the Kelid Bahr fortress—by supplying it across the Narrows from Chanak and the badly railwayed coast of Asia Minor.

But there were alternative plans open to General Hamilton, and such will always give opportunity to military strategists to debate the one adopted. What General Hamilton knew in May was that he would have 200,000 new British troops by August at his command, with 20,000 Australian reinforcements on their way and due to arrive about the middle of the same month. His army, as he commanded it then, was about 150,000 strong (including the French Expedition), and its strength might easily be diminished to 100,000 by August owing to normal wastage, Turkish offensives, and sickness that began to make itself evident. Two hundred thousand men to attack an Empire! In the days of its Byzantine glory, in the times of the early struggles for Balkan supremacy, such an army would have been considered noble. Now, though British, it was not enough. Apparently the situation on the Western front did not warrant another 100,000 men that General Hamilton had asked for more than once, to give him a safe margin, being granted him. The Turks, released from their toils against Russia on the east in the Caucasus—the Mesopotamian front not seriously threatened and the attack on the Canal being impossible—found ample men at their disposal. On the other hand, they had a long and vulnerable coastline to guard, but the 900,000 men of that German organised and commanded army, made a powerful fighting force. Nearly 400,000 troops were apportioned for service on the peninsula. I am not asserting that that number of men were facing the landed armies, but they were available, some perhaps as far away as Adrianople or the Gulf of Enos. If General Hamilton's problem was a difficult one, Enver Pasha's way was not exactly smooth. He was harassed by lack of heavy ammunition, the populace were wavering, while above all hung the terrible threat of another landing on the European or Asiatic shores.

But one factor the British leader had to ponder deeply was the submarine menace that had been threatening the very existence of the already landed armies. Two fine warships, the *Triumph* and *Majestic*, had been sunk in May while shelling and guarding the positions ashore, and the fleet had been compelled to seek shelter in the harbour of Mudros. Even though monitors, with 14-in. guns, were soon available to maintain the invaluable support that the battleships had previously given to the army, there was not the weight of artillery of a highly mobile nature, ready for any emergency, without the Admiralty were prepared to hazard a great loss. Transportation of troops and stores was dangerous and subject to irritating, and even dangerous, delays. General Hamilton sums up the situation in a masterly fashion in his final dispatch:

Eliminating the impracticable, I had already narrowed down the methods of employing these fresh forces to one of the following four:
(a) Every man to be thrown on to the southern sector of the peninsula, to force a way forward to the Narrows.
(b) Disembarkation on the Asiatic side of the Straits, followed by a march on Chanak.
(c) A landing at Enos or Ibrije for the purpose of seizing the neck of the Isthmus at Bulair.
(d) Reinforcement of the Australian and New Zealand Army Corps, combined with a landing in Suvla Bay.

Then with one strong push to capture Hill 305 [971], and, working from that dominating point, to grip the waist of the peninsula.

As to (a) I rejected that course—

1. Because there were limits to the numbers which could be landed and deployed in one confined area.

2. Because the capture of Krithia could no longer be counted upon to give us Achi Baba, an entirely new system of works having lately appeared upon the slopes of that mountain—works so planned that even if the enemy's western flank was turned and driven back from the coast, the central and eastern portions of the mountain could still be maintained as a bastion to Kelid Bahr.

3. Because if I tried to disengage myself both from Krithia and Achi Baba by landing due west of Kelid Bahr my troops would be exposed to artillery fire from Achi Baba, the Olive Grove, and Kelid Bahr itself; the enemy's large reserves were too handy; there were not fair chances of success.

As to (b), although much of the Asiatic coast had now been wired and entrenched, the project was still unattractive. Thereby the Turkish forces on the peninsula would be weakened; our beaches at Cape Helles would be freed from Asiatic shells; the threat to the enemy's sea communications was obvious. But when I descended into detail I found that the expected reinforcements would not run to a double operation. I mean that, unless I could make a thorough, wholehearted attack on the enemy in the peninsula I should reap no advantage in that theatre from the transference of the Turkish peninsular troops to reinforce Asia, whereas, if the British forces landed in Asia were not strong enough in themselves seriously to threaten Chanak, the Turks for their part would not seriously relax their grip upon the peninsula.

To cut the land communications of the whole of the Turkish peninsular army, as in (c), was a better scheme on paper than on the spot. The naval objections appeared to my coadjutor, Vice-Admiral Robeck, well-nigh insurmountable. Already, owing to submarine dangers, all reinforcements, ammunition, and supplies had to be brought up from Mudros to Helles or Anzac by night in fleet sweepers and trawlers. A new landing near Bulair would have added another 50 miles to the course such small craft must cover, thus placing too severe a strain upon the capacities of the flotilla.

The landing promised special hazards, owing to the difficulty of securing the transports and covering ships from submarine attack. Ibrije has a bad beach, and the distance to Enos, the only point suitable to a disembarkation on a large scale, was so great that the enemy would have had time to organise a formidable opposition from his garrisons in Thrace. Four divisions at least would be required to overcome such opposition. These might now be found; but, even so, and presupposing every other obstacle overcome, it was by no manner of means certain that the Turkish army on the peninsula would thereby be brought to sue for terms, or that the Narrows would thereby be opened to the fleet. The enemy would still be able to work supplies across the Straits from Chanak. The swiftness of the current, the shallow draft of the Turkish lighters, the guns of the forts, made it too difficult even for our dauntless submarine commanders to paralyse movement across these land-locked waters. To achieve that purpose I must bring my artillery fire to bear both on the land and water communications of the enemy.

This brings me to (d), the storming of that dominating height, Hill 305 [971], with the capture of Maidos and Gaba Tepe as its sequel.

From the very first I had hoped that by landing a force under the heights of Sari Bair we should be able to strangle the Turkish communications to the southwards, whether by land or sea, and so clear the Narrows for the fleet. Owing to the enemy's superiority, both in numbers and in position; owing to underestimates of the strength of the original entrenchments prepared and sited under German direction; owing to the constant dwindling of the units of my force through wastage; owing also to the intricacy and difficulty of the terrain, these hopes had not hitherto borne fruit. But they were well founded. So much at least had clearly enough been demonstrated by the desperate and costly nature of the Turkish attacks. The Australians and New Zealanders and rooted themselves in very near to the vitals of the enemy. By their tenacity and courage they still held open the doorway from which one strong thrust forward might give us command of the narrows.

From the naval point of view the auspices were also favourable. Suvla Bay was but one mile further from Mudros then Anzac, and its possession would ensure us a submarine-proof base, and a harbour good against gales, excepting those from the south-west. There were, as might be expected, some special difficulties to be overcome. The broken, intricate country—the lack of water—the consequent anxious supply questions. Of these it can only be said that a bad country is better than an entrenched country, and that supply and water problems may be countered by careful preparation.

It has been pointed out before what need there was for studying the moon at Anzac. In the fixing of the date for the new landing the Commander-in-Chief had to find a means of 'eliminating' the moon. That is, he had to find the night which would give him the longest hours of darkness, after the arrival of his forces. He found that on 7th August the moon would rise at 2 p.m. The weather might be depended on to be perfect, so that before the light would be fully cast over the movements of the troops ashore it would be almost dawn. General Hamilton would have liked the operations to have commenced a month earlier, he says, but the troops were not available. He had to fill in the time by keeping the enemy occupied and wearing them down with feints. To have waited for another month till the whole of his command had actually arrived on the adjacent islands of Mudros and Imbros, where their concentration had been planned, would have been to come too close to the approaching bad season and increase the element of risk of the Turks discovering the plans. So the die was cast.

Early in July, I was in Alexandria—the main base of the army. Even there there general opinion seemed to be that surely soon there must be an attack, for such vast quantities of stores were being sent to the peninsula. Never could one forget the sight of the wharves at that seaport, burdened to their utmost capacity with cases that contained not only the staple food of the army— beef and biscuits—but butter, cheese, jams, and vast quantities of entrenching weapons. The whole of Egypt was scoured for the last man that could be spared. Whole companies of Australians were organised from the men who had been left on guard duty— men who were keen to get away, but had been compelled to stay. Reinforcements were hurried forward to complete their training, even in the rear of the firing-line of Anzac. Hospital ships were prepared, hospitals were cleared in anticipation of the thousands of returning wounded.

At Mudros Harbour camps and bivouacs were scattered all round the harbour front. I saw a whole brigade of British troops disembarked from the massive *Mauretania* and bivouacked under the open sky. Immensely cheery bodies of ben they were, waiting for the weeks to slip by until the appointed day. This island of Lemnos lay 40 miles from the firing-line. Closer by 30 miles to the firing-line was Imbros, where thousands of other troops were gathered as far as the capacities of the island (the water supply was the problem; a ship was moored close inshore and pumped water all day into the long lines of tanks) permitted. In order to refresh the men already in the fighting-line they were rested at Imbros in battalions, the only relief they had had, since they landed, from the roar of the shells. But there came a day when this had to cease, for the resources of the naval and trawling services were strained to the utmost collecting stores and bringing forward fresh troops.

Kephalos Bay, at Imbros, was not much of an anchorage, but a boom and protecting nets kept out the submarines, and good weather favoured the operations. Gurkhas, Maoris, New Zealanders, Australians, and British troops were on the island, camped amongst the vineyards, that were just ripening. General Hamilton's headquarters were on the most southern promontory of the island, and near by were the aeroplane hangars, from which, morning and evening, patrols rose, sweeping up the Straits. Never out of sight of the land, never out of the sound of the guns, one viewed from this point the vast panorama of the peninsula. General Hamilton guided the operations from that spot, as being the most central and giving rapid access to any one of his three fighting fronts. Wharves had been built by parties of Egyptian engineers, who had been brought up specially from Cairo. The presence of Turkish prisoners in camp in a hollow and the native Greeks in their loose, slovenly garments, completed the extraordinary concourse of nations that were represented on this picturesque and salubrious island.

In the harbour were anchored some of the weirdest craft that the Navy possessed—the new heavy monitors that had been of such service already along the Belgian coast and the baby monitors that had been down the African coast and up the Tigris river. Four large and two small of these shallow-draught craft there were, whose main attribute was their unsinkableness. In the same category must be ranged the converted cruisers of old and antiquated patterns—for naval ships—from whose sides bulged a false armour-shield which was calculated to destroy the torpedo before it reached or could injure the inner shell of the vessel. And, lastly, to this extraordinary fleet must be added the armoured landing-punts, that sometimes drifted, sometimes steamed about the harbour, crammed with a thousand troops each. The motive-power was an oil-engine that gave them a speed of just 5 miles an hour. From the front there hung a huge platform that could be let down as required: across it the troops, emerging from the hold, where they were packed behind bullet-proof screens, might dash ashore. As all the weight of the craft was at the stern, its blunted prow would rest on the shore. From these strange vessels the troops destined for service at Suvla Bay practised landing assiduously.

Finally, there were the preparations on the peninsula itself. Terraces and trenches had to be prepared for the new army that was to be secretly conveyed at night to the Anzac and from which they would issue forth to the support of the Australians and form the link with the British armies to operate on the left flank at Suvla Bay. I suppose the observers in the German aeroplanes that were chased from above our lines might well have wondered why the ledges were being dug in the sides of the small valleys—that is, if they could detect them at all. What they certainly would not see would be the huge quantities of ammunition, millions and millions of rounds, that for days was being taken out through the long sap to our No. 2 outpost on the north, already strengthened with rein-forcements from the Light Horse and New Zealand Rifle regiments. Both at Imbros and at Anzac there were vast numbers of Egyptian water-cans and ordinary tins (which probably once had contained honey or biscuits), ready filled with water for the landing troops. Down at the wells in the valleys pumps had increased the capacity of the daily supply and the tanks in the gullies were kept full—except when the wretched steam-engine employed at Anzac, broke down. Why so poor a thing should have been obtained it is difficult to conceive, when more up-to-date plant might easily have been found.

But the greatest feat of all was the landing of guns, both at Helles and at Anzac. At the end of July there were a Cape Helles one hundred and twenty-four guns, composed of the following units:

VIIIth Army Corps, comprising the artillery of 29th Division, 42nd Division, 52nd Division, and Royal Naval Division. Attached were 1st Australian Brigade (Colonel Christian): 6th Australian Battery (Major Stevenson), 3rd New Zealand Battery.

At Anzac there were over seventy guns, under Brigadier-General Cunliffe Owen, when the great offensive began, from 10-pounder mountain batteries to a 6-in. battery of field guns, howitzers, and a 9-in. gun. There were guns on every available ridge and in every hollow; they were along the great northern sap, firing over it on to the northern slopes of the Sari Bair ridge, until they gradually were dragged out along the beach to the new ground won by the Australian and New Zealand Division. Owing to the closeness of the enemy positions, the small space available at Anzac, and the height of the hills, the guns were firing across one another's fronts.

In all this magnificently conceived plan of General Hamilton's, one thing that stands out above all others is the matter in which the Turks were deceived. This in some measure may be attributed to the way in which the Turkish and German observing aeroplanes were chased form the skies, for the French and British aviators had the upper hand. On a few occasions the enemy did venture forth, but only at great altitudes; invariably very swiftly they were compelled to return to their lines by the Allied aviators. The enemy's hangars behind the forts at Chanak were destroyed during one air raid, organised by Flight-Commander Sampson, from Tenedos. Now, General Hamilton determined on certain main ruses, and left the formulation of any plans to help the Anzac position to Lieut.-General Birdwood, which I shall mention in their place. As for the general scheme, the Commander-in-Chief writes:

> Once the date was decided, a certain amount of ingenuity had to be called into play so as to divert the attention of the enemy from my main strategical conception, This—I repeat for the sake of clearness—was:
> 1. To break out with a rush from Anzac and cut off the bulk of the Turkish army from land communication with Constantinople.
> 2. To gain such a command for my artillery as to cut off the bulk of the Turkish army from sea traffic, whether with Constantinople of with Asia.
> 3. Incidentally to secure Suvla Bay as a winter base for Anzac and all the troops operating in the northern theatre.
>
> My schemes for hoodwinking the Turks fell under two heads:

(a) First, strategical diversions meant to draw away enemy
    reserves not yet committed to the peninsula.
(b) Second, tactical diversions meant to hold up enemy
    reseres already on the peninsula.

Under the first heading came a surprise landing by a force
of 300 men on the northern shore of the Gulf of Saros;
demonstrations by French ships opposite Mitylene along
the Syrian coast; concentration at Mitylene; inspections
at Mitylene by the Admiral and myself; making to order
of a whole set of maps of Asia, in Egypt, as well as secret
service work, most of which bore fruit.

Amongst the tactical diversions were a big containing
attack at Helles. Soundings, registration of guns, etc., by
monitors between Gaba Tepe and Kum Tepe. An attack
to be carried out by Anzac on Lone Pine trenches, which
lay in front of their right wing, and as far distant as the
local terrain would admit from the scene of the real
battle. Thanks entirely to the reality and vigour which
the Navy and the troops threw into them, each one of
these ruses was, it so turned out, entirely successful,
with the result that the Turks, despite their excellent spy
system, were caught completely off their guard at dawn
on the 7th August.

Therefore, if I may be pardoned the term, the 1st Australian Division was to be, in this huge offensive, the 'bait' that was to be flung
to the Turks, to keep them in their trenches massed before Anzac,
while their attention was distracted at Cape Helles by the offensive
planned there. Thus there would be left a clear road round the left
flank from Suvla Bay across the Salt Lake, through Bijak Anafarta,
and so on to the northern slopes of the great crowning position of
this, the central portion of the peninsula, Koja Chemen Tepe, or
Hill 971, to give it its more familiar name. But once the Turks were
trapped, as they surely would have been, the way was clear for the
long-desired advance of the Australian and New Zealand Divisions
on to Pine Ridge, to Battleship Hill, advancing and attacking from

both its slopes up to the Sari Bair ridge, and so to possession of the plains that stretched to Maidos.

And in this carefully prepared scheme the 1st Australian Infantry Brigade, under Brigadier-General Smyth, were to make the first move—how vital a trust for a young army!—by an attack on Lone Pine trenches on 6th August.

CHAPTER XXII
LONE PINE

Lone Pine was the first big attack that the 1st Brigade had taken part in since the landing. Indeed, it was the first battle these New South Welshmen had as a separate and complete operation. It was, perhaps, the freshest and strongest infantry brigade of the four at Anzac, though barely 2,000 strong. The men had been in the trenches (except for a few battalions that had been rested at Imbros) since April. They were ripe for a fight; they were tired of the monotony of sniping at a few Turks and digging and tunnelling.

It is necessary first to go back a few days prior to this attack, to the night of the 31st July, when there had been rather a brilliant minor operation carried out by the Western Australian troops of the 11th Battalion, under Lieut.-Colonel J. L. Johnston, who had issued forth from Tasmania Post. The Turks had largely brought this attack on themselves by having tunnelled forward to a crest that lay not very many yards distant from our position. We had been unable to see what their preparations consisted of, though it was known they were 'up to mischief,' as Major Ross told me. Exactly what this amounted to was revealed one day, when they broke down the top of their tunnels and there appeared on the crest of the small ridge a line of trenches about 100 yards in extent. The enemy had come within easy bombing distance, but it was difficult for them to locate our sharpshooters and machine guns, that were so well concealed behind the growing bush.

To overcome this the Turks would creep up near to our lines—they were very skilled scouts indeed—and would throw some article of clothing or equipment near where the rifles were spitting. Next morning these garments served as an indication (that is, if we had not removed them) for the directing of fire.

On the night of 31st July at 10.15 the attack began. The Turkish trenches were heavily bombarded, and mines which had rapidly been tunnelled under their trenches were exploded, with excellent results. Four assaulting columns, each of 50 men, led by the gallant Major Leane, then dashed forward from the trenches, crossing our barbed-wire entanglements on planks that had been laid by the engineers. The men had left the trenches before the debris from our two flanking mines had descended, and it took them very few seconds to reach the enemy's line, which was fully manned with excited and perturbed Turks, who, immediately the mines had exploded, set up a fearful chattering. The Australians fired down into the enemy's ranks, and then, having made a way, jumped into the trenches and began to drive the Turks back on either side.

On the extreme right a curious and dangerous situation arose. The Turks had retired some distance down a communication trench, but before our lads could build up a protecting screen and block the trench, the enemy attacked with great numbers of bombs. While the men were tearing down the Turkish parapets to form this barricade a veritable inferno raged round them as the bombs exploded. Our supplies were limited, and were, indeed, soon exhausted. The parapet still remained incomplete. Urgent messages had been sent back for reinforcements, and the position looked desperate. By a mere chance if was saved. An ammunition box was spied on the ground between the lines. This was dragged in under terrible fire, and found to contain bombs. Very soon the Australians then gained the upper hand. The parapet was completed, and this entrance of the Turks, as well as their exit, blocked.

But in the charge a short length of the Turkish trenches (they wound about in an extraordinary fashion) had remained uncaptured, and this line, in which there were still some 80 Turks fighting, was jammed in between the Australian lines. The enemy were obviously unconscious that some of their trenches that ran back on either flank of this trench, had been captured. Scouts were sent out by Major Leane, and these men, after creeping up behind the enemy's line, that still continued to fire furiously, cleared up any remaining doubt that it was still a party of the enemy. A charge was organised, but was driven back. Then a further charge from the original lines was made direct at the trench. The Turks turned and fled down their own communication trench, but, as we held either flank, were caught by bombs and rifle fire, and killed. The Turkish dead in this attack were estimated at 100. The enemy soon turned their guns on the position, and under high-explosive shell fire all night, our troops worked with the sapper parties, under Major Clogstoun (3rd Field Company), deepening the captured trenches and transferring the parapets, which faced our lines, to the westerly side, facing the Turks. Their own trenches had been wretchedly shallow, barely 3 feet deep. By dawn our troops had ample protection. But unfortunately their brave leader, Major Leane, fell mortally wounded. Ever after the trenches were known as Leane's Trenches—one of the many men to leave an honoured name on Anzac. Machine guns shattered a Turkish attack that was being formed in a gully on the right. The Turks never attempted to retake the trench during the next days immediately preceding Lone Pine. General Hamilton regarded the action as most opportune.

Now, while the higher commands realised the scope of the pending operations, the troops knew very little. 'The 1st Brigade is for it to-morrow' was the only word that spread along the line, very rapidly, on the evening of the 5th. That it was to be the commencement of a great coup was only guessed at from various local indications. So far as was definitely known, it was to be a purely local attack. By our leaders it was rather hoped, however, the Turks would be led to believe it was but preliminary to a flanking movement from this point out towards Maidos and the plains of the Olive Grove. That was the situation on the morning of the 6th August—a bright, rather crisp morning, when the waters of the gulf were a little disturbed by the wind, and barges rocked about violently in Anzac Cove. Perhaps the arrival of the old comrade to the Australians, the *Bacchante*, that had been so good a friend to the troops during the early stages, might have been taken as a signal of hard fighting. She replaced the monitor *Humber*, that had been at work shelling the guns on the Olive Grove Plains and on Pine Ridge, 800 yards or more in front of our right flank, for some weeks.

On the morning of the 6th the heart of Anzac was wearing rather a deserted appearance, for the Divisional Headquarters of the 1st Division had been moved up to just behind the firing-line at the head of White Gully, so as to be nearer the scene of action and shorten the line of communications. Major-General H. B. Walker was commanding the Division, and was responsible for the details for this attack. The New Zealanders also had left Anzac, and Major-General Godley had established his headquarters on the extreme left, at No. 2 post, where he would be in the centre of the attacks on the left. On the beach, I remember, there were parties of Gurkhas still carrying ammunition and water-tins on their heads out through the saps. Ammunition seemed to be the dominant note of the beach. Other traffic was normal, even quiet.

Now the Lone Pine entrenchment was an enormously strong Turkish work that the enemy, while they always felt a little nervous about it, rather boasted of. It was a strong *point d'appui* on the south-western end of Plateau 400, about the centre of the right flank of the position. At the nearest point the Turkish trenches approached to within 70 yards of ours, and receded at various places to about 130 yards. This section of our trenches, form the fact that there was a bulge in our line, had been called 'The Pimple.' Their entrench-ments connected across a dip, 'Owen's Gully,' on the north with Johnston's Jolly and German Officers' Trench, all equally strongly fortified positions, with overhead cover of massive pine beams, railway sleepers, and often cemented parapets. The Turks had seen to it when constructing these trenches that the various positions could be commanded on either side by their own machine-gun fire.

Why was it called Lone Pine? Because behind it, on the Turkish ridge, seamed with brown trenches and *mia mias** of pine-needles, there remained standing a solitary pine-tree amongst the green holly-bushes. Once there had been a forest of green pines on the ridge. The others had gradually been cut down for wood and defensive purposes. Singular to relate, on the morning of the attack the Turks felled this last pine-tree.

Immediately in the rear of our trenches was 'Browne's Dip,' and it was here that the reserves were concealed in deep dugouts. Brigadier-General Smyth had his headquarters there, not 80 yards from the firing-line, and barely 150 from the Turkish trenches. It was at the head of the gully that dipped sharply down to the coast. The position was quite exposed to the Turkish artillery fire, but by digging deep and the use of enormous sandbag ramparts some little protection was obtained, though nothing stood against the rain of shells that fell on this area—not 400 yards square—in the course of the attacks and counter-attacks.

To properly understand and realise the nature of the Lone Pine achievement it must be explained that our trenches consisted of two lines. There was the actual firing-line, which the Turks could see, and the false firing-line, which was a series of gallery trenches that ran parallel to our first line beneath the ground, and of which the enemy had little cognizance. These two lines were separated by from 10 to 40 yards. The false line was reached through five tunnels. It was one of the most elaborately prepared positions on an intricate front. Three main tunnels from these gallery trenches ran out towards the Turkish line. In each of these, on the morning of the 6th, a large charge of ammonel was set by the engineers, ready to explode at the beginning of the attack. Now, the idea of the gallery trenches had been, in the first place, defensive. The ground had been broken through, but no parapets had been erected on the surface, as the enemy did not know exactly the direction of this forward firing-line. At night these holes in the ground gave the men a chance to place machine guns in position,

---

* Aboriginal word for a shelter made of gum leaves, branches, and bark.

in anticipation of a Turkish offensive. Later, however, they were blocked with barbed-wire entanglements, while *cheveaux de frise* were placed outside them, much, it may be stated, to the disgust of the engineers, who had prepared this little trap for the enemy with keen satisfaction.

Before the attack all this barbed wire was removed, and it was decided that while one line of men should dash from the parapets, another line should rise up out of the ground before the astonished eyes of the Turks, and charge for the second line of the Turkish works, leaving the men from the actual firing-line to capture the Turkish first works. All that was needed for the success of this plan was the careful synchronising of watches, and an officer stationed at every cross-section of trenches and tunnels to give the signal.

Lifeless the beach and the old headquarters may have been, but there was no mistaking the spirits of the men as I went along those firing-line trenches at three o'clock on this beautiful, placid afternoon. Lying so long without fighting, there now rose up the old spirit of the landing and fight within them. 'It's Impshee Turks now!' said the men of the 4th, as they moved along the communication trench from the centre of the position to the point of attack. Silence was enjoined on the men; isolated whispered conversations only were carried on. The seasoned troops knew the cost of attack on a strongly entrenched position. Most of the others (reinforcements) had heard vivid enough descriptions from their mates, and had seen little engagements along the line.

I was moving slowly along the trenches. The men carried their entrenching tools and shovels. At various points their comrades from other battalions, who watched the line of heroes who were 'for it,' dashed out to shake some comrade by the hand. There was a warmth about these handgrips that no words can describe. It was the silence that made the scene of the long files of men such an impressive one. It was a significant silence that was necessary, so that the Turks in their trenches, not more perhaps at that point than 100 yards away, might gain no inkling of the exact point from which the attack was to be made. As the men went on through trench after trench, they came at length into the firing-line—

the Pimple—where already other battalions had been gathered. There were men coming in the opposite direction, struggling past somehow, with the packs and waterproof sheets and impedimenta that made it a tight squeeze to get past. Messages kept passing back and forth for officers certain minor details of the attack.

Our trenches before the Lone Pine position were only thinly manned by the 5th Battalion, who were to remain behind and hold them in case of failure. These men had crept into their 'possies,' or crevices in the wall, and tucked their toes out of the way. Some were eating their evening meal. Other parties were just leaving for the usual supply of water to be drawn down in the gullies and brought up by 'fatigues' to the trenches. So into the midst of all this routine, marched the new men of the 1st Brigade, who were going out from this old firing-line to form a new line, to blaze the path, to capture the enemy's strongest post. They went in good spirits, resigned, as only soldiers can be, to the inevitable, their jaws set, a look in their faces which made one realise that they knew their moment of destiny had come; for the sake of the regiment, for the men who were around them, they must bear their share. It was strange to still hear muttered arguments about everyday affairs, to hear the lightly spoken words, 'Off to Constantinople.'

As I got closer to the vital section of trenches (some 200 yards in length), they were becoming more congested. It was not only now the battalions that were to make the charge, but other men had to be ready for any emergency. They were filing in to take their place and make sure of holding what we already had. Sections got mixed with sections in the sharp traverses. It wanted, too, but a few minutes to the hour, but not the inevitable moment. There was a solemn silence over the hills, in the middle of that dazzling bright afternoon, before our guns burst forth, precisely at half-past four. Reserves were drawn up behind the trenches in convenient spots, their officers chatting in groups. Rapidly the shells began to increase in number, and the anger of their explosions grew more intense as the volume of fire increased. Amidst the sharp report of our howitzers amongst the hills, and the field guns, came the prolonged, rumbling boom of the ships' fire.

There was no mistaking the earnestness of the *Bacchante*'s fire. Yet, distributed over the whole of the lines, it did not seem that the bombardment was as intense as one expected. In fact, there came a time when I believed that it was finished before its time. One was glad for the break, for it stopped the fearful ear-splitting vibrations that were sharking one's whole body. Yet as the black smoke came over the top of the trenches and drifted down into the valleys behind, it gladdened the waiting men, knowing that each explosion meant, probably, so much less resistance of the enemy's trenches to break down. But to those waiting lines of troops the bombardment seemed interminably long, and yet not long enough. What if the Turks had known how our trenches were filled with men! But, then, what if they really knew the exact point and moment where and when the attack was to be made! So that while in one sense the shelling gave the Turks some idea of the attack, if actually told them very little. Such bombardments were not uncommon. Their gun fire had died down to a mere spitting of rifles here and there over a line, and an occasional rapid burst of machine-gun five. A few, comparatively very few, shells as yet came over to our trenches and burst about the crests of the hills where our line extended.

It was ordered that the 2nd, 3rd, and 4th Battalions should form the first line, and the 1st Battalion the brigade reserve. The 1st Battalion was under Lieut.-Colonel Dobbin, the second under Lieut.-Colonel Scobie, the third under Lieut.-Colonel Brown, and the fourth under Lieut.-Colonel Macnaghton.

We were committed. At 5.30 came the avalanche. The artillery ceased. A whistle sharply blown was the signal prearranged. A score or more of other whistles sounded almost simultaneously. The officers, crouching each with his command under the parapets, were up then, and with some words like 'Come, lads, now for the trenches!' were over our parapets, and in a long, more or less regular line the heavily-laden men commenced the dash across the dead ground between. They ran under the protection of the intense fire from our rifles and from our machine guns that swept their outer flanks; but it was impossible to fire or attempt any shooting over our advancing lines. The sun was still high enough to be in the eyes of the Turks, but they were ready to open rifle fire on the advancing line of khaki. With their machine guns, fortunately, they were less ready. They had the range for the parapet trenches, but not the intermediate line between, from which the first line of troops, 150 men about—50 from each of the three battalions—sped across the intervening space without very serious loss, the Turkish machine guns on this, as on most occasions, firing low.

The 2nd Battalion were on the extreme right, the 3rd in the centre, and the 4th Battalion occupied the left flank, adjacent to Owen's Gully. The men ran at full speed, so far as their equipment permitted, some stumbling, tripping over wires and unevennesses in the ground; others stumbling, hit with the bullets. A thousand dashes of brown earth, where the bullets struck, were flicked up right across that narrow patch. There was no cheer, just the steady advancing, unchecked line, till the men threw themselves on the first and second trenches. Barely a minute and they were across.

It must have been with a feeling akin to dismay that the gallant line found the Turks' overhead cover on their trenches was undamaged and extremely difficult to pierce. The first line, according to the arranged plan, ran right over the top of the first enemy trenches, and, reaching the second line, began to fire down on the bewildered Turks, regardless of the fact that enemy machine guns were playing on them all the time. This was how so many fell in the early charge. A very few managed at once to drop down into the trench. I know with what relief those watching saw them gain, after that stunning check, a footing. But the greater number could be seen lying on the face of the trench, or immediately beneath the sandbags under the loopholes. Like this they remained for a few minutes, searching for the openings that our guns must have made. Gradually, sliding down feet foremost into the trench, they melted away. Each man, besides the white arm-bands on his jacket, had a white square on his back. This badge was worn throughout the attacks during the first two days, as a distinguishing mark from the enemy in the dark; a very necessary precaution where so many different types of troops were engaged. This made the advancing line more conspicuous on a bare landscape. Men could be seen feverishly seeking a way into the trenches. One man rendered the most valuable service by working along the front of the Turkish trenches beneath the parapet, tearing down the loopholes that were made of clay and straw with his bayonet.

It was still only barely five minutes since the attack had commenced, yet the Turkish artillery had found our trenches, both the firing-line and the crest of the hill behind, and down into the gully. The whole hill shook under the terrific blows of the shells. Our replying artillery, six, eight, or more guns, firing in rapid succession over the heads of the men, and passing where the enemy's shells were bursting in the air, made in a brief five minutes an inferno that it seemed a matter of madness to suppose any one would escape.

Following hard on the heels of the first men from our trenches went a second line, those on the left suffering worse than on the right. Again some did not wait at the first trench, but rushed on to the second Turkish trench. Soon there appeared a little signal arm sending back some urgent call. It turned out to be for reinforcements. It was not evident at the time they were needed, but they went. Our firing-trenches were emptying rapidly now, and only an ordinary holding-line remained.

The Turkish guns lowered their range, and shrapnel burst over the intervening ground, across which troops, in spite, and in the face of it, must pass. Signallers ran lines of wires back and forth, only to have them cut and broken, and all their work to be done again. Five times they drew the reel across from the trench where the troops were fighting. You could gain little idea of what actually was happening in Lone Pine. Occasionally butts of rifles were uplifted. On the left flank, round the edge of the trenches on Johnston's Jolly, for a few minutes the Turkish bayonets glistened in the sun as men went along their trench, but whatever they were hurrying to support their harried comrades or were the men our troops had turned in panic we could not see.

Then the wounded commenced to come back. They came back across the plateau, dripping with blood, minus all their equipment and their arms. Some fell as they came, only to be rescued hours afterwards. News was filtering back slowly. In a quarter of an hour we had won three trenches; at 6.30 we held them strongly after an hour of bloody fighting. Further reinforcements were dashing forward, taking advantage of what might seem a lull, but suffering far worse than their comrades. Shouted orders even could not be heard in the din; whistles would not penetrate.

In the midst of the whole attack one prayed that something would stop the vibrations that seemed to shake every one and everything in the vicinity. Our trenches were rent torn, and flattened, and sandbags and debris piled up, blocking entrances and exists. Men worked heroically, clearing a way where they could. Doctors were in the trenches doing mighty work. Captain J. W. Bean went calmly hither and thither until wounded. Major Fullerton had gone with the first rush, had tripped, and fell. He was thought to be wounded, but went on and reached safely the Turkish trenches, where, for six hours, he was the only doctor on the spot.

Wounded men came pouring back to the dressing-station behind the hill in 'Browne's Dip,' where friends directed them down the hill. It seemed horrible to ask the men to go farther. The stretcher-bearers were carrying cases down. I saw them hit, and compelled to hand over stretchers to willing volunteers, who sprang up out of the earth. They were men waiting their turn to go forward. The ground was covered each minute with a dozen bursting shells within the small area I could see. The dirt, powdered, fell on our shoulders. The shrapnel, luckily, bursting badly, searched harmlessly the slopes of a hill 40 yards away.

The great 6-inch howitzers of the enemy tore up the gully and hillside, sending stones and dirt up in lumps, any one of which would inflict a blow, if not a wound. They ripped an old graveyard to pieces. They tore round the dressing-station. We watched them on the hill amongst the trenches. Would our turn be next? No one knew. You could not hear except in a distant kind of way, for our guns fired at point-blank range, and their noise was even worse than the bursting shells. Yet when the call came, there rose from their dugouts another company of men of the 1st Battalion, and formed up and dashed for the comparative cover of a high bank of earth prior to moving off. The men went with their heads down, as they might in a shower of rain. A foul stench filled the air from explosives.

'Orderly, find Captain Coltman [machine-gun officer]!' called Major King, Brigade-Major. Away into the firing-line or towards it would go the messenger. 'Orderly, Orderly!' and again a message would be sent to some section of the line. The officer giving these directions was a young man (he had already been wounded in the campaign). His face was deadly white and his orders crisp and clear. He dived into his office, only to come out again with a fresh message in his hand (ammunition was wanted) and dash off himself into the firing-line. He was back again in a few minutes to meet his Brigadier. They stood there in the lee, if one may so call it, of some sandbags (the office had been blown down) asking in terse sentences of the progress of the battle. 'I think it is all right. They say they can hold on all right. They want reinforcements.' I saw the signallers creeping over the hill, feeling for the ends of broken wires, trying to link up some of the broken threads, so that information could be quickly sought and obtained. Doctors I saw treating men as they passed, halting with a case of bandages; men past all help lay in a heap across the path leading into the sap. It was, after all, just a question of luck. You kept close into a bank, and with the shells tearing up the earth round you, hoped that you might escape. After a time there was so much else to think of, especially for the men fighting, that it was no time to think of the shells. They arrived with a swish and sickening explosion and a thud. Where the next was coming, except it was sure to be in the vicinity, was a matter for the Turks and Kismet. Men ran like rabbits and half fell, half tumbled into the dugouts. Somehow the whole thing reminded me of people coming in out of a particularly violent storm. Once in the firing-line, the shells were going overhead, and curiously enough one felt safe, even in the midst of the dead and dying.

To look with a periscope for a minute over the top of the parapet. The machine guns were traversing backwards and forwards, not one, but five or six of them. I was with Captain Coltman. He went from end to end of the line, inspecting our machine guns. Some were firing, others were cooling, waiting a target, or refitting, rectifying some temporary trouble caused by a bullet or a shell. Men were watching with periscopes at the trenches. It was exactly an hour since the battle had begun, and the Turkish trenches, now ours, were almost obscured by the battle smoke and the coming night. Yet I could just see the men rushing on. The 1st Battalion reinforcement launched out at 6.20 to consolidate the position and strengthen the shattered garrison. They disappeared into the trenches. In some cases the best entrance had been gained by tearing away the sandbags and getting in under the overhead cover. I was down a tunnel that led to our advanced firing-line when I faintly heard the men calling, 'There goes another batch of men!' I could hear a more wicked burst of fire form the enemy's machine guns, and then the firing died down, only to be renewed again in a few minutes. In the captured trenches a terrible bomb battle was being fought. Gradually the Turks were forced back down their own communication trenches, which we blocked with sandbags. By 6.30 the message came back, 'Everything O.K.,' and a little later, 'Have 70 prisoners.' These men were caught in a tunnel before they could even enter the battle.

Cheerful seems hardly the right word to use at such a grim time, yet the men who were behind the machine guns, ready to pop them above the trenches for a moment and then drop them again before the enemy could blow them to pieces, never were depressed except when their gun was out of action. Soon they got others to replace them. They were watching—so were the men round them, with bayonets fixed, in case the Turks drove us back from Lone Pine. As we made our way along the old firing-line, it meant bobbing there while the bullets welted against the sandbags and the earth behind you. You were covered every few yards with debris from bursting shells. The light was fading rapidly. The sun had not quite set. The last departing rays lit up the smoke of the shells like a furnace, adding to the grim horribleness of the situation.

Of the inner fighting of those first two hours in the Turkish trenches little can be written till all the stories are gathered up and tangled threads untied, if ever that is possible. But certain facts have been revealed. Major Stevens, who was second in command of the 2nd Battalion, was charging down a Turkish trench when he saw a Turk about 2 yards from him in a dugout. He called over his shoulder to the men following him to pass up a bomb, and this was thrown and the Turk killed. Then Major Stevens came face to face with a German officer at the mouth of the tunnel. In this tunnel were some 70 Turks. The Australian was fired at point-blank by the German, but the shot missed its mark and the officer was shot dead by a man following Stevens. The Turks in the tunnel surrendered. They had gone there on the commencement of the bombardment, as was their custom, and had not had time to man the trenches before the Australians were on them. The first warning that had been given, it was learned from a captured officer, was when the sentries on duty called, 'Here come the English!'

Farther down the trench a party of Australians were advancing against the Turks, who were shielded by a traverse. The first Australian that had run down, with his bayonet pointed, had come face to face with five of the enemy. Instinctively he had taken protection behind the traverse. He had called on his mates, and then ensued one of the scores of incidents of that terrible trench fight when the men slew one another in mortal combat. Their dead bodies were found in piles.

Captain Pain, 2nd Battalion, with a party of three men, each holding the leg of a machine gun, propped himself up in the middle of one trench and fired down on to the Turks, massed for a charge, till suddenly a bullet killed one of the party, wounded Pain, and the whole gun collapsed.

The Turks had in one case a machine gun firing down the trench, so that it was impossible for us to occupy it. By using one of the many communication trenches that the Turks had dug a party managed to work up close enough to bomb the Turks from the flank, compelling them to retire. Every man and every officer can repeat stories like these of deeds that won the Australians the day; but, alas! many of those brave men died in the trenches which they had captured at the bayonet's point.

At seven o'clock, when the first clash of arms had passed, the enemy made their first violent and concerted effort to regain their lost trenches. It was a furious onslaught, carried on up the communication trenches by a veritable hail of bombs. In some places we gave way, in others we drove back the enemy farther along his trenches. From the north and the south the enemy dashed forward with fixed bayonets. They melted away before our machine guns and our steady salvos of bombs. The Australians stuck to their posts in the face of overwhelming numbers—four to one: they fought right through the night, and as they fought, strove to build up cover of whatever material came nearest to hand. Thousands of sandbags were used in making good that position. Companies of the 12th Battalion were hurried up towards midnight to strengthen the lines, rapidly diminishing under the fury of the Turkish attack. But these men found a communication-way open to them to reach the maze of the enemy's position.

Our mines, that had been exploded at the head of the three tunnels mentioned earlier, had formed craters, from which the sappers, under Colonel Elliott and Major Martyn, began to dig their way through to the captured positions. Only two of these tunnels were opened up that night, just six hours after the trenches had been won. The parties dug from each end: they toiled incessantly, working in shifts, with almost incredible speed. It was the only way to get relief for the wounded; to go across the open, as many of the gallant stretcher-bearers, signallers, and sappers did, was to face death a thousand times from the Turkish shrapnel. So part tunnel, part trench, the 80 yards was sapped and the wounded commenced to be brought in in a steady stream.

It took days to clear the captured trenches. Australians and Turks lay dead, one on top of the other, three or four deep. All it was possible to do was to fill these trenches in. That night down the tunnel on the right kept passing ammunition, bombs—some 3,000 were used in the course of the first few hours—water, food, rum for the fighters, picks, shovels, and machine guns. Every half-hour the Turks came on again, shouting 'Allah!' and were beaten back. The resistance was stubborn. It broke eventually the heart of the Turks.

Officers and men in that first horrible night performed stirring deeds meriting the highest honour. The names of many will go unrecorded except as part of that glorious garrison. It was a night of supreme sacrifice, and the brigade made it, to their everlasting honour and renown.

CHAPTER XXIII
THE HEROIC LIGHT HORSE CHARGE

So far as the 1st Australian Division was concerned, their offensive in the great battle of August began with the capture of Lone Pine, late on the afternoon of the 6th August, and ended with the desperate, heroic charge of the 8th and 10th Light Horse Regiments on the early morning of the 7th. Lone Pine had started the whole of the operations, and the Australian Division throughout the night was to carry them on by a series of offensives from their trenches right along the line. All this fighting, as has been explained, was to cover the main object of the plan, the landing of the new British force at Suvla Bay and the seizing of a base for winter operations; and, further, the capture of the crest of the main ridge, Chunak Bair and Koja Chemen Tepe, or Hill 971. So naturally the operations fall into sections. From what has been subsequently learned, the Turks, immediately after their crushing defeat at Lone Pine, hurried up reinforcements from Bogali and diverted others that were on their way to Cape Helles. It did not stay their attack at Cape Helles, however, which had been planned, by some curious chance, to take place almost at the identical hour that the British, on the 7th, were to attack the Turkish lines, which was the reason for the British being hurled back after desperate fighting.

But if there was a success for the Turk at Cape Helles, it was nothing to the blow they suffered by the loss of their declared impregnable Lone Pine trenches and the successfully accomplished landing at Suvla Bay. But in between these two operations were the long hours of the night, when the captured trenches at Lone Pine were subjected to fearful bombing attacks, and successive Turkish regiments were hurled against the closed breach, operations which lasted over all for four days. Two Divisions at least were massed by the Turks against the Anzac forces by midnight of the 6th. The enemy's trenches positively bristled with bayonets. Our green and red rocket shells showed them up; we could see them moving along the gullies and over the hills in the early dawn. The Light Horsemen on the Nek knew that the enemy were waiting to meet the charge they were in duty bound to make at grey dawn.

To retrace in detail the events of that night. On the Lone Pine section of the line the Turkish bombardment began to ease at eight o'clock, and the Turks, for a time, gave up searching the valleys of Anzac for our reserves and for the guns. Every available piece of artillery must have been trained on the position. Then the warships and our Australian and New Zealand howitzers kept up a regular, almost incessant fire. A gun banged each minute on various sections of the line. It had been determined by Major-General Walker that there should be an offensive by the men of the 2nd Infantry Brigade, occupying the trenches opposite German Officers' Trench. Our lines were but thinly held, as there had been a gradual easing off to the right towards the Lone Pine trenches, that had swallowed up the whole of the 1st Brigade, so that now the 2nd Brigade only was left to hold the position.

Lieut.-Colonel Bennett with the 6th Battalion was charged with the task of taking the almost impregnable German Officers' Trenches. Crowned with massive beams, bristling with machine guns, it had been demonstrated on more than one occasion what the Turks intended should be the fate of any men who dared attack these trenches. At eleven o'clock on the night of the 6th, the sappers

251

exploded the first mine underneath the Turkish trenches immediately in front of them. Another charge was fired at 11.30, and two at 11.40. The battalion then began to occupy the forward gallery positions that had been prepared. Unfortunately, the guns did not do the damage that was anticipated. On the contrary, they did nothing but warn the already thoroughly roused enemy of an impending assault.

The first attack was planned for twelve o'clock. At that time the bombardment of the section of the Turkish trenches ceased. From the tunnel trenches the men scrambled up, a few only from each hole, as there was little space. The enemy's machine guns raged and raked our ranks from end to end. Few of the men got more than a yard or two. The tunnels became choked with dead and dying. The attack withered at its birth. What else could be expected under such conditions? Yet a second attempt was made at 3.55 a.m., but with no better result. A score or more of machine guns firing at various angles, with the range set to a nicety, swept down the attackers almost before they had time to leave their trenches. The position was desperate. Had the whole of the attack to be sacrificed because this line of them failed to do their duty? But did they fail? They charged twice, and were preparing to go a third time, on the determination of General Walker (but against the judgment of Brigadier-General Forsyth, who saw the hopelessness of it all), when, realising that the object had already been served, as news came through of the successful landing at Suvla Bay, the third charge was cancelled at the last moment.

Dawn was beginning to steal into the sky behind the Turkish position. A thin, waning moon shed but little light over the terrible battlefields. From a forward observation station I noted the battle line spitting red tongues of flame all along to the Nek, while at Quinn's Post occurred every few minutes, terrible explosions of shell and bombs from either side. A gun a minute was booming constantly—booming from the heart of Anzac. The destroyers, the rays of their searchlights cast up on to the hill, swept the top of the Sari Bair ridge with the high-explosive shell from their 6-inch guns. Fearful as had been the night, the dawn was more horrible still, as an intense bombardment commenced on the Chessboard Trenches on the Nek. Howitzers and high-explosive shells fell thickly round those masses of Turkish trenches, so often and accurately registered in the weeks of waiting. The surmise that the Turks had brought up reinforcements had indeed proved correct, for they were waiting now in the trenches on the Nek—confidently, we learn, waiting any 'English' attack, which now seemed inevitable. It was inevitable.

At this time the 3rd Light Horse Brigade, under Brigadier-General Hughes, held the Nek. I have already described this position. It was barely 120 yards wide. The Turkish trenches were scarcely 80 yards away from our line. They sloped backward slightly up the ridge to the sides of Baby 700 and Chunak Bair. On the right of this narrow causeway was the head of Monash Gully, a steep drop into a ravine, and across it, Pope's Hill and Quinn's Post. On the left the sheer precipices fell away down into the foot-hills of the Sari Bair ridge. Row after row one could see of the enemy trenches—Chessboard Trenches; the name significant of their formation.

It fell to the 8th and 10th Light Horse Regiments to storm these enemy redoubts. They were to charge at 4.30 in the morning—the morning after the bloody battle of Lone Pine, after, as I heard Colonel Antill, Brigade-Major of that Light Horse Brigade, say, we had gone along the whole of our battle front 'ringing a bell.' Then, when that had tolled and sounded, were the Light Horse to face their certain death. The story is simply told. It is very brief. The attack was to be made in four lines. The 8th Light Horse (Victorians) were to supply the first two lines, 150 men in each. Besides scaling ladders that had been specially made to enable men to get into the trenches, these Light Horsemen each carried two empty sandbags. They had food supplies, and plenty of ammunition. But they were not to fire a shot. They had to do their work with the cold steel of the bayonet. Following them was a third line of 150 men of the 10th Regiment, and yet another line—the last—ready with picks and shovels and bombs—any quantity of bombs—and reserves of water and ammunition. They were to help to make good the trenches when they were won.

Against the sandbags of our lines thumped the bullets as the Turkish machine guns traversed from end to end of the short line. A hard purring and the whistle of bullets, then a few minutes' pause. Still the bombardment continued furiously, smashing, it was thought, the Turkish trenches to atoms. But while the communication-ways were blocked and heavy casualties were inflicted, the front Turkish trenches remained practically unharmed. In three lines of trenches, their bayonets fixed, standing one above the other to get better shooting, resting on steps or sitting on the parados of the trenches, the Turks waited the coming of the Light Horsemen. The trenches were smothered in a yellow smoke and dust from the bursting lyddite from the ships, that almost obscured from our view the enemy's position. It was a bombardment the intensity of which had never been seen yet on Gallipoli; the hill was plastered with awful death-dealing shells. Just at 4.25 the bombardment slackened significantly. Immediately there began to pour a sheet of lead from the Turkish trenches. Musketry and machine guns fired incessantly. Could anything live for a minute in it? At the end of three minutes our guns ceased.

Lieut.-Colonel A. White elected to lead the men he loved. He made a brief farewell to his brother officers. He shook them by the hand and went into the firing line. He stood waiting with his watch in hand. 'Men,' he said, 'you have ten minutes to live.' And those Light Horsemen of his regiment, recruited from the heart of Victoria, knew what he said was true. They waited, listening to the terrible deluge that rained against the parapets of their trenches. 'Three minutes, men,' and the word came down from the far end of the line, did the order still hold good? It was a sergeant who sent it, and by the time he had received the reply passed back along the waiting line, the whistle for the charge sounded. With an oath, '— him!' he leaped to the parapet of the trench; he fell back on his comrade waiting below him—dead.

The whole line went. Each man knew that to leave those trenches was to face certain, almost immediate death. They knew it no less than the glorious Light Brigade at Balaclava. There is surely a comparison between the two deeds, and shall not the last make the young Nation more honoured! Those troops, with all the knowledge, after months of waiting, of what trench warfare meant, of what they might now expect, never flinched, never presented a braver front.

Theirs not to reason why; theirs but to do—and die.

They charged.

Lieut.-Colonel White had not gone ten paces when he fell dead, riddled with bullets. The first line of 150 men melted away ere they had gone half the distance to the trenches, and yet the second line, waiting and watching, followed them. One small knoll alone gave a little protection for a few dozen paces to the advancing line from the Turkish machine guns, that rattled from a dozen different points along that narrow front, and swept from the right flank across from the enemy trenches opposite Quinn's Post. Adding to the terror of it all came the swish of the shells from the French '75' guns that the Turks had captured from the Servians, and which were now firing ten shells a minute on to the Nek. The parapets were covered with dead and dying. Stretcher-bearers rescued men where they could from just above the parapets, and dragged them down into the trenches, while over the same parapets went other men, doomed like their magnificent comrades.

Just a handful of men—how many will hardly ever be known, probably it was not ten—managed to reach the section of the Turkish line facing the extreme right of our position. At other places some few others had pitched forward and fallen dead into the Turkish trenches. But those few men that won through raised a little yellow and red flag, the prearranged signal, the signal for the second part of the attack to develop. It were better that those gallant men had never reached that position. The third line were ordered to advance, and went over the parapets. There was nothing else to do. Comrades could not be left to die unsupported. At the same time from Bully Beef Sap (that was the trench that ran down into Monash Gully from the Nek) the Royal Welsh Fusiliers attacked up the head of the gully. Their first two lines, so soon as they came under fire, fell, crumpled; at which moment the third line—Western Australian Light Horse—had gone forward from the Nek. But before the whole of the 150 men could rush to their certain destruction, Brigadier General Hughes stopped the attack. So it happened that a small party of 40 on the left managed to crawl back into the trenches. The remainder fell alongside their brave Victorian brothers who had charged and died.

For the flag in the enemy's trench soon disappeared, and the fate of the brave men who erected it was never told. Late the next night a private named McGarry crawled back from beneath the parapet of the Turkish trenches, where he had feigned dead all day. He told of the forest of Turkish steel that stood in the series of three trenches, ranged one behind the other. Another man, Lieutenant Stuart, 8th Light Horse, who, after going 15 yards, fell wounded, and managed to crawl into the crater of a shell-burst, where he lay until the signal was given to retire, returned from amongst the dead and dying lying under the pale morning light on no man's ground between the trenches.

Thus in a brief fifteen minutes did regiments perish. Only an incident it was of the greatest battle ever fought in the Levant, but an imperishable record to Australia's wounded; 50 men killed, 170 wounded, and 181 missing: and those missing never will return to answer the roll call—435 casualties in all.

What did the brigade do but its duty?—duty in the face of overwhelming odds, in the face of certain death; and the men went because their leaders led them, and they were men. What more can be said? No one may ask if the price was not too great. The main object had been achieved. The Turks were held there. It was learned that many of the enemy in the trenches had their full kits on, either just arrived or bidden remain (as they might be about to depart). And so right along the line were the enemy tied to their trenches, crowded together as they could be, packed, waiting to be bayoneted where they stood or disperse the foe. Above all, the Australians had kept the way clear for the great British flanking movement already begun. For all this, will the spot remained sacred in the memory of every Australian of this generation and the generations to come.

Now, while the 3rd Light Horse Brigade was charging from the Nek there was also a charge from round Quinn's Post by the 1st Brigade, under Brigadier General Chauvel, who held this sector of the line. The 2nd Regiment attacked the Turkish position opposite Quinn's Post in four lines. Fifty men went in each. Major T. J. Logan led one section of the first line. Led! It was only fifteen or twenty paces to the enemy, yet few of the men managed to crawl up over the parapet. They were shot down as soon as they began to show themselves, and fell back into their own trenches. Major Bourne led the other party. Both gallant leaders fell dead before they or any of their troops could reach the Turkish lines. One man only, who returned unwounded, declares that he escaped by simply watching the stream of bullets from the enemy's machine guns striking the parapets of our trenches and leaping over it; for as usual, the Turkish guns were searching low. And as this assault was launched the 1st Regiment, led by Major T. W. Glasgow, charged from Pope's Hill, on the left of Quinn's. There was in front the small ridge—Deadman's Ridge—which had been attacked on the 2nd May, and won in parts by the 4th Infantry Brigade. It was covered with trenches, dug one above the other. From all three the Light Horsemen drove the Turks. In the forward line the men for a few minutes had the awful experience of being bombed by the Turks in front and their own men behind, until the mistake was suddenly recognised by Major Glasgow, who immediately charged with his men over the parapets to the third trench, and joined up the whole of the regiment. But the Turks held the higher ground above, and from their trenches it was an easy mark to throw bombs down on to the Light Horsemen in the trenches lower on the ridge. Our bomb supplies had all to be brought forward from Pope's position under machine-gun fire. The valiant men who still clung to the trenches they had gained, suffered cruel loss from bombs that the Turks hurled overhead and along the communication trenches. After two hours' desperate fighting, at 7.30 a.m. the order was reluctantly given to retire. Then only the right section of our line ever got back, and with them the gallant commander, without a scratch. Major Reed and Lieutenant Nettleton both died in those trenches. Twenty-one men were killed and 51 were missing after the attack.

So in the course of a terrible hour the Light Horse Brigades, National Guardsmen of Australia, won deathless glory by noble sacrifice and devotion to duty, and formed the traditions on which the splendour of the young army is still being built.

It must be recognised that except for the 4th Infantry Brigade the offensive of the Australians was completed on the morning of the 7th. Part had succeeded—part had failed. Their further advance rested entirely on the success of the second phase of the great scheme, the assault of the Sari Bair ridge. This terrible task fell mostly on the New Zealanders, but partly, too, on the new British army and the Indian brigades. The Australians were the connecting link between this greater Anzac and Suvla Bay landing. When the time came, they joined in the general offensive on the crest of the Sari Bair ridge and the attempt to take Hill 971—Koja Chemen Tepe. As my story mainly rests with the Australians, if more details necessarily are given of their part in this action, it must not be considered as a slur on the brilliant achievements of the New Zealanders and Britishers. What fighting I did not see at close fighting quartets I learned from the officers of those splendid battalions, later.

The vital movement to extend the Anzac position, connecting it with Suvla Bay, enveloping and taking of the summit of the mass of hills that dominated the central part of the peninsula and the Narrows, was entrusted to the care of General Sir William Birdwood. He had prefaced it with the offensive from Anzac proper. Now, under Major-General Sir Alexander Godley, the attempt to sweep up the northern slopes was to be carried out by a mixed force of Australians, New Zealanders, British, and Indians, number in all some 12,000 men.

The complete capture of the Sari Bair ridge would have brought into action again the 1st Australian Division, whose left wing at Anzac might have been relied on to advance over Baby 700 and up to Battleship Hill. What is too often overlooked, or forgotten, is that the capture of the great Hill 971 was a separate operation, though a natural corollary to the holding of the ridge, as a deep ravine separated this peak from the Sari Bair ridge. From Hill 971 the northern slopes (called the Abdel Rahman Bair), ran back within a mile to the Bijuk Anafarta village. It was separated from the foothills that fell away to the sea by the Asma Dere. Therefore a column, it was hoped (of the British troops and the 4th Australian Brigade), would make good this ridge and advance alongside it to the main peak. The operations, owing to the nature of the ground, fell into two stages. The first was the advance over the foothills to the Sari Bair ridge, the landing at Suvla Bay and first advance. The second stage was the united effort to take the hill and main ridge. To foretell the conclusion—now alas, passed into history as a splendid failure—the second stage was only partly possible, because on the right, from the direction of Suvla Bay, the British attack never developed; that is to say, it never reached even the foot of the Abdel Rahman Bair.

I have been in the heart of all that mass and tangle of hills and ravines. The country resembled, on a less grand scale, that of the Buffalo Ranges of Victoria, or the Blue Mountains, near Sydney. It might be ideal bushranging country, but the worst possible for an army fighting its way forward to the heights; gullies and precipices barred the way. Even with expert guides, and maps compiled by the Turks themselves, which we had captured and had copied, there were many battalions that lost their way, and only by dogged perseverance and extraordinary pluck did they extricate themselves and reach pints of vantage from which they could link up their positions. I say this of all forces engaged, because I know that many miscalculations occurred even after three days of fighting as to the exact gullies in which the troops were that had linked up with the units holding 'The Farm' and Rhododendron Ridge. Gullies were cut by creeks, hills divided by spurs. Into this tangle was first hurled an army of 12,000 men—mostly fine bushmen, it is true, used either to the gum forest of Australia and its wide expanses, or to the jungles of the tropics.

General Hamilton had accepted General Birdwood's plans, that there should be two covering columns to reach the two ridges that met at the Hill 971, almost at right angles (Sari Bair, running from west to east, and Abdel Rahman Bair, running nearly due north and south), and two assaulting columns to capture the positions.

General Hamilton sets forth the plan thus:

The right covering force was to seize Table Top, as well as all other enemy positions commanding the foot-hills between the Chailak Dere and the Sazli Beit Dere ravines. If this enterprise succeeded, it would open up, at the same time interposing between, the right flank of the left covering force and the enemy holding the Sari Bair main ridge. This column was under Brigadier-General A. H. Russell, who had the New Zealand Mounted Rifles Brigade, the Otago Mounted Rifles Regiment, Colonel A. Bauchop; the Maori Contingent and New Zealand Field Troop.

The left covering force was to march northwards along the beach to seize a hill called Damakjelik Bair, some 1,400 yards north of Table Top. If successful, it would be able to hold out a hand to the 9th Corps as it landed south of Nibrunesi Point, whilst at the same time protecting the left flank of the left assaulting column against enemy troops from the Anafarta Valley during its climb up the Aghyl Dere ravine. Brigadier General J. H. Travers commanded the column which consisted of headquarters 40th Brigade, half the 72nd Field Company, 4th Battalion South Wales Borderers, and 5th Battalion Wiltshire Regiment.

The right assaulting column was to move up the Chailak Dere and Sazli Beit Dere ravines to the storm of the ridge of Chunuk Bair.

The column was under Brigadier-General F. E. Johnston, commanding New Zealand Infantry Brigade, Indian Mountain Battery (less one section), one company New Zealand Engineers.

The left assaulting column was to work up the Aghyl Dere and prolong the line of the right assaulting column by storming Hill 305 (Koja Chemen Tepe), the summit of the whole range of hills. Brigadier-General (now Major-General) H. V. Cox was in command of the 29th Indian Infantry Brigadier, 4th Australian Infantry Brigade; Brigadier-General Monash, Indian Mounted Battery (less one section), one company New Zealand Engineers.

It may be roughly estimated that there were 3,000 troops with each column. A divisional reserve was formed from the 6th Battalion South Lancashire Regiment and 8th Battalion Welsh Regiment (Pioneers), mustered at Chailak Dere, and the 39th Infantry Brigade and half 72nd Field Company at Aghyl Dere.

The two assaulting columns (*writes Sir Ian Hamilton*) which were to work up three ravines to the storm of the high ridge were to be preceded by two covering columns. One of these was to capture the enemy's positions commanding the foothills, first to open the mouths of the ravines, secondly to cover the right flank of another covering force whilst it marched along the beach. The other covering column was to strike far out to the north, until, from a hill called Damakjelik Bair, it could at the same time facilitate the landing of the 9th Corps at Nibrunesi Point (Suvla Bay) and guard the left flank of the column assaulting Sari Bair from any forces of the enemy which might be assembled in the Anafarta Valley.

Old No. 3 Post was the first objective of that right covering force which General Birdwood had prepared, and No. 2 Post was its jumping-off place. You reached this outpost, either day or night, by travelling along the great sap that for two miles wound out from the heart of Anzac. All the troops that were to take part in this new attack had come from Anzac. That night they had marched out under the cloak of darkness across the broad open flats that reached from the foothills to the water's edge. At the post they found its garrison ready to move. Major-General Godley had his headquarters there already. Here, too, had been marshalled all available water-cans and ammunition supplies.

So the first dash into what was practically the unknown was to commence at 9.30 p.m. Just in front of No. 2 Post was Old No. 3 Post, a steep-sided position which the Turks had captured from us on 30th May. They had since strengthened it by massive woodworks, protecting the avenues of advance by great stretches of thick barbed wire. Behind the post again was Table Top, very flat on the summit, and about 400 feet high. On either flank of these hills ran a gully. On the left Sazli Belt Dere, and on the right the Chailak Dere. Both entrances through the valleys so formed to the inner hills were dominated by Old No. 3 Post, a veritable fortress with its revetted earthworks and its naturally steep sides.

General Birdwood had planned a ruse to make this hill. Every night, just at the same time, the destroyer *Colne* bombarded the post. Earlier in the evening her rays had gone wandering round the hills, but always at 9 p.m. there was a steady streak of light fixed on Old No. 3 Post, and the 6-in. guns belted the position for ten minutes. There was then a pause, and the beams disappeared, only to reappear again with the shells at 9.20. The bombardment continued till 9.30 p.m. For weeks this operation had continued. The Turks, it was learned from deserters, had got into the habit of retiring to their tunnels and never worrying much about the bombardment. After it was all over the New Zealanders used to hear an old Turk (they saw him once and christened him 'Achmet'), a wiremender, who came along the front of the line to repair the damage. They would not shoot him, though an attempt was made to trap him one night.

On the evening of the 6th August the bombardment continued, as it had every night for weeks, but under the noise of it, the Auckland Mounted Rifles Regiment, under Lieut.-Colonel Mackesy, stole from the trenches down into the gully and up to the lip of the Turkish trenches on the outpost. As the bombardment ceased, they rushed into the trenches without firing a shot, and bayoneted or bombed the astonished enemy. Many of the Turks were found to have removed their boots and coats and were resting. Seventy were captured. It took several hours in the darkness to clear the hill and the trenches that ran down into the gullies; the Turks gathered in small parties, resisting.

Meanwhile the attack on the left had been launched under the gallant leadership of Lieut.-Colonel Bauchop against the hill that bore his name. It had fallen to the Otagos to clear this hill and the Chailak Dere. By one o'clock Bauchop's Hill had been stormed and won. The enemy, surprised, made a stout resistance, and it was some time before the machine guns, cunningly concealed in this hill, were located. Colonel Bauchop fell mortally wounded in this assault. The New Zealanders worked with the bayonet round and over the hill, never firing a shot until they found their further progress barred by a terrible wire entanglement and trench that the Turks had placed across the mouth of the gully, which effectively sealed it. It was a party of New Zealand Engineers, under Captain Shera, with Maories in support, who broke a way through and left the path clear for the assaulting columns, by this time following.

Simultaneously, to the east, on the right of this attacking party, a violent, almost silent struggle for the possession of Table Top was also in progress. The destroyers had been bombarding the hill, which had now to be carried at the point of the bayonet by the dismounted mounted brigades of General Russell. The Canterbury men led the attack with bayonet and bomb. Their magazines were empty, under orders. For the first hours of this hill-fight all was silence. In the gullies and amongst the wooded spurs of the hills, parties of Turkish patrols were bayoneted and gave no alarm. Then from the north echoed the cheers of the Maories as they took Bauchop's Hill. It was caught up by the Canterbury men, now on Table Top. It was flung up to the lower slopes of the Rhododendron ridge, where the Turks still were. It was the battle-cry for the assaulting columns, which were advancing now through these protecting screens to the attack on the main ridge and on 971.

The 4th Australian Brigade, under General Monash, formed the head of the assaulting column that went out from the left, followed by General Cox's Indian Brigade—the whole command under General Cox. Already the way here had been blazed by the left covering force, under Brigadier-General Travers, consisting of South Wales Borderers and Wiltshiers, who had marched out swiftly to the Damakjelik Bair—a hill that guarded the entrance to the Aghyl Dere, up which the left assaulting column of General Cox had to turn. The Turks at eleven o'clock still kept up a flanking fire from the northern slopes of Bauchop's Hill, but gradually they were driven off, and when the new columns arrived at this point—late, it is true—it was only to find isolated and terrified parties of Turks sniping from different points as they were driven back and back. The full story of this advance may be briefly told.

It was while the attention of the Turks was riveted on the fall of their trenches along the plateau at Anzac, that the Australian 4th Infantry Brigade had left Rest Gully, below the Sphinx Rock, just on the left of Anzac (where it had been for the past ten weeks), and in silence made for the seashore, actually traversing under a torrent of shell fire part of the same ground and foreshore where the troops had landed first on the peninsula. It was a start warranted to depress more seasoned troops than these browned Australians, for shrapnel fell over them, while shells skimmed above their heads on their way to the beach. But they pushed steadily on. Fortunately the casualties were light. In the far distance, from the hills on their right, came the sound of the clatter of rifles. That was the attack on No. 3 Post, for, as the troops watched the three beams of the destroyers' searchlights playing on the ridges, they saw one suddenly turned up into the sky and the noise of the ship's guns died away. The beam was the signal for attack.

Immediately the taking of the foothills by the New Zealanders was assured, the way was clear for the 4th Infantry Brigade, under Brigadier-General Monash, to advance from the outskirts of our furthermost outpost line. It was hardly a week since I had been to the edge of our flank and looked across the flats and ploughed lands, over which then it would have been instant death to have advanced. Now that the Turks had been to some extent cleared from the hills on the right, the column, with one flank exposed to the hills and the other on the seashore, set out, in close formation, from under cover of our outposts. The column worked in towards some raised land that made a sort of road running round the foot of the hills, and met with no resistance. But there was a considerable amount of shrapnel being thrown over the column, and the ranks were thinned. A mile from our outposts the brigade swung round into a gully called the Aghyl Dere, and was at once met by a hot rifle fire from the Turks, who had taken up positions behind hastily thrown-up ramparts in the gully. The nature of the country made it easy to defend the valley. General Monash found it necessary to spread out a screen. It was composed of the 15th Battalion, under Lieut.-Colonel Cannan. The advance was constantly checked by the narrowness of the defiles through which the troops had to pass. At the head of the column was a Greek, and also a Turkish interpreter.

There were evidences of considerable occupation at some time by the Turks, for a series of *mia mias* were found in the gully. But the enemy were hastily fleeing before the advancing Australian Brigade. At the junction of the gully with a branch that ran east towards the slopes of the main ridge, there came a serious halt. Already the leading battalion, the 13th, had deployed and was scouring a grassy plain out to the left—that is, the north. It was by this time eleven o'clock, and absence of any idea of the numbers of the enemy, now at bay, rendered the position critical. General Cox, with the Indian troops, had deployed to the right and was making as rapidly as possible for the slopes of the main ridge on the sector allotted to them. At this confluence of the two streams it was decided by General Monash that the 13th and 14th Battalions of the 4th Brigade, under Lieut.-Colonel Burnage and Major Rankine respectively, should be turned to the north to join up with the British force, who were holding the hills overlooking the Chocolate Hills and Anafarta Valley, the line being extended as the Battalions advanced and covered a wider front. With the 15th Battalion, under Lieut.-Colonel Cannan, and the 16th, under Lieut.-Colonel Pope, General Monash pushed on. It was soon evident that the opposition here met was the screen the Turks had placed to enable them to get away two field guns (they were the '75's' which had given so much trouble), for the emplacements were soon discovered. The advance had been series of rushes rather than a steady march forward.

I have seen no country that more resembled the Australian bush. The bushes grew very tall in the creekbed. The whole battle was a running fight right up to the head of the *dere*, where, rather than lose touch with the British on his left, General Monash halted his troops. Dawn was just appearing in the sky, and as the men reached the fringe of the foothills there lay between them and the main ridge only a broad valley and a series of smaller knolls. On this ridge, above the Asma Dere, they therefore entrenched. Knowing that their lives depended on their speed, the men dug rapidly, and when I met the brigade, just after ten o'clock on the 7th, the reports came back that the fire-trenches were completed and, except for shrapnel and sniping, the enemy had shown no signs of a counter-attack.

It is now necessary to trace the events on the right, where the New Zealand Infantry, at midnight, had started on the second great phase of this night's venture—the storming of the Chunak Bair ridge. From the Table Top to the Rhododendron spur ran a thin razorback ridge and a communication trench. The Turks had fled along this. The cheers of the army forging its way into the hills, had roused the Turks. Our infantry, in four columns, were advancing to the assault. General Monash's progress I have already described. The Indian troops of the 29th Brigade (Sikhs and Gurkhas) were on his right, having turned east where the Aghyl Dere forked, and now were approaching the foot of the main ridge, making for the hills called 'Q.' This point, in the Sari Bair ridge, was immediately to the south of the dominating peak—Koja Chemen Tepe. They held a ridge at dawn just west of 'the Farm' that nestled in a shoulder of the main ridge immediately below Chunak Bair summit.

On the right the Otago and Canterbury Infantry Battalions were forcing their way up to the Rhododendron ridge. They had fought up the thickly wooded valley of the Sazli Beit, deploying men to the right and left to clear Turks from knolls, where they gathered to impede the progress of the army. Shrapnel now began to burst over the advancing companies as the enemy gained knowledge of the assault. The din of battle grew more awful as the morning came. From Anzac there resounded the fearful crashing of the bombardment of the Turkish trenches on Battleship Hill and the eastern slopes of the main ridge and the bomb battle at Lone Pine. The Light Horse at 4.30 had charged across the Nek and perished. Two battalions of New Zealanders met on the northern slopes of the Rhododendron ridge, and gathered in a depression quite well distinguishable from the No. 2 Post, and which was promptly termed the 'Mustard Plaster.' It was the one cramped position that the Turkish guns could not reach, where the troops were now digging in along the edge of the offshoot of the main ridge. Shrapnel, in white woolly balls, began to burst over the halted column. The 10th Gurkhas had advanced to within 300 yards of the crest of the ridge, about the vicinity of the Farm, while the 5th and 6th Gurkhas had fought their way on to the ridge father to the north. There they had linked up with the 14th Sikhs on the right, who were in touch with the Australians, now brought to a standstill on the ridge above the Asma Dere.

Amongst the hills, the New Zealanders cleared the Turks from their bivouacs. Either they were bayoneted, or fled, or else surrendered. The Otagos had taken 250 prisoners before dawn. It was a curious incident, for the Turks piled their arms, cheered, and willingly left the fight. They were captured on Destroyer Hill, which was one of the knolls that had been passed in the first onward rush and left uncleared. The Canterbury Battalion, advancing up a southern gully, and the Otago Battalion, in the northern direction, swept the few remaining Turks before them, and met on the Rhododendron spur at seven o'clock. Above them lay the rugged line of Chunak Bair, 850 feet high, and just 200 feet higher than the position they held, and still some 400 yards away. This Rhododendron spur cut into the main ridge along a narrow neck. Turkish machine guns and enemy trenches, dug along the top of the crest of Sari Bair, commanded that spot. The New Zealanders were compelled to dig their trenches just below the edge of the Rhododendron spur. In support they had some light mountain batteries and machine guns, under Major Wallingford.

Having reached so near to victory early on this first morning (the 7th), they were ordered to advance again, first at 9.30 a.m. and then again at eleven o'clock, when a general assault by all the forces along the ridge took place. It was in vain that efforts were made to advance up the slopes of those terrible hills. But the Auckland Battalion gallantly charged across the bridge of land that linked the spur with the main ridge below, and to the south of Chunak Bair. It was only a narrow neck of some 30 yards wide. It was raked by Turkish fire. Up the bushy slope scrambled the gallant New Zealanders. They were checked at noon 200 yards from the crest of the ridge by a fearful musketry fire. They dug in.

At dawn, from the hills, I watched the Suvla Bay Landing spread out in a magnificent panorama before me. I saw the sea, usually just specked with a few small trawlers and a monitor or destroyer, covered with warships and transports and craft of all descriptions. I discerned through the pale morning light the barges and boats, close inshore, discharging troops round the Suvla Bay and Nebrunesi Point. As the sun mounted over the crest of Hill 971, the rays caught the rigging and masts and brasswork of the ships, and they shone and reflected lights towards the fleeing Turks. I saw, too, the British troops pouring over the hills immediately surrounding the Salt Lake. The warships were firing steadily, and, when there was light enough, the observation balloon rose steadily, and stayed in the sky, until attacked by a hostile aeroplane. But, as if anticipating this event, our aeroplanes darted up, and the

Taube fled precipitously, and descended in a terrific volplane down behind the high hills. The sea was alive with small pinnaces and boats from the ships. Hospital ships lay in a long line from Gaba Tepe to Suvla Bay. I counted six of them, and they were coming and going all day.

So during the rest of the day the two assaulting columns clung to what they had won—a great gain of 2 miles on the left of Anzac—and the new base at Suvla Bay was secured. But, while the first part of the British 9th Army Corps plans had been successful, and the Navy had achieved another magnificent feat in landing the troops, stores, water, and munitions round the shores of Suvla Bay, the newly landed army under Lieut.-General Stopford were held back all that long day on the very fringe of Salt Lake. I remember how anxiously from the various commanding positions we had gained we watched for the signs of the advance of that British column. Our line bent back sharply to the Damakjelik Hills, that had been captured early the previous night. I am not in a position to explain the delays that occurred on the beach round Nebrunesi Point. Turkish officers have stated how the first reports from their outposts at Suvla Bay, believed the landing to be only a feint. Also how two regiments of gendarmes had held back, with some few machine guns, the British Divisions advancing towards the Chocolate Hills (the first of the series of hills that ran right into Buyak Anafarta), the capture of which was so urgently needed by us to control the attack on the Abdel Rahman Bair ridge, and to protect and support the attack on the main peak, Hill 971.

The great offensive had been auspiciously launched; it had gone well till dawn, in spite of the terrible difficulties of the maze of hills that clustered beneath the Sari Bair ridge. The new expedition had been landed, and had been left an open door to pass through (if it had but had the 'punch') into the heart of the Turkish main positions. It is not too much to say that the Turks were thoroughly alarmed, surprised, and bewildered; they knew not now at which spot the great attack was to come. They had massed all their main forces at Cape Helles for an offensive there. Their supports had been hurried up to Anzac. Their reserves were still only on their way up the peninsula, coming from Gallipoli to Suvla Bay. Ignorant of the impending landing, the enemy dashed battalion after battalion against the captured Lone Pine; they recoiled before the stubborn and gallant resistance of its garrison. But by the next dawn they had recovered from the shock, and their resistance had grown powerful. Even then it was not too late. General Hamilton anxiously hastened the final assault.

CHAPTER XXV
THE BATTLE OF SARI BAIR—
THE CAPTURE OF THE RIDGE
AND ITS LOSS

As night fell on the 7th August, death and destruction was spread around the hills by the guns of the warships. It began on the farther deep-tinted purple mountain ridges overlooking Suvla Bay; it continued in a series of white shell-bursts on to the Sari Bair ridge. Grass fires lit the sky and smudged the landscape in the valley of the Salt Lake. After midnight the assault of the highest peaks was to commence. New columns had been organised. The New Zealanders, supported by British troops, were to press home their advantage on Chunak Bair. The Gurkhas were to take 'Q' Hill; the Australians and Sikhs were to attack the Abdel Rahman ridge, and advance due east along its crest and capture the crowning hill, Koja Chemen Tepe. Monitors, battleships, and destroyers covered the hills of these positions with high-explosive shell, the searchlights blazing white patches on the ridges from 3.30 a.m. till 4.15. Under this cover of screaming steel the attacks were commenced.

At a conference between the Brigadier of the 4th Brigade and General Russell it was decided to storm the slopes of Abdel Rahman

Bair. Sufficient time had elapsed to enable an inspection to be made of the country immediately in front of the ridge, but not time to reconnoitre the best route through difficult, unknown country. At 3 a.m. the brigade moved from the trenches. It was perfectly dark, and the first country crossed was the narrow crest of the bush-covered hills they held. It was barely 30 yards. Then the men slid down into the gully below, for the reverse slope was an almost precipitous sandstone ridge. Once down into the dip the brigade moved in column quietly, and swung on toward Anafarta over the crest of a low hill and down into a cornfield. The troops, lest the rustling through the corn, not yet harvested, might warn the enemy, were kept to the gully until a hedge of furze and holly, that ran east in the direction required, was reached. Following this closely, so as to pass unseen, the Australians reached a stubble field. The 15th Battalion, under Lieut.-Colonel Cannan, had spread out as a screen in front, but before this again a platoon was deployed to pick off the scouts of the enemy. The distance covered must have been nearly half a mile, and, except for a stray shot or two on the right, where the outposts of the enemy were encountered, no opposition had been offered.

The ridge of Abdel Rahman Rair was now just at right angles to the course of the advancing column as set by the guides, some 150 yards away. It rose, a black obstacle in their path. Along the back of this they were to push their way up towards the main heights, or as far as was possible with the troops at the disposal of the commander. In this general assault it was the 4th Brigade that was this time to be the decoy, or covering brigade, for the advance which the Indians simultaneously were making direct on the main ridge of Sari Bair.

To screen the troops from observation in the advance across the cropped field (it was not yet four o'clock), the column kept close to the edge of the scrubby land. No sooner had the right of the protecting screen touched the slopes of the densely scrubby hills than, at short range, there came from every nook of the hill, rising in tier after tier, a murderous fire from machine guns and rifles. At once the troops were hurried to the right. They swept back the Turks there, who retreated, under the fire of their own guns, still higher up the ridge.

But it was essential that our left flank, that faced Anafarta, should be protected. Again the platoons had to advance amidst a terrible fire from machine guns. Meanwhile the 16th and 14th Battalions, under Lieut.-Colonel Pope and Major Rankine respectively, advanced in extended platoons, trying to force a passage up the ridge. The men attacked bravely, but it was one continuous roar of musketry and machine guns they faced. Our own machine gunners in the now coming dawn, managed to locate the Turkish guns. Two were soon put out of action, but still the hills seemed alive with these terrible weapons, and the bullets tore gaps in our ranks.

At five o'clock it was apparent, unless reinforcements were brought up, the ridge could not be taken. Soon the order for withdrawal was given. It was a skilfully carried out under a covering fire from our machine guns, splendidly handled by Captain Rose, which undoubtedly saved many lives by momentarily silencing the enemy's fire, and enabling our troops to get back to the protection of our trenches. By 9 a.m. on the 8th, the withdrawal had been completed, and every man, including the wounded, was within the protection of the well-prepared trenches, left but a few hours before. It will be apparent that, great as this sacrifice was, it had necessitated a large force of the enemy being drawn away from the main objective, and gave the chance, which the New Zealanders so gallantly seized, of taking the crest of the hill; and it also enabled the Indian troops to work their way on to the uppermost slopes of the great ridge. The 15th Battalion suffered most severely, and came to closest grips with the enemy. Many hand-to-hand encounters took place, and ghastly bayonet wounds were received, but the Turks suffered quite as heavily as our lines. Looking across the valley I could see, days later, the hill covered with their dead. The brigade lost in the two days' fighting nearly 1,000 men.

In the half light of the early morning the attack began on the Sari Bair ridge. For the storming of Chunak Bair the Wellington Battalion and Auckland Mountain Rifles had been chosen, together with the Maoris—all that remained of that band—and Gloucester Battalion. The force was led by Lieut.-Colonel Malone, the gallant defender of Quinn's Post in the past months. At the head of the Wellingtons Lieut.-Colonel Malone led his men up through the long Turkish communication trench, which was perfectly visible from our outposts, to the summit of the hill. The Turks had retired during the night from this section of the ridge, leaving only a machine gun and a few men, who had come from Achi Baba, to defend the crest. The Gloucesters at the same time, in the face of heavy fire, gained a footing on an adjacent section of the ridge, and held on. It was a magnificent achievement, and only the grim determination of the troops engaged could have scaled that shell-swept slope—covered but thinly with bushes—and held it in poor shallow trenches, with short supplies, on the third day of a great battle.

Meanwhile the Gurkhas, supported by battalions of the 13th Division, pushed up the slopes of 'Q' Hill, and reached a point within 150 yards of the top. But no sooner had these position been won than the Turks directed a terrific fire on the ridge. The Wellingtons' ranks thinned rapidly, but the Auckland Mounted Rifles managed to reach the firing-line in time to reinforce it, before the enemy commenced to attack in force. The Turks poured up the reverse side of the ridge, where our Anzac guns decimated them. Colonel Malone, seeing that the Turkish plan had been carefully laid and the trenches marked for destruction, ordered the troops to dig a new trench 15 yards in the rear—a perilous operation under the shrapnel fire that was pouring on to the attackers. Yet that shallow trench was dug and held against the Turks. Bombs and waters were running low. It was two and a half miles back down through the gullies to the beach. The heat of the sun was terrific, and under it the men had been fighting for nearly three days. They were bloodstained and parched. I never have seen such appalling sights as the men who came in wounded during those days. Nevertheless there, on the top of the ridge, fluttered the small yellow and red flags, marking a section, barely 300 yards long, which had been won and held, the first foot set on the desired ridge.

A shell-burst killed Colonel Malone during that afternoon in the trenches, which he and his men had so gallantly won. Colonel Moore, who succeeded him, was wounded before midnight. Shell fire destroyed the whole of a section of the front line of the trenches. The men rebuilt them and still fought on. The next morning the remaining section of the hill 'Q' was to be charged by the Gurkhas and the South Lancashires.

So dawned the third morning of this fearful fight to dislodge the Turks from the ridge. The support that was expected from the British armies landed at Suvla Bay had failed, as now the Turks had brought up reinforcements, and all idea of a swift advance from this quarter was impossible. But General Hamilton realised that even yet there was time to snatch a victory. The chance lay in smashing a way through at the highest and most distant points gained on the crest of the ridge. So for this undertaking the flung forward a complete new column under Brigadier-General Baldwin, two battalions each from the 38th Infantry and 29th Brigades, and one from the 40th Brigade.

There began at 4.30 p.m. on the 9th, as a prelude to this supreme effort, the shelling of the whole of the Sari Bair ridge— north of the position held by the New Zealanders. The destroyers' fire was terribly accurate. From Anzac the howitzers and field guns tore up the ridge from the east where the Turkish reserves had been massing. It was as if the hill was in eruption; smoke and flame rolled from its sides. At the 'Mustard Plaster' it was intended that the assaulting column of General Baldwin should wait, and from there debouch up the hillside, prolonging to the north the crest-line held by the New Zealanders. But in the darkness the valleys and gullies of those chaotic hills, baffled even the guides. The column, advancing up the Chailak Dere to the support of the men on the hill, lost its way. The tragic result will be apparent when it is stated that already the 6th Gurkhas, led by Major C. G. L. Allanson, crept as rapidly as the steepness of the hill and the density of the under-growth would permit to the very summit of the great ridge—and gained it—at a point midway between 'Q' Hill and the Chunak Bair summit. It was, after all, only a handful of sturdy men who had to face whole battalions of the Turkish army. Still, the advantage gained was enough to stiffen the sinews of any leader and his army. There before them, at their feet one might write, lay the whole of the enemy's main position, and the road leading down the peninsula into Bogali. Beyond, glittering in tantalising fashion, were the placid waters of the Dardanelles, on which the first light of the rising sun began to pour, outlining the score of ships bringing supplies to the armies.

Into the ranks of the astonished and panic-stricken lines of Turks, the Gurkhas and the South Lancashire Regiment began to pour a torrent of lead, sweeping down the reverse slopes of the ridge. But in the very hour of their wonderful success came the first horrible check. Mistaking the target, the destroyers dropped 6-in. high-explosive shells amongst the Indian troops. The havoc was appalling. No course was open but to retire to a point of safety down the side of the ridge. The Turks were not slow to grasp the situation, and by the time that the mistake had been rectified, the Turks charged again and reoccupied the trenches they had so hastily evacuated. In spite of which disaster, even yet victory was imminent, had but General Baldwin's troops been at the moment (according to prearranged plans) swarming over the very crowning summit of the Chunak Bair position. Instead, they were still only on the sides of the ridge just above the Farm, advancing steadily, pressing up in line. But the Turks had launched their blow. They came pouring over the crest of the hill, and fired down from the commanding position into the ranks of the storming columns. A small battery placed on the very top of the summit of Chunak Bair compelled General Baldwin to withdraw his troops to below the Farm, while the enemy turned the full force of their blow on to the New Zealanders and British troops, who still stood their ground. Till night fell the Turks attacked. Our regiments clung on exhausted, desperate. They were then relieved by the 6th Loyal North Lancashire Regiment, and the 5th Wiltshire Regiment. Worn with the three days' fight, almost famished, but in good heart, buoyed by the feat of arms they had achieved, never have men deserved more the honours that have been paid them, than those New Zealanders.

Through no fault of theirs, they left to the new garrison trenches that were not deep—they were not even well placed. The Turkish fire had left little chance of that. The crest remained dead

277

ground. Even while the line was being reformed by Lieut.-Colonel Levinge, the fiercest of the Turkish counter-attacks began. To the enemy the possession of the ridge by the foe was like a pistol pointed at the very heart of their army. Unfortunately, only half our new troops were dug in when that counter-attack came (the Wiltshires finding constant checks in the gullies and hills through and up which they had marched to reach the firing-line).

It is estimated that the attacking force which the Turks launched against that garrison of 1,000 men, was a division and a regiment and three battalions. Probably 30,000 men swarmed over the crest of the hill on the 10th. In one huge effort the Turks were staking all. The German leaders found no obstacle in the loss of life. As these masses of enemy, line after line of closely formed men, came up on to the crests, the warships opened fire from Ocean Beach, while on the reverse slope the Anzac guns caught the Turks as they advanced along the communication trenches and on to the hill. From the beach our newly placed guns, near No. 2 Post, drenched the hillside with shells. The British were overwhelmed certainly. At a fearful cost did the enemy accomplish it.

Watching the commencement of the bombardment from a distance of 2,000 yards, I was more than ever convinced the Turk was a brave soldier. For thirty hours now he had been working under an intermittent fire to gain a footing on Rhododendron spur. From a range of 1,700 yards he was attacked by a group of machine guns from our position on Snipers' Nest west of the Nek, and driven from his hasty trenches by the lyddite shells that sent tons of earth and stones into the air at each explosion and cast for a moment a haze over the hill. The Turk, as he crawled away or went at a shuffle back over the ridge, was caught by the machine-gun fire. His plight was desperate. The shells fell at the rate of about ten a minute for an hour and a half, and recommenced for two hours more in the afternoon. Those shells dropped from one end of the ridge to the other, only a matter of 300 yards, and then, lowering the range, the gunners hurled shells into the hollow, drove out the Turks, and followed them as they fled back up the side of the hill. Turk after Turk came from those broken trenches, some wounded and without equipment, some still with rifles and packs. Some were moving slowly and painfully, while others were running low and quickly across the sky-lines. I watched them struggling from newly made trenches down the slope of the hill, which the gunners on the ships could see equally well with the artillery observing officers directing the field guns on the beach. I have never seen such accurate or persistent fire.

As the 8-in. or 10-in. shells from the warships struck the hillside, above the dust and dirt, one could see, almost with every shot, men blown into the air. Once three Turks went skywards, and four men, whom a minute before I had seen crawling amongst the scattered bushes, disappeared. The striking of the shells on the hill was seen before the double thunder of the guns was heard. Sometimes shrapnel, bursting just over the crest, laid low men who had escaped the larger shells. The guns of the 1st Australian Division were playing on that side as well. The Turk was caught between two fires. For hours I watched the enemy crawling out of that gully over the hill. It was appalling. The slopes were thick with their dead. Never had a hill been so dearly lost, so dearly won, and now lost again, to become, as it was for days, no man's ground; for with the continued bombardment that night and the machine gun battery playing along the ridges next morning (11th), the Turks were content to hold the trenches behind the crest on the eastern side.

But for the rat-a-tat-tat of our machine guns on this morning— the sixth day of the battle—all was perfectly still along the now extended battle front.

And all through those appalling five days of the fiercest fighting that had ever been fought on the peninsula, never for a moment did the Turks relinquish their idea of recapturing the cherished Lone Pine trenches. In the first day's fighting the Australian casualties had been nearly 1,000. By the end of the fourth day they had doubled. It was one huge bomb battle, with short respites. As the fight continued, overhead cover was erected by the sappers to prevent the Turks firing down the length of trenches. I saw men tired—so tired that they could not even stand. Yet they clung on. Colonel Magnaghten handed over his gallant 4th to Colonel Cass, only because he could not stay awake to once again refuse to relinquish his post. Relief was given to his battalion for a few hours by Light Horse regiments and infantry battalions drawn from other sections of the line. Thus the 5th, 6th, 7th, and 12th Battalions and squadrons of the 2nd Light Horse Brigade all played their share in repelling the Turks in that unforgettable four-day bomb battle. But so terrible was the position that men were only kept for short periods in the trenches. Through these rapid changes was the sting gradually drawn from the Turkish attacks. But it took five days to extract, and in that time many deeds of priceless heroism, devotion, and sacrifice were performed by men whose names will ever be associated with that fighting. I can name but a few of them.

There was Captain Shout, 1st Battalion, who could throw two bombs, and even three, in quick succession. Having charged down one of the innumerable Turkish trenches, he endeavoured to dislodge the enemy from the other end of a sap. Reckless of his life, he hurled the missiles as if they had been so many cricket balls. He killed eight Turks before he was himself killed by a bomb.

Lieutenant Symons led a charge and retook a portion of an isolated sap that the Turks had occupied. It happened at 5 a.m. on the morning of the 9th. Six officers of ours had been killed or wounded in that trench. With an extraordinary courage, Lieutenant Symons led a small party down the sap and dislodged the Turks, himself killing many. He then built a sandbag barricade under the very nose of the enemy. A somewhat similar charge was made by Lieutenant Tubb, of the 7th, backed by Corporal Burton and Corporal Dunstan, two of his men. All of these men received the Victoria Cross for their bravery.

Never before in any hundred square yards of ground have so many honours been won and such wonderful gallantry shown. Men and officers fighting in that inferno seemed to be inspired with unparalleled courage. Private Keysor (1st Battalion) threw back enemy bombs into their own trenches, and, though twice wounded, continued till the end of the engagement to act as bomb-thrower wherever there was need. Private Hamilton (1st Battalion) on the

9th sat calmly on the parados, thereby getting fire to bear on the enemy. He rallied his comrades, and they drove back the enemy.

Major Sasse (1st Battalion) won distinction by charging at the head of a small body of men down a Turkish sap, and then directing a bomb attack from the parados of the captured trenches. One has only to turn to the stories of the Military Crosses gained, to find how attack was met by counter-attack; how trenches were taken at the bayonet's point during the four days that battle lasted.

The men who sold their lives in these herculean efforts to shake off the Turks, numbered nearly 800. Officers made noble examples for their troops. Colonel Scobie, 2nd Battalion, was leading back a small section of his command from an ugly sap from which they were being bombed, when he was killed by a bomb. Colonel Brown, passing the head of one of the many dangerous saps that led to the Turkish position on the other side of the plateau, was shot through the breast and fell dead at the feet of his men.

Lone Pine on that second day, when I was through it, presented a spectacle of horror. The dead Australians and Turks lay deep in the trenches. Parapets had partly buried them.

It was at the entrance to a tunnel that I saw our lads sitting with fixed bayonets and chatting calmly to one another. There was a horrible odour in the trenches that compelled one to use the smoke helmet for some little relief. At the end of this tunnel, 40 yards away, so one of the men told me, were 30 dead Turks. In through a shell hole that had broken open a Turkish tunnel, and over these dead bodies, a wounded sapper had crawled on the day after the battle from the battlefield above, thereby saving himself from exposure and probable death. How these men had died none exactly knew. A shell may have broken through the tunnel—probably had—and those who had not been killed outright had died of suffocation from the shell fumes. It became necessary now to fill in the end of the tunel, to prevent any entry by the enemy as much as to safeguard the health of our men. The thousands of rifles, broken belts, scattered cartridges, clothing of all descriptions that were to be seen belonging to either side were being collected in order to make the way clear. One realised that there must be days before the trenches could become normal again. For all the time, simultaneously with the relief of the wounded, existed the need for the protection of the fighting troops, the changing over of the parapets, the filling of sandbags to pile up the traverses, the erection of the overhead cover. All that involved a horrible waste of men—the ruin of scores of lives—in the accomplishment. Yet never must it be forgotten that the enemy was driven from what might well have been considered an impregnable position, had been shaken, had lost five to every one of our troops.

As I walked down the trenches it was impossible to avoid the fallen men lying all around. They lay on the parapets and their blackened hands hung down over our path. While this bombing continued it was no use trying to clear the way. Amidst the horribleness of the dead, the men fought and lived. They fought, too, knowing that behind the ramparts that protected them, must lie their comrades.

It was the most touching sight in the world to see units that had won the fight being withdrawn on the second day. Perhaps only a few hundred came back. They were covered with blood; they were unrecognisable in the dirt that had been scattered over them; they were lean and haggard from want of sleep. But they bore themselves without the least touch of fatigue as they passed by British troops working behind the lines. They had in their demeanour that which showed a confidence in something accomplished and a pride in a victory won. They acknowledged modestly the tribute of those who had known the fury of battle—who had seen the charge. As they came out of the tunnel which led from the firing-line there were comrades who waited to grip their hands. For news travels in a curious manner from trench to trench of a comrade hit, wounded, or one whose life has gone. You hear it soon even down on the beach.

And amidst these brave men and those waiting to take their turn at defending, the dead bodies of the enemy were drawn, to be buried in a great pile on a hill slope. The tracks of the canvas shroud showed in the loose earth, the air polluted by the stench of the passing corpse. Not far away was a heap of Turkish equipment,

30 feet high, piled up, waiting sorting, which had been taken from the trenches. Of Turkish rifles we had enough for a battalion. Already I had seen a party of our men in the trenches handling with a certain satisfaction, and no little rapidity, the captured machine guns, which, with the ammunition also captured, gave us a splendid opportunity of turning the enemy's weapons on himself. The spoils of victory were very sweet to these men.

I have referred more than once to the bravery of the Turkish soldier. The fight he put up on these Lone Pine trenches would be enough to establish that reputation for him were there not other deeds to his credit. Not that that diminishes one degree the glory of the achievement of our arms. The fury of the fire of shots and shell was enough to have dismayed any troops. The Australians went through that with heads bent, like men going through a fierce pelting rain.

Taken all round, the Turks are by no means an army of poor physique. They may not be as well clad as our troops, but they looked healthy and well fed. A sergeant, a fine-built man, standing nearly 6 feet, who had served in the Balkan War and also the gendarmerie, when captured, accepted his fate, but showed no signs of relief that he was to be led away captive. If anything, his tone suggested that he would have liked to have gone on fighting. In this attitude he was different from the large majority of the prisoners. He never expected an attack, and the first thing that was known in the enemy trenches was a shout from the look-out. He had at once rushed to get his men out of the tunnel to line the fire-trenches. But before he could reach a position the 'English,' as the sergeant persisted in calling our troops, had arrived, and were jumping down on top of them. He believed that all his officers had been killed. It was Kismet, the will of Allah, that he should be taken.

After the constant boom of the guns, the tearing whistle of the shells overhead day and night, distant and near, the cracking of rifles for five days and nights, the morning of the sixth day broke so calm that the bursting of a shell on the beach broke a kind of peaceful meditation. The troops began to ask one another what had happened or was happening. If you listened very carefully the soft patter of a machine gun came from the distant hills across at Suvla Bay. The battle was evidently not ended there.

That evening (12th August) the quiet of the lines was broken by the appearance, in close proximity to our observation balloon over the shipping in Suvla Bay, of a German aeroplane. As it sailed overhead I could just hear the throbbing of the engine. It was heading south, when from the direction of the Narrows came one of our airmen. He was flying a little lower than the enemy. At first he apparently did not see the hostile machine. There was no mistaking the two types—the enemy, dark in colour, grey, with black crosses painted on the wings, and ours yellow, with red eyes on the wings. Suddenly the British turned directly towards the enemy, which promptly veered and fled towards the Turkish lines at Bogali, dropping behind the ridges. The Turkish aviator thus robbed us of the chance of witnessing a battle in the air.

What days of quiet followed the digging of new trenches on the Chunak Bair slopes, after the crest had been won and lost!

To complete this battle scene, there remains but to be told the position gained by the 4th Australian Brigade. Its line was spread along the crest of the range of hills practically where I first described them. Along the Asma Dere by hard digging they had secured a position, and from it I had an excellent view of Buyik Anafarta in flames. The warship shells had set it alight. From the extreme right on the plains round Suvla Bay grass fires were burning harmlessly. I watched, too, ambulances drawn by six-horse teams bringing in the British wounded across the dried Salt Lake. The headquarters of the Australian Brigade was on the side of a long, broad gully, which recently had been under cultivation. On my way there I had to pass up the bed of a creek filled with dead mules, which the Turkish shrapnel had slaughtered. I passed New Zealand engineers successfully sinking wells, and line after line of water-carriers. Ahead was a string of ten mules bringing ammunition and supplies. On my left, at the edge of a few acres of cropped land, was a German officers' camp. A well-built hut of branches and mud was concealed from the view of aircraft under the shady branches of a grove of olive trees. There were several huts like this, with a slit for a window that faced out to the sea. Immediately behind was a hill, on the slope of which were tents and a number of well-made dugouts and tracks, the remains of a considerable Turkish encampment.

I followed the telephone line, hung from bush to bush, and then came to some tall scrub, in which the brigade was camped, like a party of railway surveyors in the bush, protected from the sun by bush huts and from bullets by timber taken from the enemy's shelters. As I talked to General Monash bullets pattered against the earth walls, and he opened his case and showed me the collection he was making of the 'visitors' that dropped round him as he wrote and directed the working of his command. He was justly proud of the way his men had fought; of the running fight they had won; of their march of miles through unknown country, and the way they had established themselves in the heart of the enemy's stronghold.

In the trenches the men showed no sign of fatigue now, having rested for a few days. A much reduced brigade it was, but the men were watching the Turks digging on the hills and waiting their opportunity. Every few minutes would come the clatter of the machine gun from somewhere along the front. The firing-line was only a few hundred yards away, so the Staff was in the midst of the attacks. The firing of our artillery from the hills behind and the presence of our aeroplanes overhead made the men keen and zealous. They were then still ripe for any advance.

In the face of such achievements, was it to be wondered that General Hamilton, Lieut.-General Birdwood, Major-General Godley, all wrote of the men who fought these battles in terms of the highest admiration? 'Whatever happens,' were General Hamilton's words to General Birdwood, 'you and your brave army corps have covered yourselves with glory. Make good the crest, and the achievement will rank with Quebec.' Yes, it ranked alongside any of the fighting in history. It had been in turn trench fighting, bayonet charges, and fighting in the open, and everywhere the overseas troops had won. But at what cost! At Lone Pine the casualties were 2,000 killed and wounded men. From the captured trenches there were dragged 1,000 killed, Australians and Turks.

They were buried in the cemetery on the side of the hill in Brown's Dip. The Army Corps in four days had lost 12,000 men killed and wounded. The British casualties on the Anzac section were 6,000 out of 10,000 troops engaged. In all 18,000 casualties for a gain of 2 miles and a position on, but not the crest of, the ridge. I have omitted the casualties of the fighting at Suvla Bay.

And the Turks! Their losses? It must be one of the satisfactions of the splendid failure that they lost nearly three to our one. Over 1,000 of the enemy perished at Lone Pine. On the 10th I saw them lying in heaps of hundreds on the bloody slopes of Chunak Bair. We had captured in all about 700 prisoners, and much material and equipment. Thousands of Turkish rifles were removed from Lone Pine, and hundreds of thousands rounds of ammunition. We took seven of their machine guns and belts of ammunition, and turned them against their own army. One hundred and thirty prisoners were taken in that section. General Monash captured over a hundred prisoners, including officers, great quantities of big gun ammunition (including fifty cases of '75' ammunition, near where the Turks had their French gun), thousands of rounds of rifle ammunition, quantities of stores. The New Zealanders took in the first attack on Old No. 3 Post 125 prisoners and some machine guns, and also a nordenfeldt. As the fighting extended to the left, further plants of ammunition were discovered in the valley.

Anzac was enlarged from barely 300 acres to about 8 square miles. A base for twenty operations was gained at Suvla Bay, and though the passage along the beach to Anzac was still a hazardous one, to the joy of many Australian dispatch riders, it provided a race through a hail of bullets along that zone. If devotion and heroism could make success, then the Army Corps had indeed covered itself with glory. But it had very substantial deeds to its credit as well. It had fought, adding fresh laurels to those won in its first fight at the landing. Weakened, worn, but by no means disheartened, it was strengthened after 20th August by the arrival of the 2nd Australian Division from Egypt, under Major-General Legge, which enabled respite from trench warfare to be enjoyed by the veteran brigades. Except for the fighting on the extreme left of our Army Corps line, where the Australians linked with the Suvla Bay forces across the Chocolate Hills, the weeks after the great battles at Anzac were calm. It was only a calm that precedes a storm.

CHAPTER XXVI
HILL 60, GALLIPOLI

In the days immediately following the halting of the 4th Infantry Brigade in the Asma Dere, it would have been possible to have walked on to the top of the steep knoll marked 'Hill 60' on the maps. From the ridge that the Australians then occupied there was only a small ridge in between, and a cornfield joining a valley not many yards across. Then came the hill—not, perhaps, as famous as Hill 60 in France, nor even as bloodstained, but one that cost over 1,000 men to take—that commanded the broad plain spread inland to the town of Bujik Anafarta. A mile and a half to the north across the plain where the 'W' hills, the end spur of which, nearest the sea, Chocolate Hills, the British by this time held. Hill 60 was necessary to our plans in order to link up securely the position and give us command of the plain, on which were a number of fine wells. On the 21st August, when the first attack was made, they hill and they ridge which joined it, were strongly held by the enemy. A day attack had been determined on, following a fierce bombardment. Owing to a sudden change of plans to a general attack, the bombardment failed; it was not as intense as was intended, and in consequence the preparation for the attacking lines was inadequate.

At two o'clock the guns commenced, not only to shell Hill 60, but all along the Turkish front on the plain. For an hour scores of guns shook the earth with the concussion of the shells. Then the British advance began—yeomanry and the imperishable 29th Division.

Now, in this larger plan, Hill 60 was only an incident, but an important one for the Australians. General Birdwood had placed Major-General Cox in command of a force consisting of two battalions of New Zealand of the ground, from the stream of lead from the enemy trenches circling this Hill 60. Some of the New Zealanders worked round the end of the spur, charged across the 100 yards of open ground to the foot of the knoll also, and so into the communication trenches of the Turks. Trench fighting of desperate character continued till nightfall. The second lines that were sent to support the attacking force, faced the rapid volleys from the Turkish guns on the ridge, firing down into the valley.

The 13th Battalion, under Major Herring, and the 14th, under Major Dare, not 500 men in all, had been reduced to not more than 300 men by the time they had advanced a short distance up the slope and taken the first line of Turkish trenches. To them there was only one consolation: they could not be fired on where they were, tucked under the side of the Turks' own hill. But they could not get word back or find a means of communication, other than over the fearful bullet-swept slope that lay behind them. Messengers indeed were sent. One managed to dodge up the many folds in the hillside, chased by the machine guns. As he reached the skyline and our trench, he cried 'I have a mess—' but he got no further: a Turkish bullet struck him, and he fell, dead, into the trench amongst his comrades. Snipers rendered the situation worse. A bush fire broke out amongst the holly-bushes on the hillside, covered with the dead and wounded. No reinforcements came through till ten o'clock next morning, when a communication trench had been dug down from the ridge, which the 4th Brigade held, prolonging the line to the north.

That night was one of horror for the Australians and New Zealanders clinging to the base of the knoll. The dying men on the exposed slope of the hill were heard calling to their comrades. Many were the brave deeds performed in bringing men to safety. Captain Loughran, the medical officer of the 14th Battalion, brought in with his stretcher-bearers eight men. Yet the following morning, wounded still lay amongst the bushes, and as the fire swept up the hill, they crept out, only to be killed by Turkish bullets. One man was seen working his way on his back up a depression, the bullets flicking the earth round him, and—delirious probably—as they missed, so he slowly waved his hand back and forth. Finally the Turks turned a machine gun on him, and he lay still. The padre of the 14th Battalion, Chaplain A. Gillison, sacrificed his life in bringing the wounded from off that horrible hill. He was waiting to read the burial services over some men that had been brought in to be buried. Suddenly came a cry from over the hill, and with two stretcher-bearers—noble heroes always—he went out, creeping towards the British soldier, who was being worried by ants. Just as he had started to drag the wounded man back to safety he was shot through the spine. He died at the beach clearing station. Chaplain Grant, with the New Zealand forces, also went in search of a wounded man along a trench on the hillside. In the maze of trenches at the foot of the redoubt he took the wrong turning. As the brave chaplain turned an angle (voices had been heard ahead) a Turkish bullet struck him and he fell forward.

Thus, on the 22nd, the main Australian position was still 150 yards away down the back of the ridge to the north, while the New Zealanders held a small section of the trenches on the western side of the knoll. The Indians had been linked up with the British Suvla Bay army by the 18th Battalion, under Lieut.-Colonel A. E. Chapman, the first of the new Australian battalions of the 2nd Division to go into the fight. That Battalion was set the task, on the morning of the 22nd, or charging a section of the trenches on the upper slopes of the knoll, so as to relieve the desperate position of the New Zealanders clinging to the trenches on the side of the hill. But when they had swept clear a Turkish communication trench, they found themselves enfiladed by the enemy's rifles. A strong bomb attack at 10 a.m. shattered their ranks and drove them to the New Zealand line, where they stuck. So the position was only slightly improved to what it had been the previous evening, for there was now a linked line round the base of Kaijak Aghala, Hill 60. The Australasians had won about 150 yards of trench, while the 4th Brigade, still occupying the upper slopes, had already inflicted severe losses on the enemy, who were feverishly entrenching the top of the hill, turning it into a strong redoubt, and opening up new communication trenches. In all the operations at and round this hill the Australians had been able to terribly harass the Turks, and machine guns had caught the enemy in the open when they were attempting to dig out into the plain. The gunners let the Turks go forward with their picks and shovels and entrenching tools, and then commenced to 'stir them up,' and, as they returned, played a machine gun on them.

But the enemy made good progress in strengthening the redoubt on this knoll in the four days that elapsed before the hill was finally carried. There was no question that the first bombardment had failed to smash the trenches. General Cox, in spite of the first failure to attain the intended objective, still favoured a day attack, following on an intense bombardment. And in the closing days of August he had his way, and then began the second battle for possession of the important Hill 60. Major-General Cox was given by General Birdwood detachments of the 4th and 5th Australian Brigades, the New Zealand Mounted Rifle Brigade, and the 5th Connaught Rangers. The advance was to take place at 5 p.m. on the 27th. While the 4th Brigade was reduced to about 1,200 men, the 5th Brigade, just landed, was still some 3,500 strong, but only 1,000 men could be spared for the attack. The remainder of the command must have numbered over 2,000 men; in all, perhaps, 3,000 men.

Never, it has been declared, was there such a bombardment witnessed at Anzac as that concentrated on the Turkish position from four o'clock on the afternoon of the 27th till an hour later, when the attack began. It could be seen that the trenches were smashed and levelled, and many of the Turks slunk away, but were caught by our snipers and machine gunners from the right of the position, where the crest of the ridges commanded the communication to the hill. The main attack developed on the trench that led up the ridge to the crest on the south-east. The Auckland and Canterbury Mounted Rifles formed the first line of attack, Otago and Wellington the second, and the 16th Battalion under Lieut.-Colonel Chapman, the third. The right was still left to the 4th Brigade. On the left, adjoining the plain, were the Connaught Rangers. The attack was the most gallant affair. It was all over in very few minutes. The Turks were stunned and paralysed by the terribleness of the bombardment, and the New Zealanders, though they met with severe fire, rapidly reached the trenches with a cheer and bayoneted the enemy that remained. They found sufficient evidence here of the effect of the high-explosive shells, for the trenches were choked with dead.

On the extreme left the Connaughts had, with remarkable dash, gained a footing in the trenches from which the 18th Battalion had been driven with such heavy loss on the 22nd. But in the bomb battle that ensued till midnight they were pushed back, and the Turks retained their wedge. The 9th Light Horse at eleven o'clock, led by Colonel Reynell, charged gallantly on to the top of the hill into the heart of the Turkish position, in an endeavour to reach their communication trench, but failed to gain their objective. The Colonel was killed, and his men were bombed back until they were forced on to the New Zealand lines. Nevertheless, the hill was for the most part in our hands; there remained but the Turkish wedge driven in, with Australian and British troops on either side of the hill.

The 4th Brigade meanwhile had launched 300 men, with some of the 17th Battalion, against the trench running back along the spur, as these other violent attacks succeeded. Captain Connolly led the first of that line. He, with all other officers in the charge, was wounded, and his men were once more forced back to a line of trenches which continued the New Zealand flank round the north-east of the hill, just on the crest. All next day the Turks made desperate efforts to dislodge the New Zealand line, but without effect. At 1 o'clock on the morning of the 29th, the 10th Light Horse—part of the regiment that had stormed the Nek at dawn on the 7th August—took the remaining sector of the trenches in one gallant dash and cut the Turkish wedge. They entered the redoubt in the crown of the hill. It was filled with the Turkish dead, who had bravely sold their lives in its last defence.

In this way was the famous Gallipoli Hill 60 captured by Britons and Australasians. It was the last of the great offensives planned at Anzac. Over 1,000 men were killed or wounded in the engagement. But the Turks lost five times that number. Our gain was an important strategic point, whereby we could command the plain and the enemy lines of communications. Three machine guns and some prisoners were taken, together with 300 rifles and ammunition and bombs. The line with the Suvla Bay army was straightened, and more ground added to the land that the gallant Anzac troops had won early in the month. But by now the old army was weakening with disease. Dysentery had reduced the numbers in the last weeks even more than the fighting. So the whole of the 1st Australian Division was withdrawn, and the 2nd Division filled their places. It was not a swift movement, but one carried out gradually, battalion by battalion (200 or 300 men only in each) leaving the firing-line to their new and zealous comrades. At length the New Zealand and Australian Division was relieved, and the whole of these brave men—but how small a proportion of the original Army Corps!—who had never left the fighting zone since the day they landed, found themselves at Mudros, free from the nervous strain of watching for bombs, bullets, and shells. They were tended and properly fed. They were praised for their glorious deeds and feats of arms.

CHAPTER XXVII
THE EVACUATION OF
THE PENINSULA

While the days dragged slowly by on the Anzac front, and the armies had been brought to a standstill at Suvla Bay, events at the seat of the Allies' War Council were moving rapidly. After the last fight and the failure of the great adventure, General Hamilton estimated his force at 95,000 men. He was 45,000 men below his normal strength for the units he held. Sickness was wasting his army at an alarming rate. He cabled to the War Office for more reinforcements, pointing out that the enemy against him was 110,000. They were all fine fighters, brought up from the best regiments that had been employed against the Russians. General Hamilton writes:

> I urged that if the campaign was to be brought to a quick victorious decision larger reinforcements must at once be sent out. Autumn, I pointed out, was already upon us, and there was not a moment to be lost. At that time (16th August), my British Divisions alone were 45,000 under establishment, and some of my fine battalions had dwindled down so far that I had to withdraw them from

the fighting-line. Our most vital need was the replenish-
ment of these sadly depleted ranks. When that was done
I wanted 50,000 fresh rifles. From what I knew of the
Turkish situation, both in its local and general aspect, it
seemed, humanly speaking, a certainty that if this help
could be sent me at once, we could clear a passage for our
fleet to Constantinople. It may be judged, then, how deep
was my disappointment when I learnt that the essential
drafts, reinforcements, and munitions could not be sent
me, the reason given being one which prevented me from
any further insistence.

What could the Commander-in-Chief do under such circumstances? He might have resigned; that was not his temperament.
He would fight to a finish. What troops remained in Egypt were
reorganised, and the attack, as soon as possible, began again on
the Suvla Bay front.

All was in vain. By September the whole Gallipoli front had
settled down to trench warfare, and a winter campaign seemed
inevitable. Meanwhile events on the Balkan frontier were hastening
the Turkish plans. Additional troops were available for service
on the peninsula with the Bulgarian frontier free, and that nation
joined to the Central Powers. The failure of the Allies to save Serbia
was of enormous significance to Turkey. It meant the prolongation
of her sickness, for it left the way free from Germany to Constantinople. Big-gun ammunition, which the Turks had undoubtedly
always conserved, began to flow in freely from Austrian and
German works, across the Danube through Bulgaria. Then the
Turks, finding, too, that the attacks on Achi Baba were never likely
to be renewed in any great force, and that the Allied forces left
there were comparatively weak, removed numbers of their heavy
artillery batteries to the Anzac position and began again with
renewed fury to enfilade the beach. The Olive Grove guns and
the batteries from Mal Tepe thundered their shells on the Anzac
slopes; at Suvla Bay the plain was swept with Turkish shrapnel.
Though the weather remained fine and the Allies continued to land

stores and munitions with ease, the Navy let it be understood that after the 28th October they would guarantee no further regular communications. All September was wasted by the British Cabinet deliberating on the wisdom of continuing the Gallipoli campaign, a far longer time than it had taken to embark on the enterprise at the very beginning of the year. During that month sickness further wasted the army. By the 11th October the Cabinet came to a decision. They asked General Hamilton the cost of lives that would be involved in withdrawing from Gallipoli. Fine soldier that he is, the Commander-in-Chief refused to entertain the idea; whereupon he was recalled to London for the official reason 'that a fresh and unbiased opinion from a responsible commander might be given upon a early evacuation.'

General Hamilton's departure was a matter of the keenest regret to the Australian troops. They had often met him in the saps at Anzac, and his tall, commanding figure was well known by all on the beach. It had been the custom for various battalions and regiments to supply guards for his headquarters, situated at Imbros on the south of Kephalos Bay, and on many occasions he had inspected and complimented them on their bearing. His farewell order to the troops, and, later, the concluding words of his last report, show the affection he held for his men whom he has described as 'magnificent.' He left the Dardanelles on the 17th October on a warship bound for Marseilles.

General Sir Charles Monro, one of the ablest of the new British leaders, and a man who had come to the front since the beginning of the war, was chosen to succeed General Hamilton. It must be presumed that even his unbiased report evidently left the matter in doubt. The casualties of evacuation were put down at probably 20 per cent of the force, or even higher—20,000 men. Thereupon Lord Kitchener himself determined to visit the Levant and thoroughly investigate the situation. There were more reasons than the approach of winter and the drain on the reserves of the army, the munitions, and maintenance of lines of communication, that necessitated some very vital alteration in the action and attitude of the Allies in the Levant and Mesopotamia. Greece was wavering. There was distinctly a pro-German feeling amongst the Greek population and a widespread German propaganda on lines that ended so successfully with Bulgaria a few months before. The Serbian Army was shattered before the landing of the Allies at Salonika could prevent the free passage to Turkey of everything that the sorely harassed and depleted Ottoman Army needed.

In Egypt, British prestige was at a low ebb. There were already signs of revolt on the western frontier, where the Senussi had been organised by Enver Pasha's brother. A further attack on the Canal was threatening, while the campaign in Mesopotamia looked far from reassuring. Egypt was a vast arsenal and rapidly becoming an armed camp. The strain on the transport service and lines of communication was rapidly growing acute—in fact, the position that faced the Allies was that by some means or other their energies would have to be narrowed. Anzac, Helles, Salonika, Egypt, and Mesopotamia all needed regular supplies throughout the severe winter months, and these had to be transported by sea. Yet the submarine peril had grown more menacing, three or four ships being sunk daily, despite the greatest vigilance of the fleet. Even the Greeks were engaged in helping these under-water craft in their endeavours to starve out the armies of the Aliies. It seemed obvious one or several of the fronts had to be abandoned, or else the Galllpoli offensive completed rapidly. For Egypt had to be kept safe at all costs: so had the army in Mesopotamia, guarding the Persian oilfields. To release a grip on the Eastern theatre of Europe at Salonika would mean perhaps that the Greeks would go over to the Central Powers. There was no alternative, once the necessary forces were denied to General Hamilton to end the task which I have endeavoured to show was so near successful completion, but that the work of evacuating Gallipoli should be attempted. It was a hazardous undertaking.

Lord Kitchener's visit to the Anzac battlefields was regarded as a great compliment by the troops. So bad had become the Turkish shelling of the Anzac Cove that it was not without the greatest anxiety that the leaders watched the landing of the Minister for War. Accompanying him were General Maxwell from Egypt and General Birdwood. Though the time of arrival had been kept as secret as possible, the news spread like lightning over Anzac. Lord Kitchener went straight to Russell's Top, a climb of twenty minutes up a roughly hewn artillery road, from which he could overlook the whole of the Anzac position, across the mass of huddled foothills at Suvla Bay. He chatted to the many men and officers. 'The King has asked me,' he said to various parties he met, 'to tell you how splendidly he thinks you have done. You have indeed done excellently well; better even than I thought you would.' He was astonished at the positions won. Lord Kitchener went right through the trenches on the Nek; he saw every important position and over thirty leaders. As he returned to the beach the troops cheered lustily. The hillside had suddenly, on this wild afternoon of November, grown animated. On the beach—it was only three hours later—he turned to Colonel Howse, as he had turned to others, and asked if he wanted anything done. Colonel Howse promptly brought a number of matters regarding the medical arrangements forward. 'I think I can promise you your first and your second request,' the great War Lord assured him, 'and we will see about the third.' It is curious to note that not a shell was fired at the departing launch or the destroyer as it steamed swiftly away.

Lord Kitchener left no one long in doubt of his impressions of the Australasians and the position they had made. A man not prone to superlatives, he spoke then, and since, in the highest terms of the valour of the deeds that won those Anzac heights. In a special Army Corps order General Birdwood wrote:

Lord Kitchener has desired me to convey to the Australian and New Zealand Army Corps a message which he was specially entrusted by the King to bring to our army corps. His Majesty commanded Lord Kitchener to express his high appreciation of the gallant and unflinching conduct of our men throughout the fighting, which has been as hard as any yet seen during the war, and wishes to express his complete confidence in the determination and fighting qualities of our men to assist in carrying this war to an entirely successful termination.

The order prceeds:

> Lord Kitchener has ordered me to express to all the very great pleasure it gave him to have the opportunity, which he considered a privilege, of visiting 'Anzac,' to see for himself some of the wonderfully good work which has been done by the officers and men of our army corps, as it was not until he had himself seen the positions we captured and held that he was able to fully realise the magnitude of the work which has been accomplished. Lord Kitchener much regretted that time did not permit of his seeing the whole corps, but he was very pleased to see a considerable proportion of officers and men, and to find all in such good heart and so confidently imbued with that grand spirit which has carried them through all their trials and many dangerous feats of arms—a spirit which he is quite confident they will maintain until they have taken their full share in completely overthrowing their enemies.

'Boys,' General Birdwood adds in his characteristic way, 'we may all well be proud to receive such a message, and it is up to all of us to live up to it and prove its truth.'

The story of the last three months at Anzac may be swiftly told. It was a struggle during September and October to prepare for the coming winter months. Quantities of wooden beams, and sheet-iron, and winter equipment began to pour into Anzac. Preparations were made for the removal of the hospitals and clearing stations from the beach and from the beds of the creeks, to higher ground. For the weather could no longer be depended on, and the narrowness of the beach rendered it imperative that all the stores should be moved, as the waves would lash against the foot of the cliffs in the sudden storms that arise in the Ægean—storms that are the mariner's constant anxiety. Then at the end of October the activity suddenly was modified. The question of evacuation had brought a new commander and Lord Kitchener to this front. A winter campaign was in abeyance.

Engineers used to tell me that they did not see where the wood was coming from to shore up the trenches against the rains, and that they would all be washed down into the gullies at the first storm. The Australians had only a few days' experience of wet weather, and not very heavy showers at that, in April, when they had landed; but Turkish farmers captured told what might be expected. Ever ingenous, the troops commenced collecting tins, and anything that would keep their 'possies' and dugouts dry. In some places great caverns were dug into the side of hills by the battalions of the 2nd Division, where they might be protected from the storms and from the severest shellings. General Monash had planned for the 4th Brigade a huge barracks on the side of Cheshire Ridge—a wonderful piece of engineering. The weather, though still fine, had become decidedly colder. At night the wind was biting, and rain early in November, gave a taste of what the conditions were to be like at Christmas-time. Saps were running with water; the soft, clayey mud clung in clods to the men's boots. The 1st Division and the Australian and New Zealand Divisions came back gradually from the rest camp at Mudros—the men fit again now, but the battalions still below strength in point of numbers.

Hostilities had been confirmed almost entirely to mining operations along the whole of the front. Mines and countermines were exploded. In some places—particularly at Quinn's Post—the tunnels had met, and an underground battle had ensued. Once we had reconnoitred a whole Turkish gallery, and found the sentries nodding at their posts with the guard in a tunnel, arguing and chattering away in a rapid, unintelligible tongue. These operations were not always accomplished without loss and severe casualties. Fumes overcame a large party near Lone Pine, and many lives were lost, some in the efforts to rescue those who had been suffocated in the mine tunnel. In one instance the Turks exploded a mine that trapped some sappers in a tunnel. After three days the men dug themselves out, and appeared before their astonished and delighted friends over the parapets of our trenches.

From one end of the position to the other, right in the heart of the Turkish hills below the famous Sari Bair ridge, infantry and engineers dug down under the Turkish trenches. I remember talking to Lieut.-Colonel Martyn, of the Divisional Engineers, about his plans. He was considering the possibility of going down 40 feet, tunnelling right through the hill at German Officers' Trench, and in one great effort breaking through in the rear of the Turkish position. If they went deep enough there seemed little likelihood of the Turks hearing the picking and tapping. Whatever may have been the eventual plan, the end of November and the first week of December saw most of the energies of the men engaged in making storm shelters for themselves. That period was one fraught with misfortune for the troops.

Whether the Turkish reconnaissance on the 27th November was intended as a mere bluff, or whether the Turks were anxious to discover if an offensive was in preparation by us, they attacked in thin lines all along the Anzac position. They were driven back with severe loss, and hardly a man reached our parapets.

On the 29th November the Turks commenced a terrible bombardment with heavy howitzers—8, 9, and 10-in. pieces— of the Lone Pine trenches, which were pounded and flattened. A series of mines were exploded under them, and we had to evacuate portions of this dearly held post. But the Turks dared make no fresh attack. Our casualties were heavy.

The day previously a snowstorm had swept down on the north wind that wrought havoc with the shipping in the Cove. Pinnaces broke from their moorings and barges went ashore and were smashed. How wonderful the hills on the morning of the 29th, covered with a snow mantle, which astonished the Australians, the great majority of whom were experiencing their first snowstorm! Icicles hung from the trenches—the sentries stamped up and down. The wind howled down the gullies, that were soon turned into morasses; the trenches were ankle-deep in mud. For three days the frost continued, but the troops were in good spirits and fairly comfortable. Many of the men suffered frost-bite, but on the third day of December the sun shone and the conditions had materially improved.

And now, in this strange eventful story comes the last stage of all. Though the decision for the evacuation was taken in November, the troops guessed nothing of it even up to a week before it took place. They had no realisation that the series of very quiet evenings, when scarcely a shot was fired along the whole of the 5-mile front that Anzac now comprised, had in them any definite end. It was all part of the plan conceived by General Birdwood (now commanding the whole Gallipoli forces in places of General Monro) for beginning the education of the Turks to our leaving. But the main proposition to be faced was how to remove 200 guns and hundreds of tons of stores, equipment, and munitions and men, and keep up a semblance of normal activity of throwing supplies into Anzac. Cloudy skies and a first-phase moon helped at night, when the guns were stealthily drawn from their covered pits. There was no unusual gathering of transports by day, though the waters at night might resemble the days of the early landing, when the pinnaces and trawlers had crowded inshore with tows. The tows then removed now contained arms and munitions. More often they contained men declared not absolutely fit.

It was often remarked in the trenches, as December began, that it was an easy matter now to get a spell. The very slightest sickness was sufficient excuse to send men to the beach, from whence all the serious cases had long ago been removed, and so to the transports or hospital ships, as the case might be. Yet during the day, when Turkish aeroplanes hung menacingly over the position, observers might have seen bodies of men marching up the torturous sap to the trenches. There was more indication of permanency, even of attack, than of evacuation.

So on the 10th December there was left at Anzac barely 20,000 men—very fit, very sound, and very determined men. It wanted nine days to the day of evacuation. Still there was no hint that any unusual step was anticipated. Some regiments were removed for special duty—they anticipated another fight, even a new landing. They left by night. They arrived at dawn at Mudros, safe from the firing-line and Anzac for ever. The greater part of the army service, engineer, and hospital units had left with their equipment. They came down the deep saps from the south and from the north, right from under those hills from the crest of which the Turks could look down almost to the heart of our position. No longer could we hope to make a firm resistance to the Turkish attack, which it had been hoped would develop in November. Rearguard actions were contemplated and evolved, to resist any onslaught. On the beach the heavy ammunition was being loaded on to lighters. All except nine worn guns had gone. Two were left still, almost in the firing-line, where they had been from the first. Quantities of stores and equipment were destroyed on the 16th and 17th rather than they should fall into the hands of the Turks. The 'archives' of the brigades and divisions had been removed too, for some time. The administrative dugouts were bare of books, typewriters, and correspondence. Final orders had been issued. It was now only a question of supervision and Staff work to get the men away. And what Staff work it was on the part of General Birdwood to remove that whole army of 40,000 men (I include those troops brought out of the trenches early in December) from such a perilous position! One may write in terms of the highest praise of the demeanour and discipline of the men in those last days, but it is to the leaders that must fall inevitably the greatest praise—the leaders of the army and the leaders of the men: men such as Brigadier-General White, the Chief of Staff to General Birdwood, Brigadier-Generals Antill, Monash, Johnston, Forsyth, and Holmes, who worked on the beach till the very last.

Thousands of men were removed from Anzac during the night of the 18th. They came down rapidly through the gullies, silently, and with empty magazines. They embarked swiftly, according to a carefully adjusted timetable. By morning the sea was calm and passive. A sudden storm was the one thing now which might yet cause havoc to the plans. It was during this last day that the situation was so tense. Turkish observers might, one thought, have easily detected the thinly held lines and the diminished stores on shore. The enemy remained in utter ignorance. They would have seen—as the gunners surely saw from their observation positions on Gaba Tepe and Kelid Bahr—parties of Australians ('smoking parties,' as they were called) idling about in saps and on exposed hills, meant to attack the fire of the Turkish guns; for 'Beachy Bill' could never resist what the troops called 'a smile' at parties on the beach. The destruction of stores continued. To the enemy, Anzac firing-line was normal that day.

At dusk on the 19th began the final phase of this delicate and extraordinary operation. A force of 6,000 men were holding back 50,000 Turkish troops. The communications at Anzac were like a fan: they all led out from the little Cove in the very centre of the position. They went as far as 3 miles on the left (the north), and half that distance to Chatham's Post on the right (the south), almost to Gaba Tepe. In the centre they were short and very steep. They led up to the Nek and to Russell's Top and to Quinn's Post. From these points the Turks could have looked down into the heart of our position. If that heart were to pulse on steadily until suddenly it stopped altogether, it must be protected till the last. Therefore the flanks of the position were evacuated first.

From the Nek to the beach it was a descent of some 500 yards—a descent that might be accomplished in ten minutes. It was the head of our second line of defence that had been so hastily drawn up in the early days. There was now the last stand to be made.

Three columns, A, B, and C, held the Anzac line; 2,000 picked men in each, and the whole unit chosen men from infantry battalions and regiments of Light Horse. The last were the 'die hards.' Darkness spread rapidly after five o'clock over the front hills, wrapping them in gloom. The sea was still calm. Clouds drifted across the face of the moon, half-hidden in mist. Already men were leaving the outskirts of our line. They would take hours to reach the beach, there joining up with other units come from the centre, and closer positions to the shore. They marched with magazines empty: they had not even bayonets fixed. They might not smoke or speak. They filed away, Indian fashion, through the hills into the big sap, on to the northern piers on Ocean Beach. Their moving forms were clearly distinguishable in the glimmer from the crescent moon. The hills looked sullen and black. No beacon lights from dugouts burned. That first column began to leave Anzac shore at eight o'clock on the transports that were swiftly gliding from the shore. Another two hours and some thousands of men had gone. Parties of the 3rd Light Horse Brigade had left Destroyer Hill; most of the 1st Light Horse had evacuated No. 1 Post, the 4th Australian Brigade the line on Cheshire Ridge, the New Zealand Mounted Rifles, Yeomanry, and Maoris the famous Hill 60, position.

But still small detachments, 150 to 170 in each, belonging to these seasoned regiments and brigades remained at their post, holding quietly the Anzac line.

Midnight. The head of the second column reached the Cove and the piers so often shelled. Those on the beach knew that only 2,000 lone men were holding back the enemy along the front. They were in isolated groups: the New Zealand Infantry on the Sari Bair ridge, the 20th Infantry at the Nek, the 17th Infantry at Quinn's, the 23rd and 24th Infantry at Lone Pine, the 6th Light Horse Regiment at Chatham's Post, on the extreme right, down by the shore. On the beach there was no confusion. Units concentrated at fixed points in the gullies. They left at a certain time. They arrived just to the moment, marching hard. They found the Navy ready to clear them to the transports. There must be no hitch: there was none. On either flank could he heard a feeble rifle fire. Overhead came the answering 'psing-psing' of the Turkish bullets.

At 1.30 began the withdrawal of the 'die hards' from the points they were holding with such a terrible peril hanging over them. A bomb burst at 'the Apex,' on the slopes of Chunak Bair, with a resonant thud, with the rapid answer following from the Turkish rifles. But nothing else happened. What could happen? The New Zealand garrisons had gone from this dearly-won ridge, with a parting message left under a stone for the Turks. By two o'clock the small parties of the 19th Infantry at Pope's, the 18th Infantry at Courtney's Post, and the 17th Infantry at Quinn's Post, were still further reduced. A few hundred desperate fighters were hurrying in from the outposts of the line on the left and the right, each firing a shot as they left. The right stole away at 2.30 from Chatham's Post, men of the 6th Light Horse. Still there were 'die hards' of the 1st Brigade, and the 7th Battalion next them, in Leane's Trench up to Lone Pine, held by the 23rd and 24th Infantry of the

2nd Division. Here the Turks in their trenches were within 15 feet of them. There were a few score of determined men left at Quinn's Post, a strong party on the Nek, but yet not 800 men in all holding the whole front. Yet our line from end to end was spluttering. Ah! that was through a device whereby the running sand from an emptying bucket, fired an Australian rifle.

Swiftly the fate of Anzac was being decided now. All the trenches at Lone Pine were deserted by 3.15 a. m. The garrisons at Quinn's and Pope's Hill—the ever-impregnable post of our centre—were silently, swiftly moving down Monash Gully into Shrapnel Gully, through the sap, and towards the longed-for beach. The Anzac line was contracting rapidly. The moon slid behind some clouds as the party passed the deserted walls and tanks. Empty dugouts gaped like bottomless pits on either side of their path. Suddenly behind on the heights, like a thunderclap, there was a roar, as a vivid flash lit the sky, and tongues of flame rolled along the hills. The whole of the Nek was thus blown up by an immense series of mines. Three and a half tons of Amenol, placed there by the 5th Company of Australian Engineers, were used to throw a barrier across this entrance. The sight, awful in its meaning to the army now embarked, lent speed to the steps of those brave rearguards. From off that same Nek the Australians were rushing down the track to the boats waiting by the piers. The Turkish fire broke forth, growing, swelling in volume, as if a door were suddenly opened on a raging battle. Guns from the warships began to pound the hills. It was not yet four o'clock, but the dawn was creeping in, and with it the Turks to our trenches. Fearful of a trap, they began their exploration of Anzac as the guns of the Navy completed the destruction of our few guns on the beach (that had fired till the end) and on the piers, and swept the ranks of the advancing enemy.

Suvla Bay was also evacuated on the same evening, and with the same success, for, as the news broke on an astonished world, it was reported—and will be recorded—as one of the most extraordinary feats of naval and military history, that only three men at Anzac and two at Suvla Bay had been wounded in this astonishing masterpiece of strategy.

Before the closing days of the year, the English and French positions at Cape Helles had been abandoned also, and the Gallipoli campaign was brought to a sudden but very deliberate close. I have suggested that there were strong enough reasons for its commencement, and others for its conclusion. As to the failure, it can but be attributed to the lack of men, the lack of reinforcement, the lack of munitions. When and where these armies and reinforcements should have been landed, the campaign shows significantly enough. But in the contemplation of this failure there comes a not unpleasant feeling of achievement, the full significance of which has not yet been recognised, and will not be fully understood till the Turks lay down their arms and sue for peace. The exhaustion of the Turkish nation and its army during that Gallipoli campaign was great, and how near to collapse historians will discover. The new Russian offensive in the Caucasus found it ill prepared to resist. Over 250,000 casualties were suffered by the Turks in the Dardanelles; a great mass of the Turkish mercantile fleet was lost. And still their coast lies as open as ever to invasion, so that large armies are compelled to be kept along it.

No one can regard the evacuation (whatever relief it gave to the army) without a tinge of sadness and bitterness at relinquishing positions that had been so dearly won, to the troops engaged most of all. But it stands to the credit of the Australians that they took the situation calmly as it developed. The army made a masterly retreat, after suffering 40,000 casualties, of whom 8,000 had been killed. But the Commonwealth and the Dominion of New Zealand offered fresh battalions to the Motherland as the only sign on the changing of the tide of battle.

In one day—25th April—Australia attained Nationhood by the heroism of her noble sons. 'Anzac' will ever form the front page in her history, and a unique and vivid chapter in the annals of the Empire. The very vigour of their manhood, the impetuosity of their courage, carried slopes that afterwards in cold blood, seemed impregnable. And they held what they won, and proved themselves an army fit to rank alongside any that a World Empire has produced. But yet in all their fighting there was no bitterness—not against the

Turks—but a terrible, earnest fearlessness that boded ill for lurking enemies. They found a staunch and worthy foe, who, whatever their treatment of the people within their own borders was, abstained from the brutalities of the Germans.

Above all, the young army won its way into the hearts and confidence of the British Navy and the Indians from so near their own shores. They gained a respect for themselves and for discipline. They formed for the generations of new armies yet unborn on Australian soil, traditions worthy of the hardy, freeborn race living under the cloudless skies of the Southern Cross. Openhearted, ever generous, true as gold, and hard as steel, Australia's first great volunteer army, and its valorous deeds will live in history while the world lasts.

Text Classics

Dancing on Coral
Glenda Adams
Introduced by Susan Wyndham

The True Story of Spit MacPhee
James Aldridge
Introduced by Phillip Gwynne

The Commandant
Jessica Anderson
Introduced by Carmen Callil

Homesickness
Murray Bail
Introduced by Peter Conrad

Sydney Bridge Upside Down
David Ballantyne
Introduced by Kate De Goldi

Bush Studies
Barbara Baynton
Introduced by Helen Garner

Between Sky & Sea
Herz Bergner
Introduced by Arnold Zable

The Cardboard Crown
Martin Boyd
Introduced by Brenda Niall

A Difficult Young Man
Martin Boyd
Introduced by Sonya Hartnett

Outbreak of Love
Martin Boyd
Introduced by Chris Womersley

When Blackbirds Sing
Martin Boyd
Introduced by Chris Wallace-Crabbe

The Australian Ugliness
Robin Boyd
Introduced by Christos Tsiolkas

The Girl Green as Elderflower
Randolph Stow
Introduced by Kerryn Goldsworthy

The Suburbs of Hell
Randolph Stow
Afterword by Michelle de Kretser

Me and Mr Booker
Cory Taylor
Introduced by Benjamin Law

An Iron Rose
Peter Temple
Introduced by Les Carlyon

1788
Watkin Tench
Introduced by Tim Flannery

The House that Was Eureka
Nadia Wheatley
Introduced by Toni Jordan

Happy Valley
Patrick White
Introduced by Peter Craven

Tobruk 1941
Chester Wilmot
Introduced by Peter Cochrane

The Visit
Amy Witting
Introduced by Susan Johnson

I for Isobel
Amy Witting
Introduced by Charlotte Wood

A Change in the Lighting
Amy Witting
Introduced by Ashley Hay

Isobel on the Way to the Corner Shop
Amy Witting
Introduced by Maria Takolander

Selected Stories
Amy Witting
Introduced by Melanie Joosten

I Own the Racecourse!
Patricia Wrightson
Introduced by Kate Constable

textclassics.com.au